I0160559

HIGHER EDUCATION IN POLAND

HIGHER EDUCATION IN POLAND

PERSPECTIVES, OPPORTUNITIES, NEW IDEAS

Edited by
Zbigniew Kruszewski

PIASA Books
New York

Copyright © 2011
The Polish Institute of Arts and Sciences of America

Published by PIASA Books
The Polish Institute of Arts and Sciences of America
208 East 30th St., New York, NY 10016

All rights reserved

Library of Congress Cataloging-in-Publication Data

Higher education in Poland : perspectives, opportunities, new ideas /
edited by Zbigniew Kruszewski.
p. cm.
ISBN 978-0-940962-72-9
Includes bibliographical references.
1. Education, Higher—Poland.
2. Universities and colleges—Poland. I. Kruszewski, Zbigniew.

LA843.H54 2011
378.438–dc23   2011043644

www.polishbooks.org
Printed in the United States of America

Contents _____

PREFACE   vii
Zbigniew Kruszewski

NEW NORMATIVE SOLUTIONS FOR HIGHER EDUCATION: 1
    AN ATTEMPT AT DIFFERENTIATION
Edyta Hadrowicz

THE LEGAL STATUS OF CONTEMPORARY STUDENTS   13
    IN THE REPUBLIC OF POLAND
Elżbieta Wituska

NEW PRINCIPLES FOR STATE FINANCING OF HIGHER   57
    EDUCATION AND SCHOLARSHIP IN POLAND
Marek Tyrakowski

THE LEGAL PERSONALITY OF AN INSTITUTION OF   80
    HIGHER EDUCATION: A FEW REMARKS RELATED
    TO ONGOING LEGAL CHANGES
Agata Skorek

THE NATIONAL FRAMEWORK OF QUALIFICATIONS   99
    IN POLISH HIGHER EDUCATION AND THE
    DEVELOPMENT OF CONTINUING EDUCATION
Anna Frąckowiak

THE ROLE OF HIGHER EDUCATION IN POLAND   118
    IN CREATING ACADEMIC ENTREPRENEURSHIP
    AND THE INNOVATIVE ACTIVITIES OF STUDENTS
Rafał Marcin Borkowski

THE QUALITY OF TEACHING AT THE UNIVERSITY LEVEL   133
    IN LIGHT OF THE BOLOGNA PROCESS
Joanna Koprowicz and Kazimierz Waluch

CONTENTS

THE LEARNED SOCIETY WITHIN THE FRAMEWORK   144
   OF PERMANENT EDUCATION
Zbigniew Kruszewski

EUROPEAN UNION FUNDS FOR HIGHER EDUCATION   164
   IN POLAND: AN OPPORTUNITY FOR UNIVERSITIES
   TO IMPLEMENT SOCIAL PROGRAMS
Piotr Nasiadko and Michał Luczewski

A HISTORICAL OUTLINE OF EDUCATION   184
   IN PŁOCK, 1079–1939
Andrzej Gretkowski and Marcin Berliński

DEVELOPING SCHOOL COUNSELOR COMPETENCIES   205
   IN THE PROCESS OF HIGHER EDUCATION
Marek Borowski

THE SYSTEM OF HIRING ACADEMIC FACULTY AT   217
   UNIVERSITIES AND ITS POLITICAL IMPLICATIONS
Edyta Bogdańska

INSTITUTIONS OF HIGHER EDUCATION: AN ENVIRONMENT 229
   WHERE SCIENCE COMES INTO BEING AND KNOWLEDGE
   IS INTEGRATED WITH WISDOM AND LEARNING
Romuald Dobrzeniecki and Wiesław Wojciech Szczęsny

STUDENT SELF-GOVERNANCE IN NONPUBLIC COLLEGES AND 241
   UNIVERSITIES: CHANGES AND PERSPECTIVES, 1990–2011
Aldona Długokięcka-Kałuża

NOTES ON CONTRIBUTORS   251

Preface

ZBIGNIEW KRUSZEWSKI

Poland, a country which has thirty-eight million citizens, requires social and economic modernization. This need for modernization stems from numerous factors, the most important being the following:

- its political transformation (after the change in the political system on 4 June 1989—still unfinished),
- its adaptation to the structures of the European Union (after the accession of 1 May 2004),
- economic globalization,
- the development of a knowledge-based society.

Had it not been for the political transformation of 1989, Poland would not have joined the European Union. However, one must bear in mind that the European Union only creates chances for success, without providing any guarantees. Therefore Poland faces a great opportunity for development. Yet the said development may only be guaranteed by a properly educated and motivated people. An unquestionable chief Polish asset is a young, well-educated generation, as well as the individualism and entrepreneurship of hundreds of leaders (especially people acting within the area of economy, local authorities, and nongovernmental organizations, including learned societies and associations). In order for people to be able to deal with themselves in the future, they should acquire well-internalized knowledge as well as social, psychological and worldview self-awareness. They should be assisted by unhampered teachers, capable of dialogue, who set an example through themselves by showing that it is possible to live well and proudly even in the most difficult times.

Universities educate students to live in the future, and we know only that it will bring numerous new occupations and professions.

Poland has been seeking a model for higher education. Constant legal changes concerning the functioning of universities, employing and promoting scholars, conducting research and the state-financing of research on teaching still occur. Simultaneously, the possibilities of raising the level of education, which would satisfy European and world standards, are sought after.

Apart from the institutions which have been legally authorized to perform these tasks, the aforementioned educational processes are also supported by social institutions, such as learned societies.

The self-governance of students, voicing their opinions on all the matters related to the functioning of universities, has become increasingly significant for university structure.

This publication raises issues concerning higher education, as well as certain insoluble dilemmas. The authors of particular essays present the results of their research studies, surveys, and inquiries into these complex issues.

PREFACE

The authors are aware that they have not been able to exhaust the issues related to higher education in Poland. They are also aware of comments which may relate to their interpretations and the phenomena occurring within the area of their investigations. However, they consider the issues connected with higher education in Poland to be essential for the present social and economic life of Poland, as its future depends on their effective solutions.

HIGHER EDUCATION IN POLAND

NEW NORMATIVE SOLUTIONS FOR HIGHER EDUCATION: AN ATTEMPT AT DIFFERENTIATION

EDYTA HADROWICZ

This study is an attempt to undertake the analysis of new normative solutions in the field of higher education in Poland, focusing on selected issues currently existing in this sphere.[1]

In the current legal state, issues related to the higher education system are governed by the Law on Higher Education of 27 July 2005[2] and the Act on Academic Degrees, Title and Degrees, and Title in Art of 14 March 2003.[3] It should be noted, however, that the Polish system of higher education is internally very diverse, and some would even claim that it is very polarized.[4] The solutions that worked many years ago do not always allow us to meet new challenges de facto, as they are not adjusted for both present and future circumstances.

Consequently, the need for modernization of higher education has resulted in new regulations. On 18 March 2011, the Sejm of the Republic of Poland, at the initiative of the government, adopted (although, after consideration of Senate amendments, a relatively mitigated solution) a thorough amendment to the two laws mentioned above—a new Law on Higher Education,[5] which will be effective with the new academic year—i.e., on 1 October 2011.

Considering this matter, therefore, fundamental questions should be presented in the beginning: whether the new reform, modifying the legal environment of the institution in Poland, really set the correct direction of change in higher education, and whether innovative legislative changes are going in the right direction by creating new, better (and competitive toward other countries) conditions and opportunities for the entire academic community.

It should be agreed that the act amending the higher education system in Poland (de facto, one of most dynamically developing areas of social life) is of significant importance. Moreover, it is an important and challenging task. It also raises no serious doubts, that over the past twenty years Polish higher education has achieved significant successes (mainly quantitative ones): an increase in the number of students enrolling (nearly fivefold), and a rise in the number of universities (a result of the opportunity for new private universities to come into being and the introduction of nonpublic forms of education since 1991), which is undoubtedly proof of the huge effort undertaken by the scholarly and academic communities and the entire system of higher education. On the other hand, nota bene that there are still many problems in the abovementioned scope arising from such rapid growth. Changes are therefore necessary (analogous reforms are being carried out in all EU countries). However, it might be considered whether the current policy, including not only legislative changes, is based on a concept that could boost the development of universities and higher education in a reliable and development-supporting way. This is another question which I would like to leave without an answer at this stage of the analysis.

As a result, it seems to be a justified statement that the present time (compared to times of rapidly changing economic conditions) is an appropriate one for leading the discourse within the framework of openly and broadly reforming the learning and higher education sector. The discussions and polemics of this scope should inspire precise—as can be assumed—actions but at the same time verify some often stereotypical views of Polish universities and the whole system of learning and higher education. However, these discussions must always be preceded by debate. It is important that the debate is of good quality, and that substantive reasoning can be faced by the interests of various groups and environments, and their values, so that it is *purely* of factual nature, since encountering the external view undoubtedly adds to the value and quality of every debate.

The conclusion is therefore obvious. A huge role must be played by something which has already been stated in this subject: the achieved results of scholarly and teaching work,[6] especially as currently, the most visible consequence of the failure of the Polish higher education system (the policy has been targeted on significant improvement of quality indicators, which in fact is an undoubted success) is the lack of Polish universities among the institutions widely recognized in the world with a high quality of research and teaching.[7] Adequate efforts made by the government to stimulate a rapid development of research institutions of the highest quality and potential should constitute a priority.

II

By identifying weaknesses in the Polish higher education system (also in terms of its position in rankings of the best universities in Europe and around the world) in the general level of analysis, attention should be drawn particularly to the following aspects:

- The lack of professional quality mechanisms for a financing system;
- A generally low degree of internationalization of study;
- Often inadequate structures of specialization;
- A more complicated (long, multi- and over-formalized) scholarly career path;
- University management systems;
- Weak links between universities and the socioeconomic environment.[8]

The amendments currently suggested, acting as a kind of alternative to existing solutions, are expected to introduce mechanisms allowing eliminating the drawbacks of the Polish higher education system. Therefore, performing a more detailed analysis, it should be indicated that changes toward meeting challenges of civilization should basically focus on three pillars: first, an effective model of higher education management; second, a dynamic model for scholarly careers; and finally, an effective model of education.[9]

The specific position of Polish universities is linked to a particular responsibility related to the training of elites at the highest global level, as well as competing in the international arena to address a significant position in the European Research Area.[10] Thus, it seems that one of the key measures to achieve that purpose should be the creation of appropriate mechanisms of rational financing of Polish education, as well as higher education supported by it, based on the achieved outcomes of scholarly and teaching work. The change in the current method of funding schools might be helpful so that more funds would be distributed via a model way of transparent procedures regarding the competition. The scope of financing by state funding would ultimately depend on the quality of achieved effects, both in terms of education as well as the results of scholarly work.

Currently, the proposed legislative changes, in the scope of the main objectives of the reform, provide the concept of so-called quality-oriented funding, which (based on the outcomes of scholarly work) provides financing, for example, to the best university faculties, institutes, and research units receiving outstanding scores from the State Accreditation Committee (Polish: PKA). Every year, in accordance with the authors of the reform, the Leading National Research Centers (Polish: KNOW) can be chosen for five years, and during this time they would receive an increased subsidy for their operations and would also receive priority when applying for research grants and funding to purchase equipment.[11]

It should be noted that the effect of these new solutions will therefore depend essentially on the method of evaluation of the (public or private) unit's teaching and research activity. As a result, it is obvious that the current state of law to introduce such a system will increase (by stimulating competition and encouraging the best organizational units of public and private universities) the quality of research and teaching at Polish universities, which have often been focused on how to earn points to win, thus receiving more money.[12]

The proposed legislative amendments in this respect, therefore, give rise to statements that are intended, as they might be judged, to create better conditions for the functioning of universities in Poland, regardless of their legal status. As it seems, these amendments are based on the idea that the potential of Polish universities should be explored more fully. Also taken into account should be the innovative instruments of quality-supported financing for the highest quality higher education organizational units, those of which, however, as it was indicated, will pre-acquire the status of Leading National Research

Centers or have outstanding scores in the opinion of the State Accreditation Committee.

Staying at the level of the general analysis, it should also be noted that the current division of the spheres "learning" and "higher education" is artificial. In Poland, learning takes place at universities, which combines research and teaching processes. Changes (particularly changes of the system) should therefore aim to overcome this division, beginning the process to integrate the organizational structures of learning and higher education.

Consequently, these phenomena imply a statement that they must apply regulations to ensure the transparency of processes in this subject matter. This is especially true since the issues can be understood only when one tries to consider the matter in an exceptional way, i.e., by combining political problems with economic and social ones. And although it seems that it is obvious to understand, it is neither easy nor without controversy. More broadly speaking, it is often the result of the maturity of the society and thus requires time.

Another equally important and vital element of the reform should be the development of scholarly work, which is not only unhampered by an overly complicated and formalized procedure for obtaining degrees, but also by an extremely hermetic academic career path.[13] It is essentially an undisputed fact that the age structure, the development of subsequent stages of academic careers, and academics' salaries at Polish universities in relation to other EU countries are significantly different from the standards of the world (which suspends substantive competition and undermines the foundations for higher education in Poland). This state is reflected in reported scholarly achievements measured by the number of publications in international reviewed writings, the quantity and quality of citations, the number of patents, and the number of grants coming from domestic and foreign institutions, which largely determine the low position of Polish universities in rankings around the world.[14] However, a relatively low level of these indicators, on the other hand, does not, as it might be assumed, constitute a measure of Polish learning potential. This potential, I should emphasize, is enormous. The turning point should therefore be selective (for example, based on competitions, articulating at the same time demand where necessary), financing, which would undoubtedly increase the attractiveness of the research teaching profession and, to a significant degree, would reduce, and eventually eliminate, the previous tendencies (still common today) of the higher education sector. On the other hand, when applying for a postdoctoral degree, while maintaining substantive requirements, procedural simplifications, immanently related to the subject matter, would allow the incompatible system in a Polish scholarly career (as compared to foreign systems) to be much more transparent (which would give it a more motivational nature).

In an attempt to reach a general conclusion, it might be stated that current procedures for academic promotion mean that Polish scholarship often relies on the autotelic system, satisfying only the needs created by itself to some extent.[15] This leads to a situation where relatively few scholarly achievements are recognized internationally. Therefore, the Polish system's career incompatibility with the international system in this area is obvious. Moreover, the above observation does not present any findings.

However, it is obvious that the selection of the best, most creative people must be based on uniform principles regarding current results of individual achievement, not only in terms of training students and research work, but also in the strategic development of individuals within established frameworks, as it concerns new conditions for financing and development. The current level of funding for subsequent years of study or research is not impressive in this regard. Quite often it cannot compete with wages offered outside the development of intellectual capital area, and the development of this sector—and this should not be forgotten—in the face of the modern economy plays a key role.[16]

As a result, it is necessary to create far more attractive conditions for development in Polish higher education, particularly for the development of outstanding young academics. However, too many "rigid" barriers (deriving from the existing system's solutions, having the nature of strictly formal barriers, essentially irremovable—due to the time-consuming legislative process—in the short and medium term) in this area is a worrying fact. The removal of such barriers requires time as well as political will. The problem is also that the compromise you need to achieve, nota bene, is difficult to obtain.

Finally, the question of an effective training model, which in this context requires a bit more comment, should be analyzed. A wide access to education and comprehensive preparation of graduates for functioning in the labor market is the foundation of a knowledge-based economy. Poland still has relatively few people with university or college degrees (compared to the whole population). This is one of the principal obstacles to the transformation of the Polish economy into a modern market economy based on knowledge. Transformations in the economy are also limited by a learning structure that is inadequate for the economy, which sometimes makes well-educated graduates take classes below their qualifications. This means that the initial momentum of transformation, regardless of its strength, would never be able to cover all spheres of social life. It is inherently directed to the realm of politics, of course, and the economic sphere, in which the changes affect the effectiveness of the entire transformation process. The social sphere (including the sphere of higher education) is therefore a kind of side effect on both politics and the economy, which to some general extent determines the framework for transformations taking place within the sphere. It outlines a political model in this respect, although the dynamics, nature, and scale are clearly different. The problem is also based on the fact that political settlements should not inhibit this process and should not lead to the exacerbation of social tensions. And this is, inter alia, because the system, generally speaking, has a dual function. There are still remnants of the old system which block the disclosure of positive solutions associated with the new system. Consequently, the effect of this process involves—as it might be judged—social consciousness, and this in turn (being put in a completely different situation compared to the past) changes much more slowly, hindering and slowing the reforms.

There are of course various theoretical options in this area, which often support opposite solutions. According to some concepts, the sooner the changes take place, the better and faster the obtained results will be.[17] But there are also views emphasizing that reforms should not come too fast, that not only the interests of society as a whole should be respected, but also the interests of individual groups within that society. As a result, this approach usually results in the stretching of reforms over time. This in turn undoubtedly leads to reduced efficiency in new developments, at least over a short or even medium period of time. As it is in actual fact, in the long term, this has not yet been verified.

Regardless of that fact, it should be noted that Polish membership in the European Union is a great opportunity for Polish students, who now have a choice of their country of study, university, and major. Students also have increasingly better opportunities for training and acquiring skills needed for functioning in the European labor market. On the other hand, international competition in higher education is a serious challenge for Polish universities. The main obstacle here is difficulty in ensuring comparability of the educational process in relation to the solutions adopted in other countries (mainly Western Europe and the United States).[18]

The above analysis is obviously very general and probably oversimplified (it shows only some aspects of the proposed changes). However, as it seems, it reflects the nature of legislative amendments introduced and attempts to sketch out ways to regulate this matter. In conclusion, it is important to finally indicate that the presentation of the entire, multilayered problem is virtually impossible, and each choice of appropriate solutions is related to the subjective evaluation and interpretation of this issue.

III

Every attempt of general summary is a task neither easy nor without controversy. Indeed, theses and generalizations once formed should not be repeated. Regardless of the above, the evaluation—nota bene purely subjective—will always belong to the reader.

This study attempted to present a personal scholarly discussion on the issues raised here. However, it is impossible not to notice that new questions arise and many issues still remain—at least so far—unexplained. Hence, here has been a kind of attempt to indicate possible directions of solutions to the current status quo, but these attempts are still not very consistent.

In conclusion, the arguments presented above give rise to the statement that some of the previously proposed amendments by the Ministry of Science and Higher Education—as it might be judged—enter in the current system very deeply and even if some of them are viewed positively by academics, it is on the other hand impossible not to notice that there are many such proposals, which are—it seems—a serious threat (in particular) to public education. In fact, a large part of the amendment leaves a question mark, so to speak, and some people argue that the fact in some way disqualifies it.

Here is not the place to discuss all aspects of the proposed changes, but from the summary of these key ones two major trends arise. First—for the Polish legislature, striving to reform higher education in order to match the challenges of civilization and worldwide trends is—as it is understood—a challenge of a purely strategic nature. Second—there must be an introduction of provisions which would increase research requirements and consequently improve the quality of education. Undoubtedly, the sphere of the Polish higher education system is a success of the Polish transformation, but on the other hand, in order to fully develop, it has to face the challenges particularly connected with poor internationality (currently the number of Polish students studying abroad is rising; however, the option of Polish universities remains of little attractiveness for students from abroad); a frequently defective structure of education (the effect of this phenomenon has become a disproportionately broad expansion of the segment in certain programs, which are generally considered to be less laborious and absorbing for students and not corresponding to employers' expectations); complicated scholarly career paths (a kind of trend of aging in reaching the next levels of scholarly careers can be observed today, especially in the case of further degrees—on average after the age of forty-five); conservative management of public universities[19] (currently the Polish sector of higher education is managed in a democratically elective way,[20] which means that the management of Polish universities is inherently conservative in nature and is of unstable compromise between, for example, departmental groups and interest groups);[21] and the lack of relationship with the external environment—social and economic[22] (this aspect is particularly manifested on two basic levels—government policy and education policy; therefore, the need to bring Polish universities closer to society should be indicated, building stronger relationship between the universities and the social and economic environment, which today has very tangible consequences in the sphere).[23]

As a result, in this state of things, the conclusion might be drawn that in this background Poland looks quite poor compared to other European countries. Previous policy regarding higher education in Poland has, at first, a uniform nature, taking into consideration to a small degree the need of institutional differentiation. Secondly, it is passive, which means that it is directed for process financing in a small degree considering its effects on research, teaching, and cooperation with the social and economic environment.[24]

On the other hand, it should be noticed that the development of universities in the European Higher Education Area is conditioned by identification and appropriate use of the potential which the universities have.[25] Diversification of Polish universities by varying funding mechanisms currently often forces out the discovery of any competitive advantage or unique resources which often result from geographical location or social and economic development.[26]

New regulations should thus combine the world of higher education and the economy, creating mechanisms that become competitive in international markets due to, for example, the availability of human resources, knowledge (including constant updating, upgrading, and acquiring of new skills), and skills represented by employed graduates (who will be able—by becoming partners with the best and the largest employers—to apply for jobs in positions corresponding to their aspirations), and not—as is the case so far—because of expenses.[27]

Given the above arguments, it should be noted that due to numerous concerns about the new model of the sphere of higher education, it would be desirable—it seems—to be more flexible in this regard, through further public consultation (including meetings of the representatives of the Ministry of Science and Higher Education with the academic and student environment of individual universities, with representatives of science, and with members of organizations representing the academic and student environments), which perhaps would increase the level of real acceptance of the student environment in the legislative solutions introduced here—often innovative (although, finally, quite mitigated), which I would like to highlight again at this point. In particular, the analysis requires the content of certain provisions of a general nature for which a solution—taking into account, nota bene, the specificity of the universities—should have—as it seems—a distinct character.

Finally, it is important to identify—in the light of the subject analyzed in this publication—that the changes always constitute a certain combination. Sometimes, breaking with the future is excessive, and sometimes the future is too strongly nested in a newly emerging reality. Previous experiences in this field indicate that the appropriate balance between what is being liquidated and what is retained has been almost nowhere maintained. Roads are therefore different, and more importantly, can be tortuous. I believe that both the legacy left behind, as well as the simultaneity of a new economic system and democracy, constitutes facilitation, and at the same time a difficulty, in this process. The transformation (as well as joining the European Union), and it is one of its main specificities, is characterized by the presence of both these processes. In fact, transformations do not always produce positive developments; many groups are often harmed because of them, triggering numerous and often violent protests. A well-illustrated example of this phenomenon is a matter considered here.

Consequently, these factors affect the twists and turns of creating a new system and also are analyzed in the field of higher education. However, whether the proposed changes (for example, a second field of studies which is paid; limited multiemployment and prohibition of employment in posts connected with subordinate position of people who are blood-related or have family connections; introduction of the so-called National Qualifications Framework; changes in the scope of college staff) are favorable will be possible to judge only after several years. Currently it is difficult to conclude that following this way will bring either successes or failures, and not just in the sense that there is generally no way back regarding the adopted solutions. The influence of the state is still too large and the future defines it too much. Processes adapted to new conditions of functioning encounter numerous difficulties associated with objective reality and subjective perceptions, which—as one might think—become modern too slowly.

The degree of completeness in this regard is still too indistinct and perhaps will remain so. In addition to the lack of a clear, specific vision of the future model of the sphere of higher education and the consequences of the introduction of often elementary changes in this field, the limiting factor is still the dominant influence of internal problems, as well as the ballast of history affecting the behavior of society. Therefore, it should be noted how individual countries with essentially the same tasks to accomplish implement them in quite different situations (they had and have different conditions conducive to these changes or hindering them). Indeed the past presses heavily on the present and the future. Some states have better, and others much worse, abilities to deal with their situations. In fact, it might be stated that the change in the sphere of higher education is a difficult process to complete, because of political, social, and economic reasons. The change should therefore be kept to a reasonable compromise, but so far such compromise, *purely* practical, lacks any solid conclusions. If, therefore, the situation cannot be better, at least let it be different.

Notes

1. See more regarding this issue in the report *Diagnoza stanu szkolnictwa wyższego w Polsce*, December 2009, http://www.uczelnie2020.pl.

2. The Act of 27 June 2005, Law on Higher Education, *Journal of Laws*, no. 164 (2005), Item 1365.

3. The Act of 14 March 2003, on Academic Degrees and Title and Degrees and Title in Art, *Journal of Laws*, no. 65, Item. 595.

4. Ernst & Young Business Advisory and the Institute for Market Economics, "Strategia rozwoju szkolnictwa wyższego w Polsce do roku 2020," compiled on behalf of the Ministry of Science and Higher Education, p. 28.

5. The Act of 18 March 2011, on the Amendment of the Law on Higher Education, the Act on Academic Degrees and Title and Degrees and Title in Art, on the Amendment of Certain Other Acts, *Journal of Laws* (2011), no. 84, Item 455.

6. See Ministry of Science and Higher Education, *Założenia do nowelizacji ustawy—Prawo o szkolnictwie wyższym oraz ustawy o stopniach naukowych i tytule naukowym oraz o stopniach i tytule w zakresie sztuki*, p. 3, et seq., http://www.nauka.gov.pl/szkolnictwo-wyzsze/reforma-szkolnictwa-wyzszego/. Cf. also the governmental Draft Law on Amending the Law on Higher Education, the Act on Scientific Degrees and Scientific Titles and Degrees and Title in the Field of Art and on the Amendment of Certain Other Acts (print no. 3931).

7. See the Justification for a Government Bill on Amending the Law on Higher Education, the Act on Scientific Degrees and Scientific Titles and Degrees and Title in the Field of Art and on the Amendment of Certain Other Acts.

8. For more regarding this point, see the Justification of the Government Draft of 30 July 2010 on Amending the Law on Higher Education, the Act on Scientific Degrees and Scientific Titles and Degrees and Title in the Field of Art and on the Amendment of Certain Other Acts. Cf. also B. Galwas, "Tendencje rozwojowe współczesnego szkolnictwa wyższego," in *Przyszłość: Świat—Europa—Polska* 15, no. 1 (2007): 63 et seq.; J. Auleytner, expert opinion entitled "Uczelnie przyszłości: Czy w Polsce," prepared for the PAN Committee Polska 2000 Plus [Komitet Prognoz, 2000] at the PAN presidium; and Ernst & Young Business Advisory and Research Institute for Market Economics, "Strategia rozwoju szkolnictwa wyższego w Polsce do roku 2020."

9. Justification for a Government Bill of 30 June 2010 on Amending the Law on Higher Education, the Act on Scientific Degrees and Scientific Titles and Degrees and Title in the Field of Art and on the Amendment of Certain Other Acts.

10. See Ministry of Science and Higher Education, *Założenia do nowelizacji ustawy*, p. 45.

11. See Ministry of Science and Higher Education, *Założenia do nowelizacji ustawy*, pp. 9–17; Justification for the Government Project of 30 July 2010 of the Act on Amending the Law on Higher Education, the Act on Scientific Degrees and Scientific Titles and Degrees and Title in the Field of Art and on the Amendment of Certain Other Acts. Cf. also Galwas, *Tendencje*, p. 63 et seq.; Ernst & Young Business Advisory and the Institute for Market Economics, "Strategia rozwoju szkolnictwa wyższego w Polsce do roku 2020," p. 85 et seq.

12. See Ministry of Science and Higher Education, *Założenia do nowelizacji ustawy*, pp. 21–23; Justification of the Government Project of 30 July 2010 of the Act on Amending the Law on Higher Education, the Act on Scientific Degrees and Scientific Titles and Degrees and Title in the Field of Art and on the Amendment of Certain Other Acts. Cf. also: Ernst & Young Business Advisory and the Institute for Market Economics, "Strategia rozwoju szkolnictwa wyższego w Polsce do roku 2020," p. 89 et seq.

13. See Ministry of Science and Higher Education, *Założenia do nowelizacji ustawy*, p. 57.

14. According to the rankings in *SCImago Journal & Country*, the average number of citations of a scientific paper published by authors affiliated with Polish institutions ranks Poland thirty-eighth in a group of sixty-eight countries annually issuing a minimum of one thousand publications, and only nineteenth among the twenty-two EU countries. See more regarding this issue in Ernst & Young Business Advisory and the Institute for Market Economics, "Strategia rozwoju szkolnictwa wyższego w Polsce do roku 2020," p. 33.

15. The academic promotion path of professionals is described by the international organizations with an English term: *inbreeding*. For more regarding this issue, see Ministry of Science and Higher Education, *Założenia do nowelizacji ustawy*, p. 57. Cf. also Justification for the Government Project of 30 July 2010 of the Act on Amending the Law on Higher Education, the Act on Scientific Degrees and Scientific Titles and Degrees and Title in the Field of Art and on the Amendment of Certain Other Acts; Council of Ministers, draft of 30 July 2010, of the Act on Amending the Law on Higher Education, the Act on Scientific Degrees and Scientific Titles and Degrees and Title in the Field of Art and on the Amendment of Certain Other Acts.

16. Cf. Ernst & Young Business Advisory and the Institute for Market Economics, "Strategia rozwoju szkolnictwa wyższego w Polsce do roku 2020," pp. 91 et seq.; Ministry of Science and Higher Education, *Założenia do nowelizacji ustawy*, p. 57 et seq.

17. It is worth adding that in Poland, the public has limited qualities of perseverance in achieving long-term changes.

18. Regarding this issue, see J. Auleytner, "Uczelnie przyszłości"; Cf. also Ernst & Young Business Advisory and the Institute for Market Economics, "Strategia rozwoju szkolnictwa wyższego w Polsce do roku 2020."

19. Traditional joint management and election model currently dominate in most countries of the former Eastern Bloc (Lithuania, Czech Republic, Hungary, Latvia, Poland, Slovakia and Slovenia).

20. While in the countries of Western Europe (such as Denmark, Austria, Britain, Sweden, the Netherlands, or Ireland)—where the political context is different—more managerial models were introduced in this scope.

21. For more regarding this issue, see *Bank Światowy: Szkolnictwo wyższe w Polsce* (Warsaw, 2004), p. 29: "The management of the higher education sector is rather old-fashioned, and this means that there is a lack of strategic planning, prioritization, creating incentives, or verification of the objectives already established. The most important positions at universities (vice chancellors, deputy vice chancellors, deans) are taken by people with the largest scholarly output or by groups of interests." [Translation.]

Cf. also OECD, *Education Policy Analysis* (Paris, 2003), p. 75: "Higher education management in the twenty-first century requires a combination of the academic mission with management abilities, and not a replacement of one element by the second one."

22. See *Bank Światowy*, p. 34: "Mostly, Polish universities do not focus their attention on the needs of enterprises supplying advanced technologies or on the needs of society. There is also a lack of links (e.g., contracts or joint research, the exchange of personnel, the exchange of patents, licensing of technology, or purchase/sharing hardware) between universities and the business environment as well as the industrial sector."

23. Currently, the Polish system of higher education, largely operating within this specific isolation from the external environment is focused mainly on theoretical education (this creates the phenomenon called "overeducation"), which is not always adequate to the needs of practice, particularly with regard to the content of the curriculum, which significantly undermines education in general. See also *Bank Światowy*, p. 34: "Generally, in Poland there is no concept of participation of stakeholders, i.e., the universities, local communities, and the business community in the management of higher educational institutions."

24. For more regarding this issue, see Ministry of Science and Higher Education, *Założenia do nowelizacji ustawy*, p. 26.

25. Cf. Ernst & Young Business Advisory and the Institute for Market Economics, "Strategia rozwoju szkolnictwa wyższego w Polsce do roku 2020," p. 15 et seq.

26. Cf. Ministry of Science and Higher Education, *Założenia do nowelizacji ustawy*, p. 77; Justification of the Government Proposal of 30 July 2010 of the Act on Amending the Law on Higher Education, the Act on Scientific Degrees and Scientific Titles and Degrees and Title in the Field of Art and on Amendment of Certain Other Acts.

27. Regarding this issue, cf. "Oczekiwanie pracodawców wobec absolwentów szkół wyższych" *Perspektywy 2009*.

THE LEGAL STATUS OF CONTEMPORARY STUDENTS IN THE REPUBLIC OF POLAND

ELŻBIETA WITUSKA

In the available literature, the importance of quality and substance of knowledge and intellectual capital, which as early as the turn of the twentieth century had begun to appear as a major growth factor and a fundamental determinant of changes in the global economy, as well as a significant source of nations' wealth as embodied either by new information technologies, or biotechnology and other innovations, has been permanently raised today. Moreover, there is also an emphasis on the idea that with the growing importance of knowledge, the demand for higher education also increases, which is more desirable for an increasing proportion of the younger generation.[1] Nevertheless, with the rapid increase in the availability and mass nature of higher education's development, the quality of education at this level has significantly deteriorated and become a critical factor in lowering the competitive position of individual nations, including Poland. Therefore, the popularity of university and college study and the development of the higher education system through specific supply and demand has been observed in Poland, which has resulted in the necessity to develop strategic goals and development visions that translate to creating a strategy for an effective higher education system, targeted not only at the needs of the labor market,[2] but also characterized by very high quality, as well as being as one of the leading strategies for national development,[3] in which students also see an opportunity for development.[4]

This article was prepared in parallel with several years' legislative process toward creating a multidimensional reform of higher education in Poland. This resulted, therefore, in a need to explore not only systemic higher education changes, but primarily in an attempt to identify the legal status in Poland of the contemporary student, whose rights and obligations are formed out of the specific legal situation, conditioned by the forthcoming entry into force of new, relevant legal regulations in that regard. Therefore, the aim of this essay is to illustrate not only current legislation relating to the legal situation of students, by establishing their legal relationship with their higher educational institutions, but also an explanation of this relationship's character, which is also necessary, as well as its consequences in terms of the substantive legal reforms of the higher education system.

The Process of Legislative Changes in Higher Education in Poland in Recent Years

As a result of the Republic of Poland's transformation in the 1990s, higher educational institutions faced new challenges and needed to create a market for educational services for potential students that had a revised legal status as well as various other academic qualities. Also, an important role in this respect began to be played by nonpublic schools, which by becoming an increasingly important component of the higher education system broke the former state monopoly, both in providing educational services and developing the higher education system in Poland.[5]

After fifty-seven years, the Act of 12 September 1990 on a wide range of higher educational institution autonomic and academic freedoms was restored, which was also a manifestation of the emerging democratic state.[6] It allowed for the gradual creation of a model system of higher education in parallel with the ongoing political, economic, and social changes in Poland, as well as involvement in the Bologna Process and Poland's seeking of its own place in the European Higher Education Area.[7] The entry into force of the above act of 1990 resulted in an unexpected rise in enrollment rates at the higher education level, and thus an impulsive quantitative increase in the number of higher educational institutions, especially private ones, not necessarily supported by proper development of qualitative changes and uniformity of laws,[8] which led to the inevitability of further work being put in on the next Act on Higher Education.

This phase was completed with the entry into force on 1 September 2005 (with the exception of certain regulations), of the provisions of the Act of 27 July 2005 Law on Higher Education,[9] which repealed the provisions of the Act of 31 March 1965, on Military Higher Education,[10] the Act of 12 September 1990 on Higher Education[11] and the Law of 26 June 1997 on Higher Vocational Schools.[12] The Law on Higher Education[13] was passed by the Parliament of the Republic of Poland as a result of a legislative initiative by the RP president, which was presented to the Sejm in the spring of 2004. A draft of the act was developed on the initiative of the Conference of Rectors of Polish Academic Schools by a team of experts, established by and operating in the Presidential Chancellery of the Republic of Poland. Although the introduced legislation created a number of dilemmas both in the context of the evolutionary concept of higher education and at the RP educational policy level, and in the light of EU integration,[14] the implemented changes were evidence of the fact that legal regulation concerning the matter of higher education is extremely dynamic and requires systematization and adaptation to the ever-changing sociocultural and economic conditions as well as changing political systems. One of the aims of this legislation was an attempt to organize and gather solutions related to the functioning of higher education in Poland in a single legal act,[15] and was primarily an expression of the need for transformation of quantitative changes into qualitative changes.[16]

However, more and more new challenges and tasks were imposed on Polish higher education by the global education market, the demand for modern education focused on the future, innovation, and progressivism,[17] as well as the development of the European "knowledge society." All these factors forced the need to take further measures to reform higher education in Poland. Two important aspects coincided with the need for these changes: Polish membership in the European Union, which supports and complements the activities of member states to contribute to an increase of the education level by generating European added value resulting from international cooperation,[18] and also the need to adapt Polish higher education to the foundations resulting from the Bologna Declaration signed on 19 June 1999,[19] the main goal of which was to create a unified, completely modernized European Higher Education Area (known in Poland as Europejska Przestrzeń Szkolnictwa Wyższego) by 2010.[20] Work on the strategic documents for research and higher education was included in the "Plan for the National Development Strategy," that the Council of Ministers adopted on 24 November 2009. Within the next few months a Long-Term National Development Strategy was created, along with nine integrated strategies, which replaced the forty-two existing sectoral strategies and development policy. This synergistic and supraministerial approach, coordinated by the Coordinating Committee for Development Policy in the Chancellery of the Prime Minister, was designed to ensure consistent and systematic action in key areas for national development. In order to effectively carry out public policy by Poland in the field of higher education, it was necessary to clarify both medium and long-term objectives, which would set the direction for the modernization process. The lack of development goals for higher education in Poland had also been noted in the OECD Report of 2007.[21] On 30 March 2010, a draft amendment to the Law on Higher Education and Act on Academic Degrees and Academic Titles, covering degrees and titles in articles adopted the year before by the Council of Ministers, was presented for wider public consultation, which ended in June of that year. The project had taken into account, for example, more autonomy for higher educational institutions, greater financial and system support for the best higher educational institutions, researchers, and students, as well as an aversion to favoritism in higher education. On 4 August 2010 the above project of the act prepared by the Ministry of Science and Higher Education was sent for consideration to the Standing Committee of the Council of Ministers, which adopted it by 1 September 2010. As a result, it was approved by the Council of Ministers a few days later. Then, on 6 October 2010, during a plenary meeting of the Sejm of the Republic of Poland, the government project of this act was read for the first time. At that point, the Minister of Science and Higher Education highlighted the need to reform the higher education system in Poland, by quoting the governmental proposal and stressing at the same time the "pro-qualitative nature of the proposed changes resulting from the need to adapt the Polish higher education system to an unprecedented increase in the range of tasks that it was facing, as well as the need to harmonize the system with solutions implemented in the European Higher Education Area."[22] On 9 November 2010, in the Sejm of the Republic of Poland, a public hearing was held on a governmental act amending the existing legislation, which was initiated by the Parliamentary Commission for Education, Science, and Youth. Participants in the hearing included, among others, representatives of the Central Commission for Academic Degrees and Titles, the Council for Higher Education, the National Accreditation Commission, the Council of Young Scientists, the Student Parliament of the Republic of Poland, the National Council for Doctoral Students, the National Academy of Sciences Section of the Solidarity Trade Union, the Conference of Rectors of Academic Schools in Poland, the Conference of Rectors of Public Vocational Schools, and the Conference of Rectors of Vocational Polish Schools. Also, the Undersecretary of State at the Ministry of Science and Higher Education was listening to the speeches. After completing the public hearing procedure, the draft was sent for work to the permanent Subcommittee on Science and Higher Education of the Sejm, which met six times, and then, on 4 January 2011, adopted a report on the work on the project. The project then went back into the deliberations of the Committee for Education, Science, and Youth of the Sejm and was approved by it on 19 January 2011, by taking into account the minority's amendments and proposals. This complex legislative process was finalized on 18 March 2011, when the Sejm, after the Senate work on the project, accepted the revised Law on Higher Education and Act on Academic Degrees and Academic Title and Degrees and Title in the Arts.[23] After the president's signature, crowning three years of work on the reform of higher education, new legislation in this field will come into force (with some exceptions) on 1 October 2011. The Ministry of Science and Higher Education emphasizes that the new law is designed primarily to affect not only a new quality of teaching and combining of the academic world with the labor market, but above all, to exert a significant influence on students' legal status, as they are seen as the most important beneficiaries of this reform. The act is in fact intended to create new, better conditions and opportunities for students and young scholars.[24]

Undergraduate and Graduate Students as Members of a Public-Law Corporation

Although in the light of traditional postwar theories of administrative law a higher educational institutions were recognized as administrative or public facilities,[25] the latest doctrine[26] inclines to classifying them as public-law corporations,[27] mainly because of the latest scholarly achievements of E. Ochendowski, which deal precisely with the problems of higher education.[28] Moreover, the argument for higher educational institutions' recognition as public-law corporations is not only that they perform the kinds of public administration tasks credited to these types of entities,[29] but also because of the legal status of higher educational institution staff, students, and doctoral students. This idea provides the opportunity for these entities to manage higher educational institutions and allows for selection of their authorities, which further allows recognition of academic staff, students, and doctoral students as a specific personal substrate of a higher educational institution, which also has a decisive influence on the basis of its actions.[30]

Consequently, academics and other higher educational institution staff who are not academic teachers (inner core), as well as undergraduate and graduate students (outer core)[31] should be regarded as members of public-law corporations entitled to a number of rights in the management of their higher educational institution.[32] On the other hand, it is also thought that the participants of undergraduate and postgraduate courses should be treated differently, as these entities do not have the status of public-law corporation members, and their status is only *similar* to that of a user of an administration facility or public establishment.[33] This follows from the fact that these people do not have an impact on managing their higher educational institution, and their roles are limited to the use of benefits or services offered by their higher educational institutions.

Given the factual framework of this essay and the fact that higher education activity is aimed mainly at the education of undergraduate and graduate students who form the fundamental member group of a corporation, I would like to refer only to the legal status of these entities.

In accordance with current law and following a three-leveled education path,[34] these entities include students of: 1) first-degree study (leading to a bachelor's degree or professional title of Engineer),[35] 2) second-degree study or uniform master's degree study[36] (leading to a professional title of MA or equivalent title),[37] 3) third-degree study, or so-called doctoral study[38] (leading to a doctoral degree).[39]

It is worth mentioning here, after Ł. Błąd, that although in the legal definition of "uniform master's degree studies," the Polish legislature until now has clearly indicated that completion of such study entitles one to apply for admission to third-degree study, it has not mentioned this in relation to other types of studies,[40] On the other hand, this issue was regulated in the amendment of this act,[41] because it clearly points to the fact that the qualifications obtained at a given level of study entitle one to apply for admission to the next study level.[42] However, the legislature does not include any more detailed nomenclature which precisely defines the types of acquired qualification at different stages of education (professional title of bachelor, engineer, master or equivalent degree, or PhD). Within current legal definitions, only terms such as "qualifications of the first, second and third degree" exist, which are vastly insufficient and can only be understood after looking at the legal definitions of these terms.[43] Such a legal solution introduces unwanted chaos and unnecessary detailing of so-far obvious terms.

In accordance with Article 163 and Article 195.4 in relation to Article 2.1 Points 12–13 of the Law on Higher Education,[44] and in consideration of the amendment of the act,[45] studies at each level can be conducted full-time or part-time. Students may also study according to individual study plans and curriculums.[46] Nevertheless, there is an emphasis in the literature that, in principle, the type of study cannot affect the position of an undergraduate or graduate student as a member of the public-law corporation.[47]

As a result of the Bologna Process, the duration of study at different levels of academic education was standardized in Poland, which affects the time a member belongs to the public-law corporation. So far, first-degree study should last six to eight semesters, with engineering degrees lasting seven to eight semesters.[48] Second degree study lasts three or four semesters,[49] and the uniform master's degree about nine to twelve semesters.[50] The legislature also pointed out that part-time study may take one or two semesters longer than the corresponding full-time studies in the same faculty.[51] It should also be noted that if the educational standards provide for a professional internship of first-degree students, then the period of these studies may be extended by their duration—although the senate of the higher educational institution may determine the conditions for releasing students from the requirement to perform such internships.[52] However, the new provisions state that the first-degree study should last at least six semesters, and the engineering at least seven semesters, without defining more precisely their upper duration limit.[53] In addition to the duration of first-degree study and uniform master's degree study, professional internships are also included.[54] The time frames for the duration of studies shall be from the date of acceptance of members of the public-law corporation until the date of their graduation.

Following this principle, and in accordance with current regulations and their amendments, lectures in higher educational institutions at the first- and second-study levels are open, unless the statute of the higher educational institution states otherwise.[55] Classes may be conducted in the form of language courses, classes, conservatories, lectures, and in the form of classes using the methods and techniques of distance learning through the use of computer technology,[56] as well as opportunities based on use of the Internet, which significantly expands access to this type of teaching to a wider range of graduate and undergraduate students.[57] The doctrine also raises the point that, "due to the lack of detailed regulations for studies which are partially based on learning via the Internet, e-studies must meet all requirements governing the class conducted using traditional methods. Thus, they correspond to part-time studies or extramural studies, and students have the same rights and responsibilities as students of other modes of education."[58]

Currently valid regulations of the Law on Higher Education also permit conduct of classes at higher education facilities, as well as tests of knowledge or skills, or diploma examinations in a foreign language. Still, the details of such activities must be defined more closely in the study regulations,[59] and additionally Polish language courses for foreigners should be made available.[60]

Although a provision of Article 70.2 of the Constitution of the Republic of Poland clearly indicates the constitutionally guaranteed right to free education in public higher educational institutions,[61] at the same time the basic law permits that the current act allows for the provision of certain educational services by public higher educational institutions for a fee.[62] This, however, does not equate to recognition of public higher educational institutions as entrepreneurs in the strict sense, with those receiving the education being consumers of educational services.[63]

While the need for a tuition fee in the case of nonpublic higher educational institutions does not raise any doubts,[64] the adopted regulations of public higher educational institutions have raised many controversies.[65] The first disputes in this regard have already appeared about the existing (at the time) provision in article 23.2.2 of the Act on Higher Education,[66] on the basis of which a constitutional complaint was made. In this case, the Constitutional Tribunal of the Republic of Poland took a position allowing for payment for classes in public higher educational institutions,[67] with the case law designating some standards relating to this issue. Therefore, the Law on Higher Education allows for the collection of fees from undergraduate and graduate students in public higher educational institutions for the provision of educational services related to 1) education of undergraduate and graduate students on a part-time study basis, 2) re-takes of certain classes of full-time studies due to unsatisfactory academic performance, 3) conduct of studies in a foreign language, 4) carrying out of activities not covered in the curriculum, 5) conduct of post-graduate studies and retraining courses.[68] At the same time it should be noted that the amount of such fees shall be fixed by the rector of the public higher educational institution, and may not exceed the actual costs necessary to initiate and conduct the undergraduate or graduate studies (taking into account depreciation and hard maintenance costs).[69] The terms of the tuition fees are determined by written civil-law contracts conducted between the higher educational institution and the undergraduate or graduate student.[70] This type of contract acts as a kind of guarantee that the specified entities will receive good quality educational services in exchange for paid tuition fees, while providing legal protection to students of private and public higher educational institutions. However, this does not mean that agreements don't sometimes contain clauses and phrases which are inconsistent with the provisions of the law.

Even more controversial in the analyzed issue are concerns resulting from the legislative solution adopted by the Polish legislature in the amendment to the law. These further restrict the constitutional right to free public higher education in Poland, and are already raised in the doctrine as a negative solution interfering with the rights of undergraduate and graduate students.

This amendment anticipates the framework of legal standards contained in Article 99.1. It extends the standard disposition in relation to the already cited possibility of collecting higher fees by public higher educational institutions for the provision of educational services related to the education of full-time students, if they are in their second or subsequent majors on a full-time basis,[71] in cases where they are taking extra classes outside the ECTS[72] credits limit that are assigned to a student after completing a course or educational program.[73] This is because, according to Article 170a of the amended act, full-time students in public higher education have the right to take classes without paying fees only when they acquire the following number of ECTS credits:[74] 1) student of first-degree study—at least 180 ECTS credits to receive a diploma, 2) student of second-degree study—at least 90 credits to receive a diploma, 3) student of a uniform master's degree study—at least 300 ECTS credits to receive a diploma in a five-year study system and 360 ECTS credits for a diploma in the six-year study system.[75] Apart from the designated credit limit, the same students have the same right to attend classes free of charge at a particular level of study, for which they can obtain an allowance of 30 or 90 ECTS credits for pursuing an education within individual inter-area studies.[76] At the same time, with the reservation that public higher educational institutions may not charge fees related to full-time students' education who, after completion of first-degree study, continue studying a full-time second-degree study in order to obtain a professional title of master or equivalent,[77] as well as students or graduates of the first full-time major who can take up studies free of charge at their next major,[78] because they received a scholarship for the best students from the rector of their higher educational institution.[79] While the exemption of such fees is a one-off authorization and their rector made the decision on awarding such an authorization,[80] students should make an appropriate statement on their application, which is evaluated by the head of the basic organizational unit,[81] to which the candidate should also submit an appropriate statement.[82] Neither are fees collected for academic education from students studying subjects related to artistic disciplines, which, because of their specificity and the level of required knowledge and skills obtained from an earlier completion of second-degree study can be studied on a full-time basis in a public higher educational institution at a second department without paying fees.[83] Students will also not incur registration charges for the next semester or year of study by virtue of exams, including re-sit exams, exams conducted before an examination board, or diploma exams, and also for the issuance of an internship log, submission and evaluation of a diploma thesis, or the issuance of a diploma supplement.[84]

The entries to new regulatory rights mentioned above refer to the introduction of payments for the use of academic learning opportunities for full-time students and, on the one hand, are seen in the literature as an opportunity to balance access to studies to the first and second majors and ensure guaranteed state funding of the second major only for the best students. This will provide not only an opportunity to study for a larger number of candidates, especially from poorer areas and small towns, but will also eliminate the problem of places being taken in the various fields of study by students who do not study hard enough, or do not discharge their duties properly, because the reason for their studying is just to obtain a diploma and not for the pursuit of knowledge itself. On the other hand, the restrictions introduced are seen as a violation of the right to free education, already quoted here, within full-time study which had been absolutely free so far.[85]

Establishing a Corporate Relationship by Undergraduate and Graduate Students

Although in the doctrine of Polish administrative law there were disputes over the legal nature of combining administrative or public-establishment administration with its users,[86] from the point of view of the adopted position defining a higher educational institution as a public-law corporation, and undergraduate and graduate students as members of the above corporation, it seems more appropriate to quote the position of P. Przybysz.[87] The adoption of his views allows us to see the comprehensive position of corporate members, both in respect of the administrative and legal relationship determined by public law enforcement, and in light of the possibility of application by the authorities of higher educational institutions of both public and private forms of activities under civil law against these entities, which is confirmed by the previously mentioned Article 160.3 Law on Higher Education.[88] According to this law, tuition fee conditions are determined by the written civil-law contract concluded between the higher educational institution and undergraduate or graduate student.

One of the groups of so-called second generation of human rights is the constitutionally guaranteed right to education,[89] related to access to higher education and the possibility to obtain education at an academic level, which is seen as a primary legal provision allowing for the voluntary legal relationship between an undergraduate or graduate student and a higher educational institution.[90] Currently, this right was regulated by Article 70.1 of the Constitution of the RP.[91] It states that everyone has the right to an education, which means that not only are citizens of the Republic of Poland entitled, but everyone residing on its territory.[92] This is because under current law, foreigners can also study or use other forms of education conducted by higher educational institutions—on the same terms as Polish citizens—if they meet certain conditions.[93] Other foreigners can conduct studies and participate in scholarly research and training only based on certain international agreements, civil law agreements, or the decisions of specified authorities, which the legislature expressly enumerated in Article 43.3 of this act.[94]

Nevertheless, it should be noted that the right to education in relation to higher education does not constitute an automatic scheme that requires absolute acceptance of anyone as a member of a higher educational institution. Under existing law there are two basic criteria for admission: the substantive and the procedural.[95]

Among the mandatory substantive criteria that must be met by each candidate, the literature primarily indicates conditions that have to be met in order to apply for admission to a higher educational institution.[96] A natural person holding a high school diploma *(matura)*[97] and fulfilling the conditions laid down by a higher educational institution's recruitment process,[98] may become a student of first-degree study or the uniform master's degree, while a natural person holding a professional title of master, bachelor, engineer, or the equivalent, and meeting the admission criteria established by the higher educational institution,[99] may become a student of second-degree study. To study at the third-degree study (PhD) level, a natural person who holds a master's degree or equivalent and meets the admission criteria set by a higher educational institution may be permitted.[100]

Results of the matriculation examination or equivalent as recognized,[101] and an exam conducted under the International Baccalaureate Diploma Program,[102] are the bases for admission to first-degree study or uniform master's degrees.

The second set of criteria includes the formal conditions to be met by the prospective undergraduate or graduate student. The senate of the higher educational institution is entitled to its own determination, and first determines what results of the matriculation examination are to be the basis for admission to its uniform master's degree and first-degree study programs. According to the case law, this does not violate the principle of equal treatment of candidates.[103] Secondly, the senate shall determine the general conditions and procedures of recruitment and the form of the uniform master's degree and first-to-third-degree studies in each of its departments, and this resolution shall be made public not later than 31 May of the year preceding the academic year of which the resolution is concerned.[104] In relation to doctoral studies, the senate's or the academic unit's scientific council resolution should be made public no later than 30 April of the calendar year in which the academic year begins, of which the resolution is concerned.[105] In the cases of police, military, and other academies for training of national and state services, the conditions and procedures for admission of candidates for professional soldiers and state officers are established, upon the senate's proposal,[106] by the Minister of National Defense[107] or the minister for internal affairs,[108] respectively. The responsibility of the indicated ministers is related to the type of higher educational institutions over which they exercise supervision. The admission conditions to those types of higher educational institutions are similar to the above-mentioned senate resolutions; they do not constitute acts of the current law, only specifically designate admission conditions for students as members of the public-law corporation and should comply with applicable law.[109] The senate is also empowered to issue a resolution setting out detailed rules for the admission to uniform master's degree study and first-degree study in public higher educational institutions of the winners and finalists at the central-level contests for at least three years,[110] because this is a duration of a series of school contests in a subject that a candidate can participate in.

A unique situation is that the formal recruitment conditions on uniform master's degree study, or first-to-third-degree study may provide an optional opportunity to carry out additional entrance exams by higher educational institution with the approval of the minister responsible for higher education, expressed as an administrative decision. At the same time, the conduct of entrance exams can take place purely and simply in cases enumerated in the provisions of the act, i.e., when it is necessary to test knowledge or skills not verified during their *matura* examination (final high school graduation exams), or when an applicant applying for an admission has a diploma obtained abroad, or when the bases for admission are the results of their *matura* exams.[111]

Formal conditions also include issues related to the deadline and submission mode of properly completed applications for admission for any type of study by a candidate seeking to become a member of a public-law corporation. Enrollment in the form of consideration of the above applications is carried out by enrollment committees, appointed by the head of a basic organizational unit or other authority specified in the statute of the higher educational institution.[112] These committees issue administrative decisions in cases of acceptance or refusal of admission of candidates.[113] The results of the recruitment procedure are public,[114] which gives full transparency to admissions. In cases of admission refusal by the enrollment committee, an undergraduate or graduate student may appeal to the higher educational institution's enrollment committee within fourteen days from the date of notification of the decision.[115] The basis for an appeal can only be an indication of a breach of the terms and procedure for admissions.[116] However, the enrollment committee is not a competent authority for determination of the appeal. The decision on the appeal is made by the rector, after reviewing the judgment of the higher educational institution's enrollment committee in this regard. The rector's decision is final,[117] and subject to review by an administrative court.[118] The aim is to control verification of this decision by the supervisory authority, which is a barrier protecting the right of a candidate applying to become a member of a higher educational institution.

The amended provisions of this act in terms of the above-presented issues do not bring any significant changes, except to emphasize that the enrollment conditions and procedures, which are set by the higher educational institution's senate, should be formulated by considering the special needs of disabled persons,[119] and the actual recruitment may also be carried out electronically.[120] In the case of free doctoral study (full-time study), enrollment is conducted through a competition.[121] Moreover, the authority empowered to issue decisions on admission is still the enrollment committee,[122] except where access to study is free and the enrollment committee is not required. In that case, the head of a basic organizational unit or other authority specified in the statute takes responsibility.[123] Also—and this is an additional entry and valid as well as the previous one—candidates are entitled to appeal the head's decisions or the decision of another authority specified in the statute regarding admission refusal.[124] Since 1 October 2011, after consideration of an appeal in relation to the decision of the enrollment committee, a decision will be made by the same enrollment committee of the higher educational institution, and in the event of an appeal against a head of the basic organizational unit's decision or the decision of another designated authority in the statute, the final decision is made by the rector and only his decision is defined as final.[125]

I think that the above-mentioned regulation may raise serious doubts because, on the one hand, it destroys the principle of appealing to the competent authority of a higher degree through the authority that issued the decision,[126] which guarantees the objectivity needed to issue a supervising authority's resolution on the subject. On the other hand, it is inconsistent to clarify the last resort only with reference to supervising authority's resolution issued by the rector of the higher educational institution.

Rights and Obligations of Members of Public-Law Corporations

The legislature clearly indicates that a person admitted to study at any level acquires the rights of a student upon matriculation and the taking of an oath, the content of which is defined in the statute of the higher educational institution or scholarly unit he or she is attending,[127] and the student's rights and obligations as defined by the regulations of study.[128]

New provisions for this statement only add student entitlements on every level for the right of training in the scope of the rights and responsibilities of the student who goes on to lead the Students' Parliament of the Republic of Poland, in consultation with a student government of individual higher educational institutions.[129]

The basic undergraduate and graduate students' rights include, in particular, the entitlements which I've already enumerated, entitlements related to the right to study at an academic level and entitlements associated with establishing a corporate relationship at every level with a higher educational institution, including a controversial new entitlement to free higher education in selected aspects.

In addition, students have the right to transfer from one higher educational institution to another and the right to transfer and have recognition of the credits earned by them in the organizational unit of their home higher educational institution or other educational institution,[130] including a foreign one,[131] after completing all obligations under the regulations in force in the higher educational institution left by the student and in accordance with the principles of achievement transmission system.[132] The reference literature points to a number of benefits for a student resulting from this entitlement.[133] The importance of the diploma supplement is highlighted, which provides evidence of student achievement reached in the previous institution.[134]

Under current law, students at every level are entitled to dean's leave from classes in higher educational institutions, based on the principles and procedures specified in the study regulations, and what is important to note here is that, during the use of such leave, the student retains his or her student rights,[135] unless the higher educational institution's regulations or rules on financial aid state mandate otherwise.[136] In addition, it is stressed that doctoral students have the right take a rest break for a period of not more than eight weeks a year, during which there should be no classes.[137]

In relation to third-degree students, the legislature clearly specifies that they are fully entitled to social security and general health insurance on the principles defined in separate provisions, and it is also emphasized that post-doctoral students have the length of their doctoral studies' duration included in their work duration (no more than four years), including full-time doctoral study, dropped upon taking up employment as an educator or research fellow in scholarly institutions.[138] This is important in terms of employee rights.

Students of every level are also entitled to join student governments and student organizations,[139] which significantly interact and participate in the management of their higher educational institutions, and which also supports the thesis identifying the higher educationl institution as a public-law corporation. Student government bodies, created by students of first- and second-degree study and uniform master's degree study, are their exclusive representative in higher educational institutions and outside them.[140] Both undergraduate and graduate student governments operate under the provisions of the current act, and based on regulations adopted by an institution's legislative body of student government,[141] which are entered into force after confirmation of its compliance with the law and the statutes of the higher educational institution by the higher educational institution's senate. The first regulations of undergraduate and graduate student government of a newly created higher educational institution are adopted by a senate at the request of the Students' Parliament of the Republic of Poland or the National Representation of Doctoral Candidates.[142] These regulations form a fundamental document setting out the framework for undergraduate and graduate student governments' functioning, which operate on campus and conduct activities related to student affairs, including sociocultural and living conditions.[143] In particular, the undergraduate and graduate student governments decide on the distribution of funds allocated by their higher educational institutions for student purposes.[144] Rectors of higher educational institutions have the right to revoke resolutions of the student government body that are incompatible with the law, higher educational institution statutes or regulations, or undergraduate or graduate student government regulations.[145] Representatives of all the Polish higher educational institutions (both public and private) of student governments form the Students' Parliament of the Republic of Poland, which is the only institution empowered to represent all students in the country.[146] Doctoral student government is entitled to similar rights and can form the National Representation of Doctoral Candidates.[147] The highest authority of the Students' Parliament of Republic of Poland[148] and the National Representation of Doctoral Candidates[149] is the Convention of Delegates representing undergraduate and graduate student governments, which has adopted a statute defining the rules of organization and procedure of the Students' Parliament of the Republic of Poland and the National Representation of Doctoral Candidates, including the types of bodies and procedures for their appointment as well as competence. Their statute shall enter into force once its compliance with the law has been confirmed by the minister responsible for higher education.[150] Both the Students' Parliament of the Republic of Poland and the National Representation of Doctoral Candidates have the right to express opinions and present proposals in matters relating to all undergraduate and graduate students, including giving opinions on normative acts concerning those entities. Projects of such normative acts shall be submitted by the minister responsible for higher education to representatives of undergraduate and graduate students, and the deadline to express such an opinion comes to an end in a month from the date of submission of a normative act.[151] Moreover, under applicable law, both undergraduate and graduate students also have the right to associated higher educational institutions' student organizations, in particular, scholarly clubs, artistic groups, and sports teams. These associations are entitled to apply to higher educational institution authorities or undergraduate or graduate student government bodies in matters concerning higher educational institution students.[152] It is also worth noting that undergraduate and graduate student government, including the Students' Parliament of the Republic of Poland and National Representation of Doctoral Candidates as well as a national association affiliating only undergraduate or graduate students, can support their claims regarding important students' issues or interests or take the form of a protest (student strike), without violating current provisions.[153]

According to Article 207.1 of the Law on Higher Education[154] the appropriate provisions of the Act of 14 June 1960, Code of Administrative Proceeding,[155] and provisions on legal actions against an enrollment committee's decision in an administrative court[156] should apply regarding acceptance or refusal of a candidate to a specific academic department (as already mentioned), as well as in relation to the committee for students grants' decisions or decisions taken by higher educational institution authorities, the head of doctoral study, or the director of a scientific unit in individual undergraduate or graduate students' matters, in supervising matters over the activities of a higher educational institution's student organizations and undergraduate and graduate student government. This provision indicates the need to emphasize the administrative and legal aspects of the relationship between undergraduate and graduate student and the higher educational institution as a public-law corporation.

The amended provisions of the Law on Higher Education here introduce the obligation to prepare and promote a student ethics code by the higher educational institution's undergradatue and graduate student governments.[157] Above all, they make the Students' Parliament of the Republic of Poland and the National Representation of Doctoral Candidates legal entities[158] and dictate applying the provisions of Articles 10.1 and 2,[159] Article 11,[160] Article 25,[161] Article 29,[162] and Articles 33–35[163] of the Act of 7 April 1989 Law on Associations in relation to these entities,[164] which is an equivalent to a regulation granting even greater powers to the indicated entities, arising from the opportunity to be a private law entity and acting on one's own behalf.[165]

It is worth mentioning that the contemporary literature on the subject in the new regulatory entries cited above see the development of undergraduate and graduate student governance as a great opportunity for civil society development and a specific incubator of eminent personalities, who in later life may become devoted citizens, fulfilled businesspeople, good organizers, leaders, and members of local governments.[166] However, the authors see a certain pathological danger of an unworthy and misused energy uptake of active entities involved in the activities of analyzed subjects. It is emphasized that in the new legal situation, where student governments are provided with substantial powers and can use the entries quoted here of the Act on Associations and have a lot of opportunities for profitable activities (e.g., photocopying points, Internet cafes, sponsorship agreements, etc.), there may be opportunities for financial fraud. Moreover, local governments were given significant opportunity to use and obtain EU subsidies, which may also lead to a disgraceful abuse. However, it must be acknowledged that such situations can only occur in isolated and in sporadic cases in the absence of adequate supervision from the higher educational institution, as well as in corrupt situations or by the indifference of local government initiatives.[167]

As a result of the commodification of educational services and the introduction of payments for receiving an academic education, serious problems of the scholarship system for undergraduate and graduate students were revealed as well as a natural desire of students of nonpublic higher educational institutions and part-time students of public higher educational institutions to obtain the appropriate scholarship entitlements because nowadays the scholarship system is the most important and the most comprehensive category of undergraduate and graduate students' rights, and the lack of previous regulations in this regard was the source of a sense of injustice and discrimination. Based on current legal provisions, both full-time and part-time students of the public and private sector have been appropriately equated for purposes of collecting different kinds of scholarships, which the Polish legislature has normalized to some degree.

A student of the uniform master's degree program and first-to-second-degree studies may apply for financial support from the funds allocated for this purpose in the state budget in the form of 1) a social scholarship, 2) a social scholarship for the disabled, 3) a scholarship for academic performance or sport, 4) a minister's scholarship for achievements in academics or athletics, 5) a food allowance, 6) a housing scholarship, or 7) relief.[168] However, a student of third-degree study (PhD student) may receive a much more limited pecuniary assistance in the form of 1) social scholarships, 2) social scholarships for the disabled, 3) a scholarship for academic performance, 4) a food allowance, 5) a housing scholarship, and 6) relief.[169] Additionally, students— except for doctoral students—may apply for accommodation in the higher educational institution's dormitory or for board in the student canteen, as well as accommodation for a student's spouse and child in a higher educational institution's dormitory.[170]

Until now an undergraduate or graduate student in a difficult financial situation was entitled to receive a social scholarship,[171] food,[172] and housing scholarship.[173] The last two types of scholarship have been isolated from the social scholarship because of the variety of life situations and disproportionate hierarchy of students' needs. However, they are conditioned from it, because granting a social scholarship is a condition for the granting of housing and board allowance.[174] A full-time undergraduate or graduate student may receive a housing scholarship with accommodation in a dormitory or in a facility other than dormitory, if his or her daily journey from his/her place of permanent residence[175] to the higher educational institution would prevent or significantly interfere with his/her studies.[176] In addition, such an undergraduate or graduate student can receive the specified provision for residence of a nonemployed spouse or child in a dormitory or other building.[177] A determinant conditioning the granting of the above benefits is the amount of net income obtained for the previous calendar year, per person in the student's family. The rector of the higher educational institution determines this amount, in consultation with the school's undergraduate or graduate student government body.[178] In accordance with Article 179 Law on Higher Education,[179] the amount of income referred to may not be less than the amount indicated in Article 8.1.2 of the Act of 12 March 2004 on social scholarship,[180] and greater than the sum of the amounts referred to in Article 5.1 and Article 6.2.3 of the Act of 28 November 2003 on family benefits.[181] At the same time when determining this income, the rector should take into account incomes obtained by 1) an undergraduate or graduate student; 2) the undergraduate or graduate student's spouse and underage children receiving education up to age of twenty-six, and children with disabilities regardless of age, maintained by the undergraduate or graduate student and his/her spouse; 3) parents, legal guardians, or the actual undergraduate or graduate student and their siblings until twenty-six years of age or any age for students with disabilities.[182] If a student (first–third-degree studies), or his/her spouse, at the end of the tax year had a regular source of income and monthly income that was not less than the minimum salary, s/he is considered to be a financially independent person;[183] and then in income calculation and at the same time if there is no statement that s/he maintains domestic dependency, income earned by the student's parents[184] is not included. However, if for calculation of qualifying income of an undergraduate or graduate student entitled to apply for social scholarship or scholarship for food and housing, income from a farm is used, this income is determined by the area of agricultural land in conversion to hectares and the average amount of income from work in private farms of 1 calculated hectare, as published under Article 18 of the Act of 15 November 1984, on agricultural tax.[185] In the case of earning an income from farm and non-farm sources, this revenue is added up.[186]

From 1 October 2011, as a result of amendments to the act, on the one hand, the letter of the law will highlight even further the integrity and mutual dependence of benefits of a social nature, and on the other, student rights in respect to social benefits allocated to date will be deducted from the food allowance because in the new legal regulation, the legislature adopted only the term "social scholarship,"[187] which can only be increased by an amount in respect of residence in a dormitory or other place,[188] which is identical with the housing scholarship. The new version of the provision's entries regarding board scholarship is clearly omitted. However, the procedure for calculating the amount of income entitling an undergraduate or graduate student to receive a social scholarship is also changing; it cannot be less than 1.30—the amount referred to in Article 8.1.2 of the Act of 12 March 2004 on social security,[189] and higher than 1.30 of the amounts referred to in Article 5.1 and Article 6.2.3 of the Act of 28 November 2003 on family benefits,[190] which could significantly expand the circle of persons entitled to collect this benefit. However, in order to verify real student income, in justifiable cases, the head of the basic organizational unit or appropriate scholarship committee or scholarship appeal committee will be aided with the right to ask for an appropriate opinion from a unit in the social welfare system responsible for the determination of the actual situation of an undergraduate or graduate student's income and assets.[191]

An undergraduate or graduate student can also get a one-off social benefit twice a year in the form of relief, in cases when he will find himself in a difficult situation caused by force majeure.[192]

Students of first-to-third-degree studies with disabilities may receive a special scholarship after a disability is confirmed by the decision of the competent authority.[193]

In the catalogue of scholarships for academic achievements, the act provides a possibility for students of first-to-second-degree studies to be awarded with a grant for academic or athletic performance and a scholarship to be administered for the same achievements which should be motivating,[194] and for which a student may apply no earlier than after completing the first year of study[195] or in the first year of the second cycle started in the year after the graduation from first-degree study and if the student meets certain criteria.[196] A scholarship for academic performance or sports can be awarded to a student who received a high grade point average (GPA)[197] for the previous year of study or achieved high results in sports on the international- or national- competition level.[198] Further, a scholarship for academic achievements may be awarded to a student with particularly outstanding achievements in scholarship and having scholarly achievement,[199] and a minister's scholarship may be awarded for outstanding achievements in sport for a student who has achieved high results in sports on the international- or national-competition level,[200] and completed another year of study.[201] At the same time the legislature clearly emphasizes that the above entitled benefits are alternatives,[202] which means that a student cannot collect them all simultaneously in a given academic year. This does not preclude the possibility of taking other scholarships paid by nonpublic higher educational institutions, for example, or by various foundations.[203] In addition, case law emphasizes the discretionary nature of decisions on the granting of a scholarship for outstanding achievement in sport, which means that the mere fact of meeting the criteria specified in the regulations does not genuinely merit a scholarship to the person concerned.[204] This allows for assuming that a scholarship for academic performance is leading the way in relation to a scholarship for achievements in sports, which also has an indirect impact on the imbalance of powers entitled to individual grantees.

Amendments to the act also add artistic achievement[205] to the group of determining conditions for granting the student the above entitlements, but above all, introduce the possibility of a student's simultaneously receiving both a rector's scholarship for the best students, and a minister's scholarship for outstanding achievements. Receiving these scholarships does not preclude a student the right to financial aid and the right to receive a scholarship awarded by other entities or originating from EU structural funds.[206]

A slightly different situation occurs in matters with reference to granting of scholarships for academic performance in the case of third-degree students (PhD students). Such an allowance may be awarded for the first year of a study to a doctoral student who achieved very good results in academics or good results in an admission procedure, as well as in the second and following years of study, if in the previous academic year the doctoral student also proved progress was made in research work and in the preparation of the dissertation and particular involvement in teaching.[207] In addition, a full-time doctoral student is entitled to receive a doctoral scholarship, where its minimum amount may not be less than 60 percent of the minimum of an assistant's basic salary, set forth in the provisions on the remuneration of academic teachers. The decision to award a scholarship, the duration of its collection, and the amount is made by rector,[208] and implementing provisions in this area are contained in the relevant regulations.[209]

The current scholarship system for doctoral students, through the amendment, will be extended for a minister's scholarship for outstanding achievements.[210] In addition, an increase of a doctoral scholarship also becomes possible for a full-time doctoral student from professional quality grants[211] which will be given to a doctoral student who has outstanding research and teaching work. The procedure regarding increased granst will be defined by the relevant regulations established by the rector, after obtaining an opinion from a competent body of doctoral student government, and by taking into consideration that no more than 30 percent of the best doctoral students in subsequent years of doctoral study of both public or private higher educational institutions are entitled to receive the scholarship.[212]

In principle, benefits to which undergraduate and graduate students are entitled, except for ministerial ones, are awarded from the funds of financial support for students and graduate students and the rector in consultation with a body of the higher educational institution's undergraduate and graduate student government, which distributes these funds on the assumption that the resources devoted for scholarships and other social benefits may not be lower than those for scholarships for academic or sports performance.[213]

The amount of a scholarship is a personal matter of authorities of the individual higher educational institutions and other entities authorized to grant them, because both undergraduate and graduate students may also receive financial support granted by a local government unit[214] or scholarships for academic performance given by natural or legal entities other than state or local government legal persons.[215]

An undergraduate or graduate student may be granted the above benefits, except for ministerial ones, from the head of a basic organizational unit or the rector upon application, while scholarship for academic performance may be granted with or without application.[216] A student may appeal a head of the basic organizational unit's decision to the rector within fourteen days of receipt of the decision,[217] and if the rector's decision given at first instance is unsatisfactory, s/he is entitled to apply to the rector again for reconsideration within fourteen days of receiving the decision.[218] At the proposal of a competent body of a student government, either the head of the basic organizational unit or the rector may delegate their powers in the above range to the scholarship committee or scholarship appeal committee.[219] These are appointed by the head of a basic organizational unit, or the rector from among students delegated by the competent body of the student government and the higher educational institution's staff, and students constitute the majority of such committees. For purposes of proceedings in specific cases, the law grants the scholarship appeal committee and faculty scholarship committee the status of public administration bodies with all its consequences in rights and obligations.[220] Supervision of a committee is performed by the entities forming them and under this supervision they may revoke a committee's decision that does not comply with the provisions of the act or the regulations.[221] The rector in consultation with the higher educational institution's body of undergraduate or graduate student government through detailed regulations establishes details regarding the amount, terms for financial aid payment for undergraduate and graduate students, including specific criteria and procedures of financial aid grants for students, the application form for applying for a social scholarship as well as methods of submission of documentary evidence regarding a student's financial situation.[222] Detailed terms and procedures of granting and paying of a minister's scholarship, its maximum amount, and an application form for scholarship grants are regulated by the relevant order.[223] A student may receive scholarship benefits in an academic year for a period of up to ten months, paid on monthly basis. Scholarships are awarded on a semester or academic-year basis; ministerial scholarships are granted only for the academic year, except when the final year of study lasts for one semester only. When studying several for several majors at the same time, a student may receive specified benefits and a scholarship for his/her achievements in sports only in one major designated by him, whereas a social scholarship for the disabled and scholarships for academic performance in each of the majors. However, the total monthly sum of received scholarships by a student (that is, social, for performance in academics or sports, or for food and housing) cannot be greater than 90 percent of the lowest basic salary received by an assistant in the previous month, established in regulations on academic teachers' salaries. A student who has already completed one faculty and started studying at the next one, is no longer eligible for social scholarships, or for board and housing, unless s/he had completed his/her first-degree study and continued education at the second degree in order to obtain the professional title of master, but for no longer than for a period of three years.[224]

Under new provisions in force, benefits in the form of social scholarships, social scholarships for the disabled, the rector's scholarship for academic performance, scholarships for artistic achievement or in sports, and scholarships for relief will continue to be granted from the means of financial aid for graduate and undergraduate students, but the rules for distribution of scholarship allocation for a specific purpose will be much more strict. The means for rector's scholarships for the best students, awarded to a number of students not higher than 10 percent of majors in each academic department at the higher educational institution, cannot serve more than 40 percent of the total funds allocated for rector's scholarships for the best students, social scholarships, and relief,[225] which on the one hand may undermine the principle of equal treatment of students, but on the other is to increase the motivating factor for research fellows. Moreover, all benefits will be awarded to students by application,[226] and given that it is justified in the case of financial support benefits, it does not however gain, in my opinion, adequate reasons for rector's scholarships for best students. Also the mode of payment of the minister's scholarship for outstanding achievements will change, which will no longer be paid in monthly installments, but as a single payment no later than until 15 December of a given year.[227] A significant change is also the student's obligation to submit a statement that s/he is not collecting financial support benefits for more studies in than one faculty, because as of 1 October 2011, a student will be entitled to receive all cited benefits only in one faculty, which should be specified by him/her.[228] By using this type of regulation, the Polish legislature has significantly depleted the existing rights of persons with disabilities, and research fellows. However, an entry was added to the current law that entitled no more than 100 highly gifted graduates of bachelor's studies, engineering studies, and students who completed the full three-year cycle of the uniform master's program, to apply for a competition conducted under a "Diamond Grant," funds for scholarly research from funds provided in the state budget on education.[229] This legal solution is an opportunity for development and support of the brightest young scholars.

Students of uniform master's studies and first-to-second-degree study may also be entitled to use the 50 percent discount on fees for travel by public transport,[230] and the details in this respect are regulated by the relevant act.[231]

Amendments to the act in the cited above range clarify the entitlement, putting it within a time frame and clearly indicating that it is entitled until 31 October of the year in which the student has completed the studies mentioned above,[232] which had already been used in practice anyway. Another solution, which was taken from practice, was a legal regulation concerning the decision-making process by local government bodies in respect of identical allowances for doctoral students.[233]

On the other hand, students' primary responsibilities in each type of study are to follow the oath and study regulations, and in particular they are obliged to 1) participate in didactic and organizational classes in accordance with study regulations, 2) take examinations, perform internships, and meet other requirements provided in the curriculum, 3) follow provisions of the higher educational institution, 4) conduct doctoral studies programs and scholarly research and submit reports on their progress (only doctoral students), 5) teach classes for a maximum of ninety hours per year (only doctoral students).[234]

Disciplinary Responsibility of Undergraduate and Graduate Students

In the literature on the subject, disciplinary responsibility qualifies as one of the important characteristics of a corporate relationship, linking a higher educational institution as a public-law corporation with its members, which also allows the institution to influence the attitude of its members, that is, undergraduate and graduate students.[235]

Due to the fact that the standard system of regulating disciplinary proceedings in relation to undergraduate and graduate students is relatively large and results not only from the provisions of the act in question, but also from regulations on a detailed investigation and disciplinary procedure against students[236] and the Code of Criminal Procedure,[237] this is an extremely expensive and complex issue. Thus, given the constraints of this essay's framework, I will refer only to a narrow discussion of legal regulation in this area, which are contained in the analyzed act and significantly affect the legal position of an undergraduate and graduate student.

Authors of papers on higher educational matters allow themselves to include disciplinary proceedings against undergraduate and graduate students in the category of professional responsibility, and not against the criminal proceedings, and in making procedural solutions closer to a criminal procedure model and extensive references to the Code of Criminal Procedure, they only see the attractiveness of the high standards of this regulation process.[238]

The basis of being liable to disciplinary action in student matters is to have the legal status of an undergraduate or graduate student as a result of entering into a corporate relationship with a higher educational institution at the time of the oath until the cessation of the above relationship. The expiration of disciplinary punishment enforcement occurs one year after completion of the student's studies,[239] which also means conduct processing in relation to a person who no longer has the status of undergraduate or graduate student.

In accordance with Article 226 and Article 211 of the Law on Higher Education,[240] an undergraduate or graduate student or is liable to disciplinary action for violation of the higher educational institution's rules, binding legislations, or internal regulations, as well as for acts of offenses against the dignity of an undergraduate or graduate student. While it is relatively easy to better define the list of binding provisions in the higher educational institution, the range of acts offending student's dignity and the very idea of the "dignity of the student" has been designated by law.[241]

An undergraduate or graduate student is liable to disciplinary action before the disciplinary committee or before peer disciplinary committee of undergraduate and graduate student government, but for the same act can be punished simultaneously by both entities.[242] The disciplinary committee (in the first instance) and the disciplinary appeals committee (in the second instance) are appointed in the manner specified in the statutes of the higher educational institution from academic staff and undergraduate or graduate students for a term of office also designated by statute. These committees are independent regarding the case law and settlement of all factual and legal issues on their own and are not bound by previous rulings of other authorities applying the law, except the final judgment of the court.[243] However, the rector on his own initiative or at the proposal from a competent body of undergraduate or graduate student student government may also refer the matter to a peer disciplinary committee rather than to a disciplinary representative,[244] who acts as prosecutor before the disciplinary board and follows the rector's orders.[245] Nevertheless, only the disciplinary committee is empowered to render a judgment against an undergraduate or graduate student with the penalties listed by the legislatur[246] in the form of admonition, reprimand, reprimand with warning, suspension of certain student rights for a period of up to one year or expulsion from the institution of higher education.[247] For minor offenses, the rector may also try to punish a student with an admonition after hearing the person out, and an undergraduate or graduate student may appeal this decision to a disciplinary committee or peer disciplinary committee within fourteen days of receipt of the penalty notice. Then these entities can only delay the penalty of reprimand.[248] On the other hand, if an undergraduate or graduate student is suspected of committing an act of plagiarism, the rector immediately instructs a disciplinary representative to carry out a disciplinary investigation; in cases of reasonable suspicion of this crime he may even suspend the student from their students' rights until issuance of a decision by the disciplinary committee.[249] If evidentiary materials collected as a result of the above proceedings confirm criminal plagiarism, then the rector will suspend the proceedings for awarding the student's professional title and give notice of the crime.[250] After the completion of an explanatory investigation, the disciplinary representative may also revoke the proceedings by order approved by the rector, or refer a proposal for punishment to the disciplinary committee. He may also submit a proposal to the rector for administering an ad-monishing punishment or refer the case to the peer court.[251] On suspicion of an undergraduate or graduate student of committing an act of a greater weight other than plagiarism, disciplinary proceedings shall be initiated by the disci-plinary committee at the proposal of a disciplinary representative.[252] However, disciplinary proceedings may not be initiated after six months from the day the rector receives the information about the commission of this act or after three years from the date of its commission, and if the act is a crime, this period may not be shorter than the period of the statute of limitations for such a crime.[253] In addition, limitation provisions are not applied in respect of disciplinary pro-ceedings against an undergraduate or graduate student who is alleged to have committed plagiarism.[254]

The doctrine stipulates that disciplinary proceedings against an under-graduate or graduate student should adhere to the following rules: information transparency for the parties, adversary, independence of case law, speed, ma-terial truths, honest and fair trial, control of process decision and accusatory and, above all, the presumption of innocence and the right to a defense,[255] be-cause an undergraduate or graduate student suspected of having committed a particular act has the right to counsel (either of his choice or publicly appointed from the academic staff or students).[256] The hearing before the disciplinary committee or peer court is open, but has the possibility of being closed in whole or in part, with the exception of the announcement of the decision.[257]

The disciplinary committee shall give its decision after hearing the par-ties,[258] and disciplinary proceedings terminated by a legally binding decision may be resumed in the abovementioned cases.[259] Such a motion/proposal can be submitted by the punished person or the disciplinary representative within thirty days of becoming aware of the reason justifying the renewal.[260] The par-ties are entitled to appeal the decision of the disciplinary committee or peer court, and this appeal is made to the disciplinary appeals committee, or peer court of the second instance within fourteen days of receiving the decision.[261] However, an undergraduate or graduate has the right to appeal from the legally binding decision of the disciplinary appeals committee to the administrative court.[262] Both the resumption of proceedings and the measure in the form of a complaint to the administrative court are ways to move the legally binding disciplinary decisions.

The erasure of disciplinary punishment occurs by virtue of law after three years from the decision after validation of the punishment, and a punished person may request a blurring of the penalty decision to the authority that has decided the punishment, one year after the validation of the decision on pun-ishment.[263] The blurring of disciplinary punishment is, in practice, the removal of the person's entries having to do with his/her sentence of punishment from his/her personal files.

At the end of the deliberations on a student's disciplinary problems, it should be stressed that the legislature does not exclude the possibility of disciplinary action in cases of overlapping disciplinary and criminal liability for the same act.[264]

The amended provisions do not make even a single change in relation to the issues discussed above. As a result, the provisions which are already in force are still valid in that regard.

The Termination of the Corporate Relationship of the Undergraduate or Graduate Student

In accordance with applicable law, the termination of the corporate relationship of the undergraduate or graduate student occurs at the moment of 1) achievement by an undergraduate or graduate student of the aim which prevailed during his/her accession to the public-law corporation, i.e., the higher educational institution, 2) the deletion of an undergraduate or graduate student from the list of the higher educational institution's members, 3) the liquidation of the higher educational institution, or 4) the death of the undergraduate or graduate student. The termination of the corporate relationship of these entities is also associated with the loss of rights to various benefits and services offered by a higher educational institution to the undergraduate or graduate student, and also with a loss of the potential impact on the management of the public law corporation by the quoted member entities.

The first group of circumstances determining the termination of the corporate relationship of the undergraduate or graduate student is unquestionably linked to the achievement of an aim, which is manifested by 1) obtaining a higher education diploma by a graduate of the uniform master's degree programs and the first-to-second-degree studies or confirming the receipt of the appropriate professional title, or 2) obtaining a study completion certificate by of a doctoral graduate and the obtainment of the academic title of doctor.[265] It should be noted that the detailed conditions and procedures for determining the manner of receipt of a diploma or a certificate of higher educational completion at a given education level must be consistent not only with the provisions of study regulation decisions,[266] but above all, with the provisions contained in the relevant regulation.[267] In addition, detailed rules for obtaining the academic degree of doctor are determined by a separate law that I quoted previously.[268] The doctrine[269] and case law[270] emphasize that that the submission of the final/diploma exam and the decision by the committee to grant an appropriate professional title and the resolution to grant a doctoral degree are the final administrative decisions under the provisions of the Code of Administrative Procedure,[271] where the resolution to grant a doctoral degree becomes final upon its adoption with one exception.[272] Therefore, these decisions are of an exceptional nature, because they cannot be challenged in the course of the administrative instance, and are not subject to judicial review as final decisions, which, however, does not mean the exclusion of the possibility of verifying the above decisions under emergency procedures, such as by the resumption of the proceedings and the annulment of the decision. There is no doubt about the date of graduation, for which the legislature requires acceptance of the date of passing the final/diploma exam, (in the case of medical, dental, and veterinary schools) the date of passing the final exam required by the curriculum, or (in the case of pharmacy school) the date of passing the last internship required in the curriculum.[273]

In this respect, the provisions of the amended act do not introduce revolutionary changes with the exception of a provision stipulating that the fact that graduates of the uniform master's and first-to-second-degree studies will no longer receive state diplomas but the higher educational institution's diploma with a diploma supplement, approved by the Senate and the competent supervisory authority.[274] The legislature does not mention doctoral diploma completion, which may indicate either a deliberate omission or a striking weakness on the part of the legislature.

The second category of circumstances determining the termination of the corporate relationship of an undergraduate or graduate student may, on the other hand, refer to the following circumstances: 1) the resignation from membership by an undergraduate or graduate student, 2) the exclusion of an undergraduate or graduate student from the corporate affiliation as a result of not fulfilling obligations, or 3) the exclusion of an undergraduate or graduate student from the corporate affiliation as a result of decisions of the disciplinary committee.

Due to the voluntary nature of the corporate relationship, each member of the public-law corporation has the right to cancel the membership by an appropriate declaration of intent. Such a resignation submitted by an undergraduate or graduate student results in issuing a compulsory decision on deletion from the list of undergraduate or graduate students.[275] Students are entitled to appeal the above decision of the head of the basic organizational unit or the head of a division of the higher educational institution to the rector, and his decision is final.[276] An undergraduate or graduate student has the right not to undertake studies in spite of a positive decision on admission. Such a circumstance obliges the head of the basic organizational unit or a faculty advisor to issue a decision to remove them from the corporation's participants.[277]

Under current law, both the head of the basic organizational unit and a faculty advisor of doctoral studies are also authorized for mandatory or optional issuance of the decision to delete an undergraduate or graduate student as a result of their not fulfilling obligations, which have already been discussed here, arising from the oath and study regulation.[278] Among those circumstances, the legislature primarily mentions failure to submit a doctoral desideration or diploma exam[279] (obligatory)[280] on time, stating no progress in learning,[281] failure to pass a semester or a year in a specified deadline,[282] failure to pay fees related to the conducted study (optional),[283] and with regards to doctoral students the legislature mentions noncompliance with the oath or study regulations,[284] not completing the study program and failure to perform

37

scholarly research, and failure to perform internships in the form of classes[285] (optional).[286] The undergraduate or graduate student is also entitled to appeal this decision to the rector,[287] and using up all methods of appeal results in the possibility to appeal to an administrative court.[288]

The last condition in this category, which entitles an undergraduate or graduate student to mandatory removal from the list of participants, is the disciplinary penalty punishment of expulsion from the higher educational institution.[289] The legally binding decision of the disciplinary committee in this regard is the basis for the head of a basic organizational unit or the faculty advisor of doctoral studies for the removal from the list of undergraduate or graduate students. As already mentioned, that decision may be appealed to the rector and the administrative court.[290]

Another circumstance that causes the termination of the corporate relationship of an undergraduate or graduate student is a situation where the institution is liquidated. In that situation, the corporate relationship expires by virtue of law due to lack of an entity with which it has been established, and this situation does not require the issuance of a relevant administrative act.

A similar situation occurs in the case of the death of an undergraduate or graduate student, which is the last of the conditions determining the termination of the corporate relationship of the specified entities with a higher educational institution. The amended provisions do not make even a single change to the discussed matters. As a result, the provisions already in force are valid in that regard.

Conclusion

The ongoing reform of higher education and legislative changes which we are witnessing is, in a significant way, changing the conditions under which knowledge comes to be acquired by young people. The amendment of provisions on higher education is leading in the designated direction. Although the higher educational institution's gates are wide open and there is a commercialization and marketization of educational services at the university level today, and "the knowledge-based economy" has already entered our daily vocabulary, yet, in the Republic of Poland efforts are being made, despite the transfer of the higher education sector to the service sector, to maintain an adequate education level. At the same time the amended law on higher education in the field of regulation of undergraduate and graduate students and their learning process is taking shape in accordance with the Bologna Process and the directions of the desired changes. Currently, an undergraduate or graduate student's status is being enhanced by awarding this group of entities with a valid public interest and social development. Thanks to which, an important role played by undergraduate and graduate students in the functioning of higher educational institutions as public-law corporations is still being highlighted. Appropriate entities are being awarded with more rights which raise both their legal and social position. All this today results in the group's receiving not only a status permitting it to govern itself, but also a formal mechanism to assess the merits for including members and eliminating those whose behavior is not in harmony with the dignity of a member of the corporation. Moreover, young scholars are given more and more opportunities for growth through comprehensive financial support and students themselves have a lot of opportunities today not only to decide their own destiny and the functioning of the higher educational institution, on which they have an impact, but also they can acquire modern knowledge and skills in the framework of a real, reformed higher education on a Western level. Of course, the assumptions and trends are correct; however, the practice and implementation resulting from the background of the new competency standards of executive regulations will provide a true picture of the real reflection of an accurately adopted Polish legal solution by the legislature.

Notes

1. For more on the subject, see J. Thieme, *Szkolnictwo wyższe*: *Wyzwania XXI wieku. Polska. Europa. USA* (Warsaw, 2009), pp. 19–22.

2. J. Garniewicz, "Proces Boloński w systemie szkolnictwa wyższego w Europie—główne postulaty," *Wychowanie na co dzień*, no. 12 (2004): 6.

3. Thieme, *Szkolnictwo wyższe*, p. 314.

4. Quoted in K. Denek, "Ku szkolnictwu wyższemu XXI wieku," in *Przemiany szkolnictwa wyższego u progu XXI wieku*, ed. Z. Kruszewski (Płock, 1999), p. 32.

5. For more on the topic, see, e.g., E. Szczepanik, *Szkolnictwo wyższe i edukacja kadr menedżerskich w Polsce* (Warsaw, 2006).

6. Law of 12 September 1990 on Higher Education, *Dz. U.*, no. 65, Item 385 as amended.

7. S. Waltoś, "Korzenie współczesnego szkolnictwa wyższego—ścieżki tradycji," in *Szkolnictwo wyższe w Polsce: Ustrój—prawo—organizacja*, ed. S. Waltoś and A. Rozmus (Rzeszów, 2008), pp. 46–47.

8. See M. Rocki, "Szanse i zagrożenia wynikające z nowej ustawy o szkolnictwie wyższym z dnia 27 lipca 2005 r.," in *Edukacja wobec rynku pracy i integracji europejskiej*, ed. K. Szczepańska-Woszczyna and Z. Dacko-Pikiewicz (Dąbrowa Górnicza, 2007), p. 9.

9. *Journal of Laws*, no. 164, Item 1365 as amended.

10. Single text. *Journal of Laws*, no. 10 (1992), Item 40 as amended.

11. *Journal of Laws*, no. 65, Item 385 as amended.

12. *Journal of Laws*, no. 96, Item 590 as amended.

13. Act of 27 July 2005 Law on Higher Education, *Dz. U.*, no.164, Item. 1365 as amended—further as of the Law on Higher Education. See Rocki, "Szanse i zagrożenia," p. 10.

14. Quoted in B. Żechowska, "Dylematy w obszarze reform szkolnictwa wyższego," in Kruszewski, *Przemiany szkolnictwa*, pp. 45–55.

15. Quoted in T. Brzezicki, *Ustrój szkolnictwa wyższego w Polsce* (Toruń, 2010), pp. 43–44.

16. See Rocki, "Szanse i zagrożenia," p. 10.

17. See J. Zieliński, "Uwarunkowania i założenia przemian edukacyjnych w XXI wieku," in Szczepańska-Woszczyna and Dacko-Pikiewicz, *Edukacja*, p. 21.

18. See Art. 165 and 166 of the Treaty on European Union, Wersje skonsolidowane Traktatu o Unii Europejskiej i Traktatu o funkcjonowaniu Unii Europejskiej, *Dz. Urz.* UE C 83 z 30 marcu 2010 [Consolidated version of the Treaty on the European Union and Treaty on the Functioning of the European Union, *Official Journal* EU C 83, of 30 March 2010], which indicate the need for action by member states in their efforts to promote mobility of students and academic teachers, the development of higher education inter-institution cooperation, encouragement in the learning of foreign languages, and the recognition of titles and scholarly degrees, professional qualifications, and competence in universities and workplaces; to promote open learning and distance learning; and, above all, to adapt the education system to labor market needs and enhance the attractiveness and competitiveness of higher education in Europe. For more information on the subject, see E. Chmielewska, A. Kraśniewski, and J. Woźnicki, *Korzyści i koszty związane z przystąpieniem Polski do Unii Europejskiej w sferze szkolnictwa wyższego* (Warsaw, 2003), p. 5.

19. The Bologna Declaration was approved by twenty-nine signatories through the ministers of those countries responsible for higher education, including the fifteen EU member states, the three EFTA member states (Iceland, Norway, Switzerland) and eleven of the then candidate countries to the European Union (including Poland). The initiative was also joined by the European Commission, the European Council, university associations, rectors, and students as rightful partners in higher-education governance. The main objectives of the Bologna Process were set, and foremost among them were the following: 1) the introduction of a comparable system for diplomas along with supplements, clearly showing the comparable degrees, as well as a system of mutual diploma nostrification by European universities; 2) a study system development structure based on two to three levels of education (undergraduate, MA, and PhD); 3) the introduction of a point accreditation system for crediting student achievements (the ECTS—European Credit Transfer System); 4) the development and promotion of the mobility of students and higher educational institution teachers, researchers, and administrative staff (development of scholarships, exchange programs, and joint research systems, etc.); 5) the development of European cooperation in quality-assurance systems and the initiation of systems for assessment of that quality at the same time; 6) the promotion of a European dimension of higher education,

especially in terms of professional development, mobility, and integrated curricula, training, and research; and 7) the emphasis on the importance of cooperation with higher educational institutions and students. Poland joined the implementation process of the Bologna Declaration by taking steps to promote the widespread use of the Diploma Supplement, developing a two-level system of studies and using the ECTS credit point system, as well as citing the State Accreditation Committee to promote mobility within, for example, the Socrates/Erasmus program or bilateral international agreements, etc. Additionally, international conferences were organized on the quality of education in 2005 and on doctoral studies in 2010. Poland also participated as a member state in the European Consortium for Accreditation register. More on this topic can be found at the website of the Ministry of Science and Higher Education, Bologna Process, http://www.nauka.gov.pl/szkolnictwo-wyzsze/sprawy-miedzynarodowe/proces-bolonski/ (accessed 2 May 2011); Ł. Błąd, "Organizacja studiów, stypendia oraz funkcjonowanie samorządu i organizacji studenckich," in Waltoś and Rozmus, *Szkolnictwo wyższe*, pp. 345–47; A. Frąckowiak, "Proces Boloński w szkolnictwie wyższym," in *Szkolnictwo wyższe w Płocku na tle tendencji rozwojowych współczesnej edukacji akademickiej*, ed. Z. Kruszewski and J. Półturzycki (Płock, 2006), pp. 212–19; A. Kraśniewski, *Proces Boloński: dokąd zmierza europejskie szkolnictwo wyższe?* (Warsaw, 2004), pp. 3–4; U. Malarz, "Europejski wymiar szkolnictwa wyższego: stypendia zagraniczne—droga do przyszłości," in *Nowe prawo o szkolnictwie wyższym a podmiotowość studenta*, ed. A. Szadok Bratuń (Wrocław, 2007), pp. 101–11; R. Mossakowski, *Szkolnictwo wyższe w krajach Unii Europejskiej: Stan obecny i planowane reformy* (Gdańsk, 2002), pp. 252–53; A. Wójtowicz Dawid, "Ustroje szkół wyższych: Rozważania modelowe," in Waltoś and Rozmus, *Szkolnictwo wyższe*, pp. 75–76.

20. Cf. Chmielecka, Kraśniewski, and Woźnicki, *Korzyści i koszty*, p. 5; Z. Kruszewski, "Dobre kształcenie studentów i rozwój kadry naukowej drogą do nowoczesności i atrakcyjności miasta Płocka," in Kruszewski and Półturzycki, *Szkolnictwo wyższe*, p. 13; B. Sitarska, R. Droba, and K. Jankowski, eds., *Dylematy edukacyjne współczesnego człowieka a jakość kształcenia w szkole wyższej* (Siedlce, 2008), p. 12.

21. O. Fulton, P. Santiago, C. Edquist, E. El-Khawas, and E. Hackl, "OECD Reviews of Tertiary Education POLAND 2007," 2 May 2011, http://www.oecd.org/dataoecd/23/31/39321279.

22. Ministry of Science and Higher Education, "Reform on Higher Education," 2 May 2011, http://www.nauka.gov.pl/szkolnictwo-wyzsze/reforma-szkolnictwa-wyzszego/.

23. Act of 18 March 2011 on the Amendment to the Law on Higher Education, Act on Academic Degrees and Academic Title and Degrees and Title in the Arts and Amendments of Some Acts, *Dz. U.*, no. 84, Item. 455—further as an amendment of the Law on Higher Education.

24. See Ministry of Science and Higher Education, "New Law on Higher Education Signed by President," 2 May 2011, http://www.nauka.gov.pl/min isterstwo/aktualnosci/aktualnosci/artykul/nowe-prawo-o-szkolnictwie-wyzszym-podpisane-przez-prezydenta/.

25. In the position adopted by E. Ochendowski and M. Elżanowski, it was crucial to define more precisely in the doctrine of postwar Polish administrative law the concept of "the Department of Administration," which resulted in the elaboration of three definitions of the term, i.e., the formal, material, and mixed definitions. See M. Elżanowski, *Afterkład państwowy w polskim prawie administracyjnym* (Warsaw, 1970); E. Ochendowski, *Zakład administracyjny jako podmiot administracji państwowej* (Poznań, 1969). Ochendowski, taking into account the changes in the system already initiated during the 1990s, in the literature suggested the term "Administration Institution" instead of "Public Institution" as being a "unity of persons and goods, appointed by public authorities or by their permission by others for the purpose of lasting implementation of a specific public task." For more on the topic, see E. Ochendowski, "Pojęcie Afterkładu publicznego," *Studia Iuridica*, no. 22 (1996): 205. A similar position was taken by P. Fundowicz and J. Zimmermann. Compare P. Fundowicz, "Afterkłady publiczne," in *Prawo administracyjne ustrojowe: Podmioty administracji publicznej*, ed. J. Stelmasiak and J. Szreniawski (Bydgoszcz and Lublin, 2002), p. 175; J. Zimmermann, *Prawo administracyjne* (Cracow, 2005), p. 134.

26. Compare Brzezicki, *Ustrój szkolnictwa wyższego*, pp. 76–77; Zimmermann, *Prawo*, p. 134.

27. See W. Chrzanowski, *Zarys prawa korporacji: Część ogólna* (Warsaw, 1997), p. 15; S. Fundowicz, "Osoby prawne prawa publicznego w prawie polskim," *Samorząd Terytorialny*, no. 3 (2000): 5.

28. See E. Ochendowski, "Pozycja prawna studenta uniwersytetu użytkownik zakładu publicznego czy członek korporacji," in *Jednostka w demokratycznym państwie prawa*, ed. J. Filipek (Bielsko-Biała, 2003), pp. 455–63.

29. See Brzezicki, *Ustrój szkolnictwa wyższego*, p. 85.

30. See ibid., p. 81.

31. Originally, in the Polish doctrine of administrative law, the category in question was classified as a category of members of an administrative or public facility who used its services. Usually, this category included natural persons and, in exceptional cases, also legal persons who, from the moment of being acceepted into the establishment, were entitled to exercise their rights, but were also bound to respect the obligations arising from this relationship. For more on this topic, see W. Klonowiecki, *Zakład publiczny w prawie polskim* (Lublin, 1933), p. 201; Ochendowski, *Zakład administracyjny*, p. 235.

32. Ochendowski, "Pozycja prawna studenta," pp. 455–63.

33. See Ochendowski, *Zakład administracyjny*, p. 122.

34. See Article 159 of the Law on Higher Education. The provisions of

that article were introduced as a result of the Berlin Communiqué of 2003, which was a determinant in expanding the two-leveled educational structure adopted in the Bologna Declaration, for the third degree of studies, i.e., doctoral studies. For more on this topic, see Ł. Błąd, "Organizacja studiów, stypendia oraz funkcjonowanie samorządu i organizacji studenckich," in Waltoś and Rozmus, *Szkolnictwo wyższe*, pp. 335–36.

35. See Article 2.1.7 of the Law on Higher Education.

36. Although the standard should no longer be the basic two-level educational structure, as a result of the Bologna Process implementation in Poland, many higher educational institutions are not moving away from an integrated study model, which leads directly to the professional title of master's or equivalent without the intermediate diploma of bachelor's or engineer. This is a condition of the specific course of study and remains relevant to Poland, especially for the medical and legal fields. It is now permissible in the case of six faculties of the uniform master's degree indicated in para. 4 of the Ordinance of the Minister of Science and Higher Education of 19 December 2008 concerning the types of professional titles awarded to graduates and diplomates as well as certificate templates issued by higher educational institutions (*Journal of Laws*, no 11.61 [2009]). For other faculties, a two-level education system is mandatory under Article 159 of the Law on Higher Education. For more on this topic, see J. Woźnicki, "Studia trójstopniowe europejski i polski wybór," in *Dylematy studiów dwustopniowych*, ed. J. Dietl and Z. Sapijaszka (Łódź, 2005), pp. 22–23.

37. See Article 2.1, Points 8–9, of the Law on Higher Education.

38. The academic degree of doctor in a specific academic field, in a scientific discipline, or in a specified field in an artistic discipline, confirmed by the relevant diploma is obtained by a doctoral proceeding conducted on the basis of Article 11.1 of the Act of 14 March 2003 on Academic Degrees and Academic Title and on Degrees and Title in Art (*Journal of Laws*, no. 65, Item 595, as amended).

39. See Article 2.1.10 of the Law on Higher Education.

40. Ł. Błąd, "Organizacja studiów, stypendia oraz funkcjonowanie samorządu i organizacji studenckich," in Waltoś and Rozmus, p. 336.

41. Act of 18 March 2011 on the Amendment to the Law on Higher Education and the Act on Academic Degrees and Academic Title and Degrees and Title in the Arts (*Journal of Laws*, no. 84, Item 455).

42. Article 2.1, Points 7–10 Amendment of the Law on Higher Education.

43. See Article 2.1, Point of 18f–18h of the Amendment to the Law on Higher Education.

44. *Dz. U.*, no. 164, Item 1365 as amended.

45. Act of 18 March 2011 on the Amendment to the Law on Higher Education and the Act on Academic Degrees and Academic Title and Degrees and Title in the Arts.

46. Article 171.2 of the Law on Higher Education.

47. See Ł. Błąd, "Organizacja studiów, stypendia oraz funkcjonowanie samorządu i organizacji studenckich," in Waltoś and Rozmus, *Szkolnictwo wyższe*, p. 354; Brzezicki, *Ustrój szkolnictwa wyższego*, p. 123.

48. Article 166.1 of the Law on Higher Education.

49. Article 166.4 of the Law on Higher Education.

50. Article 166. 5 of the Law on Higher Education.

51. Article 166. 6 of the Law on Higher Education.

52. Article 166, Passage 2-3 of the Law on Higher Education.

53. Article 166.1 Amendment to the Law on Higher Education

54. Art. 166.2 Amendment to the Law on Higher Education

55. Article 164.1 and Article 195.3 of the Law on Higher Education.

56. Article 164.3 of the Law on Higher Education.

57. However, such classes may be conducted only after certain conditions are met, as specified in the Ordinance of the Minister of Science and Higher Education of 25 September 2007, on the conditions that must be met so that the methods and techniques of distance learning could be used in classes at institutions of higher education (*Journal of Laws*, no. 90, Item 551).

58. Quoted in Ł. Błąd, "Organizacja studiów, stypendia oraz funkcjonowanie samorządu i organizacji studenckich," in Waltoś and Rozmus, *Szkolnictwo wyższe*, p. 361.

59. See Articles 160–62 of the Law on Higher Education.

60. Article 164.2 of the Law on Higher Education.

61. Constitution of the Republic of Poland of 2 April 1997 (*Journal of Laws*, no. 78, Item 483 as amended).

62. See Article 99.1 and Article 195.9 of the Law on Higher Education.

63. See the Judgment of the Court of Appeals in Warsaw of 19 June 2007, VI ACa 186/2007, *LexPolonica*, no. 388433.

64. Thieme, *Szkolnictwo wyższe*, p. 257.

65. See, e.g., Rocki, *Szanse i zagrożenia*, p. 15.

66. Act of 12 September 1990 on Higher Education (*Journal of Laws*, no. 65, Item 385 as amended).

67. See, e.g., the Judgment of the Polish Constitutional Tribunal of 8 November 2000, SK 18/99, OTK 2000, no. 7, Item 258; the Judgment of the Polish Constitutional Tribunal of 5 October 2005, SK 39/2005, OTK ZU 2005/9A, Item 99.

68. Article 99.1 of the Law on Higher Education.

69. Article 99.2 and Article195.9 of the Law on Higher Education.

70. Article 160.3 of the Law on Higher Education.

71. Article 99.1.1a in relation to Article 99.1b, the amendment to the Law on Higher Education.

72. Article 99.1.1b amendment to the Law on Higher Education.

73. Article 164 a.1 amendment to the Law on Higher Education.

74. See Article 170a.1 with reference to Article 2.1.8d Amendment to the Law on Higher Education.

75. Article 164a.2 Amendment to the Law on Higher Education.
76. Article 170a.2 Amendment to the Law on Higher Education.
77. Article 99.1a.1 Amendment to the Law on Higher Education.
78. Article 170a.3-4 Amendment to the Law on Higher Education.
79. See Article 181.1 Amendment to the Law on Higher Education.
80. Article 170a.7 Amendment to the Law on Higher Education.
81. Article 170a.8 with reference to Article 2.1.29 Amendment to the Law on Higher Education.
82. Article 170a.9 Amendment to the Law on Higher Education.
83. Article 170b.1 Amendment to the Law on Higher Education.
84. Article 99a Amendment to the Law on Higher Education.
85. See U. Mirowska-Łoskot, "Płatny drugi kierunek studiów w Trybunale Konstytucyjnym," *GazetaPrawna.pl*, 5 April 2011, http://praca.gaze taprawna.pl/artykuly/502193,platny_drugi_kierunek_studiow_w_trybunale_k onstytucyjnym.html.
86. The legal relationship was placed either exclusively within administrative law, or its complexity was pointed out, which included both administrative and legal components and those under civil law, or components subjected to another legal regime. A representative of the first view was, e.g., J. Filipek, while P. Przybysz took the second view. See J. Filipek, *Prawo administracyjne: Instytucje ogólne. Part I* (Cracow, 1995), p. 173; P. Przybysz, "Sytuacja prawna jednostki w Zakładzie oświatowym," in *Jednostka wobec działań administracji publicznej* (Rzeszów, 2001), p. 368.
87. Ibid.
88. *Journal of Laws*, no. 164, Item 1365 as amended.
89. In the general view in the literature, the right to education is conceived as a "right to use education in all its forms by each person, given that education indirectly serves human rights, by conditioning their development, and that it opens a possibility for each entity to benefit from their rights and provides them with specific content." Quoted in H. Saba, "L'UNESCO et les droits de l'homme," in *Les dimensions internationales des droits de l'homme*, ed. K. Vasak (Paris, 1978), p. 480, cited in J. Mikosz, "Prawo do nauki," in *Prawa człowieka:Model prawny*, ed. Wieruszewski (Wrocław, Warsaw, and Cracow, 1991), p. 979, cited in Brzezicki, *Ustrój szkolnictwa wyższego*, p. 51.
90. The doctrine draws attention to the peculiar characteristic of a corporation that is manifested by being based on the relationships of people deciding about its system. At the same time it is stressed that members of a public-law corporation are bound by rights and obligations resulting from membership, under the statute or founding act, while membership in this corporation is, in principle, voluntary. For more on this topic, see Brzezicki, *Ustrój szkolnictwa wyższego*, p. 78.
91. Constitution of the Republic of Poland of 2 April 1997.
92. See O. M. Rudak, "Prawo do nauki," in *Prawa and wolności obywatelskie w Konstytucji RP*, ed. B. Banaszak and A. Preisner (Warsaw, 2002), p. 489, cited in Brzezicki, *Ustrój szkolnictwa wyższego*, p. 52.

93. Article 43.2 of the Law on Higher Education.

94. Article 43.3 of the Law on Higher Education.

95. Quoted in J. Borkowski, *Organizacja Zarządzania szkołą wyższą* (Wrocław, Warsaw, Cracow, and Gdańsk, 1978), p. 261.

96. Brzezicki, *Ustrój szkolnictwa wyższego*, p. 125.

97. Article 9.1.3 of the 7 September 1991 Act on the Educational System regulates the detailed procedure for obtaining of a high school diploma (Single text, *Journal of Laws*, no. 256 [2004], Item 2572 as amended).

98. Article 169.1.1 of the Law on Higher Education.

99. Article 169.1.2 of the Law on Higher Education.

100. Article 196.1 of the Law on Higher Education.

101. Article 169.3 of the Law on Higher Education.

102. Article 169.5 of the Law on Higher Education.

103. Judgment of the Voivodship Administrative Court [WSA] in Szczecin of 30 May 2007, II S/Sz 1277/2006, *LexPolonica*, no. 2144333.

104. See Judgment of the Supreme Administrative Court of the Republic of Poland [NSA] of 25 Novermber 2010, and OSK 1550/2010, *LexPolonica*, no. 2428992.

105. Article 196.2 Amendment to the Law on Higher Education

106. A service academy, as a military unit, does not have the full range of autonomy as its normative limitation is a separate procedure determining the conditions and procedures for admission of candidates as defined in Article 169.10 of the Law on Higher Education. See Judgment of the Voivodeship Administrative Court in Wrocław of 1 November 2009, IV SA/Wr 410/2008, *Gazeta Prawna* 50 (2009): 13.

107. See, e.g., Ordinance No. 21/MON Minister of National Defense of 29 May 2009 on establishing the conditions and procedure for admission of cadets to a service academy for the academic year 2010/2011, *LexPolonica*, no. 2324604; Ordinance No. 26/MON Minister of National Defense of 28 May 2010 on establishing the conditions and procedure for admission of cadets to a service academy for the academic year 2011/2012, *LexPolonica*, no. 2324604.

108. Article 169.10 of the Law on Higher Education.

109. Quoted in Brzezicki, *Ustrój szkolnictwa wyższego*, p. 128.

110. Article 169.6 of the Law on Higher Education.

111. Article 169.3–4 of the Law on Higher Education with reference to Article 93.3 of the 7 September 1991 Act on the Education System.

112. Article 169.7 of the Law on Higher Education.

113. Both in doctrine and case law there is no doubt that this type of decision is an administrative decision shaping the individual factual and legal situation of a student candidate. This view had been formulated under the 4 May 1982 Act on Higher Education (*Journal of Laws*, no. 14, Item 113 as amended) and was distributed, e.g., by J. Filipek, "Glosa do wyroku NSA z 29 czerwca 1982 r., II SA 532/82," *Państwo i Prawo*, no. 8 (1983): 148; J. Homplewicz,

"Glosa do wyroku NSA z 29 czerwca 1982 r., II SA 532/82," *OSPiK*, no. 1 (1983), Item 20, p. 53; E. Ochendowski, "Zakres stosowania kodeksu administracyjnego w szkołach wyższych" in *Zagadnienia proceduralne w administracji*, Scientific Papers of the Silesian University, no. 646, (Katowice, 1984), pp. 8–9. They are also reflected in contemporary case law, which obliges both authorities of higher educational institutions to maintain at least a minimum of administrative procedure necessary to settle matters and guarantee the party's legal rights (See Judgment of the Administrative Court in Warsaw of 21 January 2010, and SA/WA 1324/2009, *LexPolonica*, no. 2239911), as well as the appropriate application of the Code of Administrative Procedure to the decisions of admission committees and appeals from those decisions. (See Judgment of the Administrative Court in Lublin, 16 March 2010, II, SA / Lu 562/2009, *LexPolonica* no. 2265696.)

114. Article 169.9 of the Law on Higher Education.

115. In the reference literature the point is raised that it is an unnecessary regulation, which constitutes a repetition of the provision of Article 129.2 of the Code of Administrative Procedure, while representing a specific provision against the provision of Article 128 of the Code of Administrative Procedure. For more on this topic, see *Ustrój szkolnictwa wyższego*, p. 133. In one of the judgments of a Voivodeship Administrative Court it was decided differently: it was found that this provision is not a detailed rule in relation to the provision of Article 128 of the Code of Administrative Procedure. Cf. Judgments of the Voivodeship Administrative Court in Olsztyn of 16 December 2008, II SA/OI 770/2008, *Gazeta Prawna* 40 (2009): 13; Article 128 and Article 129, para. 2 of the act of 14 June 1960 Code of Administrative Procedure (Single text, *Journal of Laws*, no. 98 (2000), Item 1071 as amended)—further as CAP.

116. In this aspect of the case law, the lack of unanimity of the administrative courts is coming under scrutiny because on the one hand the courts confirm the statutory basis for an appeal against the decision to refuse admission (see Judgments of the Voivodeship Administrative Court in Olsztyn of December 16, 2008, II SA/OI 770/2008, *Gazeta Prawna*, no. 40 [2009]: 13), and on the other, one of the judgments of the Supreme Administrative Court raises the point that the candidate who did not get in can use any arguments in the appeal (see Judgment of the NSA, 14 May 2009, and I OSK 154/2009, *Rzeczpospolita*, no. 114 (2009): C2).

117. See Order of the VAC in Lublin of 27 December 2006, III SA/Lu 427/2006, *LexPolonica*, no. 2419886; Order of the VAC in Olsztyn of 30 March 2006, II SA/OI 133/2006, *LexPolonica*, no. 2112720.

118. Article 169.8 of the Law on Higher Education.

119. Article 169.5 Amendment to the Law on Higher Education.

120. Article 169.2 Amendment to the Law on Higher Education.

121. Article 196.2 Amendment to the Law on Higher Education.

122. Article 169.10 Amendment to the Law on Higher Education.

123. Article 169.11 Amendment to the Law on Higher Education.

124. Article 169.13 Amendment to the Law on Higher Education.

125. Article 169.15 Amendment to the Law on Higher Education.

126. See Article 129 § 2 CPA.

127. Article 170 of the Law on Higher Education. and Article 196a Amendment to the Law on Higher Education.

128. Article 160.1 of the Law on Higher Education.

129. Article 170.2–3 Amendment to the Law on Higher Education.

130. The amended provisions of this Act emphasize the need for transfer and recognition of ECTP points collected by a student in a previous higher educational institution. See Article 165.2 Amendment to the Law on Higher Education.

131. The issue in question is governed by the Ordinance of the Minister of Science and Higher Education of 3 October 2006 on the conditions and procedures for the transfer of student achievements (*Journal of Laws*, no. 187, Item 1385) and issued pursuant to Article 192.4 of the Law on Higher Education and the Ordinance of the Minister of Education and Science of 24 February 2006 on nostrification of higher education diplomas obtained abroad (*Journal of Laws*, no. 37, Item 255).

132. See Article 165.1 and Article 171.3 of the Law on Higher Education.

133. See T. Wojciechowski, "Porozumienia uczelni," *Forum Akademickie*, no. 5 (2006): 44–45.

134. See M. Poliwka-Pacyna, "Internacjonalizacja studiów and badań naukowych," in Waltoś and Rozmus, *Szkolnictwo wyższe*, p. 390.

135. See Judgment of the WSA in Szczecin of 30 December 2009, II SA/Sz 1260/2009, *LexPolonica*, no. 2322184. However, in the case law it is also emphasized that applying for leave and waiting for a decision in this matter does not relieve the student from fulfilling his/her duties, particularly from crediting a semester. See Wyrok WSA w Warszawie [Judgment of the WSA in Warsaw] of 4 February 2010, and SA/Wa 496/2009, *LexPolonica*, no. 2238312.

136. Article 172 of the Law on Higher Education.

137. Article 198.1 of the Law on Higher Education.

138. Article 198.2–4 of the Law on Higher Education.

139. Article 202.1 and Article 208.1 of the Law on Higher Education.

140. Article 202.2 of the Law on Higher Education.

141. Article 208.2 with reference to Article 202.3 of the Law on Higher Education.

142. Article 208.2 with reference to Article 202.4 of the Law on Higher Education.

143. Article 208.2 with reference to Article 202.5 of the Law on Higher Education.

144. Article 208.2 with reference to Article 202.6 of the Law on Higher Education.

145. Article 202.7 of the Law on Higher Education.

146. Article 203.1 of the Law on Higher Education.

147. Article 209.1 of the Law on Higher Education.

148. Article 203.3 of the Law on Higher Education.

149. Article 209.2 of the Law on Higher Education.

150. Article 203.4 of the Law on Higher Education.

151. Article 203.2 and Article 209.3 of the Law on Higher Education.

152. Article 210.2 with reference to Article 204.1–2 of the Law on Higher Education.

153. Article 208 with reference to Article 206 of the Law on Higher Education.

154. *Journal of Laws*, no. 164, Item 1365 as amended.

155. Single text. *Journal of Laws*, no. 98 (2000), Item 1071 as amended.

156. The case law is rich with examples of individual cases of an under-graduate or graduate student, to which the appropriate legislation of the Code of Administrative Procedures is applied by settlement of such cases by administrative decisions, or examples of cases excluded from the applicability of the specified administrative procedure. Compare, e.g., Judgment of the WSA in Szczecin of 19 July 2006, II SA/Sz 424/2006, *LexPolonica*, no. 2144300; Judgment of the WSA in Szczecin of 19 July 2006, II SA/Sz 323/2006, *Lex-Polonica*, no. 2144299; Judgment of the WSA in Białystok of 7 November 2006, II SA/Bk 474/2006, *LexPolonica*, no. 2419886; Judgment of the NSA of 6 September 2007, and OSK 877/2007, *LexPolonica*, no. 2144342; Judgment of the WSA in Poznań of 19 September 2007, IV SA/Po 357/2007, *Lex-Polonica*, no. 2215746; wyrok WSA w Bydgoszczy z 19 sierpnia 2009, II SA/Bd 373/2009, *LexPolonica*, no. 249886; Judgment of the WSA in Gliwice of 18 January 2010, IV SA/Gl 482/2009, *LexPolonica*, no. 2237569; Judgment of the WSA in Lublin of 16 March 2010, III SA/Lu 562/2009, *LexPolonica*, no. 2265696; Judgment of the NSA of 6 August 2010, and OSK 673/2010, *LexPolonica*, no. 2373442.

157. Article 202.5a and Article 208.1a Amendment to the Law on Higher Education.

158. Article 203a.1 and Article 209.2 Amendment to the Law on Higher Education.

159. That provision specifies, in particular, mandatory norms, which should contain status, which translates into components of the Students' Parliament of the Republic of Poland or the National Representation of Doctoral Candidates.

160. This article emphasizes that the supreme authority of an association is a general assembly of members or meeting of delegates, and the association is obliged to have a board and an internal control body, which is a reference to the organizational structure of the Students' Parliament of the Republic of Poland or the National Representation of Doctoral Candidates.

161. The provision of that article should be interpreted with reference to Article 203a.3 of the Amendment to the Law on Higher Education, and then

it shall be presumed that in relation to the Students' Parliament of the Republic of Poland or the National Representation of Doctoral Candidates, the supervisory authority is not a competent governor to the office of the entity, but the minister responsible for higher education, which may require providing copies of resolutions of the most important authority of those entities (General Assembly of Members or Meeting of Delegates) and a request for the necessary clarifications.

162. According to the letter of Article 28, if established by the supervisory authority that the activities of legal persons are unlawful or violate the provisions of the statute, depending on the type and degree of irregularities, it may apply for their removal within a specified period, give warning to an association's authority, or apply to court to use the measure specified in Article 29. Then, the court may, at the proposal of a supervisory authority or the prosecutor, 1) give a warning to the authorities of the legal person, 2) repeal a resolution of a legal person which does not follow both law and status, 3) dissolve the indicated legal person, if their operations possess a serious or persistent violations of law or provisions of the statute and have no conditions for the resumption of activity in accordance with the law or statute.

163. With this regulation it should be concluded that property of the specified legal persons arise from membership fees, donations, legacies, bequests, incomes from their own operations, the legal person's incomes from properties, and public generosity, which is tantamount to the fact that the legal persons cited here can run a business, the revenue from which is to serve the statutory purposes, and they are eligible for grants, which can occur even in the form of grants from the European Union.

164. Single text. *Journal of Laws*, no. 79 (2001), Item 855 as amended.

165. Article 209.5 with reference to Article 203a.2 Amendment to the Law on Higher Education.

166. Cf. Ł. Błąd, "Organizacja studiów, stypendia oraz funkcjonowanie samorządu and organizacji studenckich," in Waltoś and Rozmus, *Szkolnictwo wyższe*, pp. 384–85; J. Stawska, "Organizacje studenckie drogą do kariery," in Szczepańska Woszczyna and Dacko Pikiewicz, *Edukacja*, pp. 160–71.

167. Ł. Błąd, "Kultura studencka—przeszłość a teraźniejszość: od pokolenia kataryniarzy do pokolenia gadu-gadu," in *Uniwersytet—społeczeństwo—gospodarka*, ed. J. Chłopecki (Rzeszów, 2006), p. 191, cited in Ł. Błąd, "Organizacja studiów, stypendia oraz funkcjonowanie samorządu and organizacji studenckich," in Waltoś and Rozmus, *Szkolnictwo wyższe*, p. 385.

168. Article 173.1 of the Law on Higher Education.

169. Article 199.1 of the Law on Higher Education.

170. Article 173.1 of the Law on Higher Education.

171. Article 179.1 and Article 199.1 of the Law on Higher Education.

172. Article 182.3 and Article 199.1 of the Law on Higher Education.

173. Article 182.1–2 and Article 199.1 of the Law on Higher Education.

174. M. Pawełczyk, "Ustawa efektywna czy tylko efektowna," *Forum Akademickie*, no. 4 (2005): 36–37.

175. In line with Article 25 of the Civil Code Act of 23 April 1964 (*Journal of Laws*, no. 16, Item 1993 as amended) a permanent residence of a natural person shall mean the place where he lives with the intention of permanent residence. See Judgment of the WSA in Gorzów Wielkopolski of 25 June 2009, II SA/Go 157/2009, *LexPolonica* , no. 2271807.

176. See Judgment of the NSA of 19 February 2010, and OSK 1446/2009, *LexPolonica*, no. 2230077.

177. Article 182.1–2 of the Law on Higher Education.

178. Article 199.3 with reference to Article 179.2 of the Law on Higher Education. From the standpoint of a student's legal position this entry is significant not only because of the guaranteed benefit, but primarily because of the necessity of consultation and the obtaining of consent from undergraduate or graduate student government to the proposed rector's solutions in terms of rules for the granting and paying of scholarship benefits, which translates to emphasizing the importance of the powers conferred to and by the Polish legislature. See Judgment of the WSA in Cracow of 3 December 2008, III SA/Kr 623/2008, ONSAiWSA 2011/1, Item 15; Judgment of the WSA in Rzeszów of 25 August 2006, II SA/Rz 245/2006, *LexPolonica*, no. 2144302; Judgment of the WSA in Białystok of 3 August 2006, II SA/Bk 129/2006, *LexPolonica*, no. 2211741.

179. *Journal of Laws*, no. 164, Item 1365 as amended.

180. *Journal of Laws*, no. 64, Item 593 as amended.

181. *Journal of Laws*, no. 228, Item 2255 as amended.

182. Article 199.3 with reference to Article 179.4 of the Law on Higher Education.

183. See Article 179 .6 of the Law on Higher Education. The case law has raised the issue that the concept of "financial independence"adopted by the legislature is a criterion to apply for a social scholarship and was used only to determine how to calculate the amount of income received by an undergraduate or graduate student . Furthermore, it is even being stated that the term is used inappropriately, because it violates the essence of the nature of a social scholarship granted to an undergraduate or graduate student who, because of the difficult financial situation of his or her family, is unable to support him/herself on his/her own. See Wyrok WSA w Białymstoku of 16 October 2007, II SA/Bk 420/2007, *Gazeta Prawna*, no. 34 (2008): 22.

184. See Article 179.5 of the Law on Higher Education.

185. Single text. *Journal of Laws*, no. 94 (1993), Item 431 as amended.

186. Article 179.7 of the Law on Higher Education.

187. See Article 179.2–7 Amendment to the Law on Higher Education.

188. See Article 182 Amendment to the Law on Higher Education.

189. *Journal of Laws*, no. 64, Item 593 as amended.

190. *Journal of Laws*, no. 228, Item 2255 as amended.

191. Article 179.8 Amendment to the Law on Higher Education
192. Article 199.3 with reference to Article 183 of the Law on Higher Education.
193. Article 199.3 with reference to Article 180 of the Law on Higher Education.
194. The case law also stresses this. See Judgment of the WSA in Poznań of 28 May 2008, IV SA/Po 403/2007, *Zeszyty Naukowe Sądownictwa Administracyjnego*, no. 4 (2009): 155; Judgment of the WSA in Warsaw of 10 June 2008, and SA/Wa 365/2008, *LexPolonica*, no. 2144323.
195. Article 181.3 of the Law on Higher Education.
196. Article 181.4 of the Law on Higher Education.
197. See Judgment of the WSA in Gorzów Wielkopolski of 10 June 2009, II SA/Go 289/2009, *LexPolonica*, no. 2052584.
198. Article 181.1 of the Law on Higher Education.
199. In accordance with Article 178 of the Law on Higher Education, appropriate scholarships are granted by the minister responsible for higher education. And as for the service, state services, artistic, medical, and marine academies, by the relevant ministers who carry out supervisory activities over them.
200. As above.
201. Article 181.2 of the Law on Higher Education.
202. See Article 181.5–6 of the Law on Higher Education.
203. For more on this topic, see J. Induska, "Fundacje reformują edukację," *Forum Akademickie*, no. 1 (2005): 54–55.
204. See Judgment of the WSA in Warsaw of 2 December 2008, and SA/Wa 1201/2008, *LexPolonica*, no. 2259944; Judgment of the NSA of 21 March 2007, and OSK 2032/2006, *LexPolonica*, no. 2144323.
205. Article 181.1–2 Amendment to the Law on Higher Education
206. Article 181.6 Amendment to the Law on Higher Education. Polish students, as citizens of the EU, are fully entitled to choose from a number of scholarships offered by EU institutions and programs. For these studies, students of all modes and degrees are entitled to receive financial aid from any public or nonpublic higher educational institution. Primarily they are intended for people living in the so-called preferential areas and in difficult living conditions. In addition to benefits of a social nature, students can also benefit from the internships and scholarship programs for exchange students based on academic achievement criteria.
207. Article 199.4 of the Law on Higher Education.
208. Article 200.1–3 of the Law on Higher Education.
209. Ordinance of the Minister of Science and Higher Education of 19 December 2006 concerning doctoral study carried out by organizational units of higher education (*Journal of Laws*, no. 1 [2007], Item 3).
210. Article 199.1.5 and Article 199c Amendment to the Law on Higher Education.

211. See Article 94b.1.5 Amendment to the Law on Higher Education.

212. Article 200a.1 Amendment to the Law on Higher Education.

213. Article 199.2 with reference to Article 174 of the Law on Higher Education.

214. Article 199a with reference to Article 173a of the Law on Higher Education. Where no provision of the act commented on authorizes a body of local government to establish principles to award a student scholarship by means of a local legal act. See Judgment of the WSA in Lublin of 18 November 2008, III SA/Lu 309/2008, *Nowe Zeszyty Samorządowe*, no. 3 (2009), Item 53.

215. Article 199b with reference to Article 173b of the Law on Higher Education.

216. Article 175.1 and Article 176.1 of the Law on Higher Education.

217. See Judgement of the WSA in Szczecin of 30 December 2009, II SA/Sz 793/2009, *LexPolonica*, no. 2421627.

218. Article 175.2 and Article 176.2 of the Law on Higher Education.

219. Article 175.3 and Article 176.3 of the Law on Higher Education.

220. See Judgment of the WSA in Gorzów Wielkopolski of 30 June 2009, II SA/Go 268/2009, LexPolonica No. 2066906; Judgment of the WSA in Olsztyn of April 5, 2007, II SA/Ol 114/2007, *Orzecznictwo Sądów w Sprawach Gospodarczych*, no. 7 (2007): 71, Item 1.

221. Article 177.1–6 of the Law on Higher Education. Due to the fact that the legislature did not specify the form that this kind of settlement should be made, the case law raises the possibility of the application of the provision of Article 104 of the Code of Administrative Procedure providing for this decision settling the matter, in the form of an administrative decision. See Judgment of the WSA in Bydgoszcz of 6 December 2006, II SAB/Bd 55/2006, *LexPolonica*, no. 2144311.

222. Article 200.3 with reference to Article 186.1 of the Law on Higher Education. As provided for by law, rectors' empowerment to interpret this regulation does not, however, include the authorization to introduce principles other than legal statutes, with regards to the definition of determinants conditioning a student's application for financial aid benefits. See Judgment of the WSA in Cracow of 3 December 2008, III SA/Kr 623/2008, ONSAiWSA 2011/1, Item 15; Judgments of the WSA in Szczecin of 22 June 2006, II SA/Sz 204/2006, *LexPolonica*, no. 2144293; Judgment of the WSA in Bydgoszcz of 31 May 2006, II SA/Bd 389/2006, *LexPolonica*, no. 2144298. Moreover, in case law, it is stated that the terms contained in the regulation of principles and procedures of awarding financial aid to students are the terms of procedural law and uncomplicated terms of substantive law, and consequently should provide students with an opportunity to apply for their restoration. Further, the situation that allows students only to apply for scholarships or special aid for the disabled, or to submit applications for restoring the terms, constitutes a clear violation of the principles of equality through diversity of student

status. See Judgment of the WSA in Szczecin of 12 July 2006, II SA/Sz 475/2006, *LexPolonica*, no. 2144298; Judgment of the WSA in Szczecin of 7 September 2006, II SA/Sz 452/2006, *LexPolonica*, no. 2079480; Judgment of the NSA of 5 December 2006, and OSK 646/2006, *Przegląd Prawa Publicznego*, no. 12 (2007): 69; Judgment of the WSA in Szczecin of 6 December 2006, II SA/Sz 495/2006, *LexPolonica*, No. 2144310; Judgment of the WSA in Wrocław of 28 March 2007, IV SA/Wr 803/2006, *LexPolonica*, no. 2144324; Judgment of the WSA in Białystok of 9 August 2007, II SA/Bk 363/2007, *LexPolonica*, no. 2144298.

223. Issued under Article 187 of the Law on Higher Education. The Ordinance of the Minister of Science and Higher Education of 16 August 2006 on detailed conditions and procedures for awarding Minister's scholarships for achievements in academics and Minister's scholarships for outstanding achievements in sports (*Journal of Laws*, no. 153, Item 1093).

224. Article 184.1–6 of the Law on Higher Education.

225. Article 174.1 and 4 Amendment to the Law on Higher Education

226. See Article 175–76 Amendment to the Law on Higher Education

227. Article 184.3 Amendment to the Law on Higher Education

228. See Article 184.4 and 7 Amendment to the Law on Higher Education

229. Article 187a Amendment to the Law on Higher Education

230. Article 188.1–2 of the Law on Higher Education. See Wyrok WSA we Wrocławiu z 10 lutego 2010, III SA/Wr 595/2009, *LexPolonica*, no. 2239151; Judgment of the WSA in Wrocław of 10 February 2010, III SA/Wr 596/2009, *LexPolonica*, no. 2239152.

231. Act of 20 June 1992 concerning authorization for a discount for a journey by collective means of public transport (Single text. *Journal of Laws*, no. 175 [2002], Item 1440 as amended).

232. See Article 188.1 Amendment to the Law on Higher Education

233. Article 188.1a Amendment to the Law on Higher Education

234. See Article 189 and Article 197 of the Law on Higher Education.

235. Brzezicki, *Ustrój szkolnictwa wyższego*, pp. 154–56.

236. Wydane na podstawie Article 224 of the Law on Higher Education rozporządzenie Ministra Nauki and Szkolnictwa Wyższego z 6 grudnia 2006 w sprawie szczegółowego trybu postępowania wyjaśniającego and dyscyplinarnego wobec studenta (*Journal of Laws*, no. 236, Item 1707).

237. Act of 6 June 1997 Kodeks postępowania karnego (*Journal of Laws*, no. 89, Item 555 as amended).

238. See K. Kurczewska, "Odpowiedzialność dyscyplinarna studentów," in Waltoś and Rozmus, *Szkolnictwo wyższe*, p. 302.

239. Article 217.4 of the Law on Higher Education.

240. *Journal of Laws*, no. 164, Item 1365 as amended

241. In terms of case law, "the dignity of a student" refers to any student's behavior toward other people who do not bring reproach upon the higher educational institution of which a student is a member, and which proves a sense

of responsibility for respecting the rights of another person. See Judgment of the WSA in Cracow of 24 September 2008, III SA/Kr 449/2007, *LexPolonica*, no. 2244529.

242. Article 211.1–2 of the Law on Higher Education.

243. See Article 213.1–4 of the Law on Higher Education.

244. Article 214.1 of the Law on Higher Education.

245. Article 215.3 of the Law on Higher Education.

246. See Article 214.1 of the Law on Higher Education.

247. Article 212 of the Law on Higher Education.

248. Article 214.2–3 of the Law on Higher Education.

249. The suspension of a student on this basis is a measure different in character from the suspension of certain rights of a student for a period of one year as a disciplinary penalty. See Judgment of the WSA in Lublin of 27 February 2007, III SA/Lu 598/2006, *LexPolonica*, no. 2144321.

250. Article 214.4–6 of the Law on Higher Education.

251. Article 216.1–3 of the Law on Higher Education.

252. Article 217.1 of the Law on Higher Education.

253. Article 217.3 of the Law on Higher Education.

254. Article 217.5 of the Law on Higher Education.

255. Quoted in K. Kurczewska, "Odpowiedzialność dyscyplinarna studentów," in Waltoś and Rozmus, *Szkolnictwo wyższe*, pp. 312–18.

256. Article 218.1–2 of the Law on Higher Education.

257. Article 219.1–2 of the Law on Higher Education.

258. Article 219.3 of the Law on Higher Education.

259. Article 217.6 of the Law on Higher Education.

260. Article 217.7 of the Law on Higher Education.

261. Article 220.1–2 of the Law on Higher Education.

262. Article 221 of the Law on Higher Education.

263. Article 222.1–2 of the Law on Higher Education.

264. Article 217.2 of the Law on Higher Education.

265. See Article 167.1 of the Law on Higher Education.

266. See Article 160.1 of the Law on Higher Education.

267. Issued pursuant to Article 167.3 of the Law on Higher Education. The Ordinance of the Minister of Science and Higher Education of 19 December 2008 on the types of professional titles awarded to graduates and diploma templates and certificates issued by higher educational institutions (*Journal of Laws*, no. 11 (2009), Item 61).

268. A doctoral degree in a specific scholarly in the discipline of scholarship or a specified field of art in an artistic discipline, confirmed by the relevant diploma obtained by a doctoral student according to procedures conducted on the basis of Article 11.1 of the Act of 14 March 2003 on Academic Degrees and Academic Title and on Academic Degrees and Academic Title in Art (*Journal of Laws*, no. 65, Item 595 as amended)—further refered to as Act on Scientific Degrees

269. See Brzezicki, *Ustrój szkolnictwa wyższego*, p. 141.

270. See Judgment of the Voivodeship Administrative Court in Opole of 11 October 2007, II SA/Op 341/2007, *LexPolonica*, no. 1934290.

271. Act of 14 June 1960 Kodeks postępowania administracyjnego [Code of Administrative Procedure] (Single text. *Journal of Laws*, no. 98 [2000], Item 1071 as amended)

272. See Article 15.2 Act on Scientific Degrees

273. Article 167.2 of the Law on Higher Education.

274. See Article 167.1 and 1a Amendment to the Law on Higher Education

275. While the above statement is referred to in a provision of the laws on students of the uniform master's study and first- and second-degree study (Article 190.1.2 ppw), there is no such regulation for doctoral students. Therefore, it is presumed that such issues should be regulated by internal acts of higher educational institutions in order to achieve consistency of organizational and behavioral principles of equal treatment of students of each level. Likewise for the other mandatory and optional conditions for removal from the list of participants, as expressed in Article 190.1 and 2 of the Law on Higher Education.

276. Article 190.3 of the Law on Higher Education.

277. Article 190.1.1 of the Law on Higher Education.

278. This decision is issued on the basis of the institutions' administrative discretion and the head of the basic organizational unit or the director of doctoral studies is responsible for it. See Judgement of the WSA in Lublin of 7 February 2008, III SA/Lu 531/2007, *LexPolonica*, no. 2052550.

279. Article 190.1.3 of the Law on Higher Education.

280. Article 190.1.3 of the Law on Higher Education.

281. Article 190.2.1 of the Law on Higher Education.

282. Article 190.2.2 of the Law on Higher Education. See Judgment of the NSA of 24 February 2010, and OSK 1107/2009, *LexPolonica*, no. 2226899.

283. Article 190.2.3 of the Law on Higher Education.

284. Article 197.4 of the Law on Higher Education.

285. Article 197.3 of the Law on Higher Education.

286. See Judgment of the WSA in Wrocław of 9 February 2007, IV SA/Wr 107/2006, *LexPolonica*, no. 2144317.

287. Article 190.3 and Article 197.5 of the Law on Higher Education.

288. See Judgment of the Court of Appeal in Katowice of 28 March 2008, and ACa 117/2008, *Gazeta Prawna*, no. 226 (2008): 12.

289. Article 226.1 with reference to Article 190.1.4 p.p.w

290. See Brzezicki, *Ustrój szkolnictwa wyższego*, p. 147.

NEW PRINCIPLES FOR STATE FINANCING OF HIGHER EDUCATION AND SCHOLARSHIP IN POLAND

MAREK TYRAKOWSKI

The globalization of the contemporary world both forces and facilitates civilizational, technical, and cultural progress. In this context, the significance of research cannot be overestimated. Apart from human resources, an adequate financial basis constitutes the main requirement for a high level of teaching and education as well as the further development of research. The functioning of research and education is also directly influenced by their finances. Without financial resources they are unable to perform their tasks. Finance also constitutes the most fragile point of the organizational system of education and higher education, the supervision of which may be easily exercised through finances; therefore financial matters, as well as a broadly defined academic environment, remain an area of interest of the national strategy.[1]

Research and education at the university level are particular assets which are of both a private and public nature. Therefore the state supports their popularization and use through its tax system, subsidies, or suitable legal regulations. Education is a key factor in increasing human capital, which in turn is the most significant factor in economic development. Furthermore, it contributes to the development of democracy and results in numerous positive effects.[2]

The existing education system in Poland is distinguished by considerable fragmentation (e.g., within its organization), sectoral divisions (research and development units, research units of the Polish Academy of Sciences, higher educational institutions), and the predominance of cognitive studies over industrial research. Globalization-related challenges, Polish membership in the European Union, and alterations in the priorities within particular functions of research resulted in the necessity of effecting a number of changes to this system. In order to create optimal conditions for the development of a knowledge-based society in Poland, the strategic aim of the development of research is to use research for enhancing Polish civilizational development, particularly through its more extensive application in education, the economy, and culture.[3]

The development of a knowledge-based economy, which constitutes a strategic target of the state's policy on research, technology, and innovation, requires channeling the stream of the financing of scholarly research and development works into those fields and scholarly disciplines which influence the country's social and economic development. Thus arose the National Program for Scholarly Research and Development Activities, the principal objective of which is to accelerate the sustainable development of the economy, as well as improve the living standards of Polish society. Under priorities determined in this program, budget financing applies first of all to that scholarly research which contributes to achieving the aforementioned objective. The strengthening of cooperation between research and the economy requires significant budget outlays, which results in the fact that scholarly research issues in a contemporary country may not be governed by free market rules only. Therefore the government, as the creator of the country's reserch, technical, and innovative policy, as well as researchers and entrepreneurs, need to participate in the decision-making process.[4]

Professional quality financing of research institutions, a more efficient use of resources for research and improved cooperation between scholarship and the economy constitute the basis of six acts reforming the education system, i.e., "We Build on Knowledge—The Reform of Scholarship for the Development of Poland." The above package of acts includes the following legal regulations:

- regulations implementing acts reforming the education system,[5]
- the Act on Principles for Financing Research,[6]
- the Act on the Polish Academy of Sciences,[7]
- the Act on the National Science Center,[8]
- the Act on the National Center for Research and Development,[9]
- the Act on Research Institutes.[10]

The primary target of the aforementioned reform was to develop a modern, transparent system for financing scholarly institutions and rewarding the research conducted by them. The new law is supposed to allow for a more effective use of budget resources for scholarship as well as their concentration in research institutions, which guarantee the highest world-class level of research. Public funds for research will be distributed with the use of transparent competition procedures by two independent agencies. The first of them, the National Center for Research and Development, will support applied research, while the other one, the National Science Center, will finance basic research. The previous research and development units will be transformed under the new law into research institutes. Their essential task will be to conduct implementation research and development works for the benefit of the economy and also the transfer of technology and the adaptation of research results to the expectations of the industry. The Act on the Polish Academy of Sciences also constitutes part of the package of education reform acts. On the one hand, the Academy is a corporation of academics, on the other hand it is a network of jointly managed public institutes which are aimed at conducting scholarly research at the highest possible level. The education reform will be followed by a package of acts reforming the system of higher education effective as of 1 October 2011, which will present the opportunity to combine two sectors—that is, research and higher education.[11]

Entities Associated with Scholarship versus the Sector of Public Finance

Contemporary scholarship, in order to rise to the challenges and tasks it faces, requires huge amounts of financial outlay. Thus the state (the government), as one party, and entrepreneurs, as the other party, need to participate in this financing. State financing of research and higher education stems from the fact that entities dealing with these areas belong to the public finance sector. In order to point this out one needs to briefly describe the following terms: public finance, entities of the public finance sector, and finally, organizational and legal forms of the public finance sector units as well as their relationships with the sector of research and higher education.

Public Finance

The Act on Public Finance (APF) does not include a comprehensive legal definition of public finance.[12] This has been replaced with a description of its scope. Under this act, public finance involves processes related to accumulating public funds and distributing them, particularly:

1. accumulating public revenues and income,
2. disbursing public funds,
3. financing the loan requirements of the state's budget,
4. contracting liabilities investing public funds,
5. managing public funds,
6. managing public debt,
7. apportioning the EU budget.[13]

It is pointed out, in the relevant literature, that public finance relates both to the accumulation and disbursement processes of financial assets by entities of public law and to the organizational solutions supporting the aforementioned processes as well as enacting the applicable laws.[14]

Public finance fulfills diverse functions which are often understood in different manners depending on the historical period, the political and economic system, the development level of particular countries, and similar considerations. This principle incorporates a number of such functions, yet four basic ones are the most frequently indicated:

1. The fiscal function. This is a classic function, the oldest and the most relevant, combining the collection and accumulation of financial assets by the state. It is conducted in order for the state to perform its obligations;
2. The stimulus function. In democratic countries the state may not influence ecnomic activities directly; therefore this is achieved in an indirect way, through influencing particular entities (e.g., entrepreneurs), or through promising financial benefits (e.g., tax deductions), or through financial sanctions;[15]
3. The redistribution function. This is an "intentional, conscious use of lega and financial institutions for the redistribution of a country's gross national product." On

the one hand, the redistributive function may be fulfilled through the tax system, while on the other hand, through a system of grants, subsidies, allowances and the like for specific entities;[16]

4. The informative and supervisory function. This is rather of an informative and record-keeping nature, as, substantially, it does not involve supervision, but signaling positive or negative outcomes of economic processes. This information may be relevant when performing various activities aimed at streamlining public finance.[17]

Public Finance Sector

In the APF it has been indicated which units constitute this sector. These are the following:

1. public authority bodies, including government administration bodies, state supervisory and legal protection bodies, and courts and tribunals,
2. local government units and their associates,
3. budgetary units,
4. self-government budgetary entities,
5. executive agencies,
6. institutions of budgetary economy,
7. funds earmarked by the state,
8. the Social Insurance Company (ZUS) and the funds it manages, as well as the Agricultural Social Insurance Fund and the funds managed by the president of Agricultural Social Insurance Fund,
9. the National Health Fund,
10. independent public health care institutions,
11. public universities,
12. the Polish Academy of Sciences and organizational units established by this institution,
13. state and self-government cultural institutions as well as state film institutiions,
14. other state or self-governmental legal persons established under separate acts in order to perform public obligations.[18]

As may be inferred from the above list, the Act on Public Finance includes an extended list of the units belonging to the public finance sector. They differ in terms of possession of civil-law subjectivity and organizational and financial separation.[19] It may also be noticed that in the APF it was mentioned that public universities and the Polish Academy of Sciences, along with the organizational units it establishes, belong to the public finance sector. As newly established institutions such as the National Center for Research and Development and the National Science Center were created as executive agencies under the stipulations of the Act on Public Finance, thus they also belong to the public finance sector.[20] This diversification of entities belonging to the public finance sector, from the sector of research and higher education as well, is also reflected in the legal and organizational forms of the activities conducted by them. In this case, two organizational and legal forms used by the entities of the research sector and the sector of public universities in relation to the public finance sector, i.e., an executive agency and public legal persons established under separate acts. The Act on Public Finance indicates basic regulations applicable to the aforementioned units.

An executive agency is a public legal person established under a separate act in order to conduct the tasks of the state. The principles for the activities of an executive agency are determined by the act under which said agency is established as well as by its statute.[21] Its financial policy is based on the principles set out in the Act on Public Finance as well as in the act establishing it. The basis of the financial management of an executive agency is its annual financial plan. A draft of this plan is elaborated by a competent body in concert with the minister supervising the said executive agency. On approval by the minister supervising the draft, the plan is transferred to the Minister of Finance, under the procedures and deadlines applicable to the elaboration of a draft of a budgetary act. In the income and expenditure schedule of an executive agency, its expenditure should not exceed its expected income. It is also allowed to alter the income and expenditure with the approval of the minister supervising the said agency, issued on the basis of the opinion of a Sejm (Parliament) committee competent to decide on budgetary issues. It is necessary to inform the Minister of Finance of such changes immediately. Changes to the financial plan of an executive agency may not cause an increase of the agency's liabilities, or failure to meet its planned financial results, unless separate acts provide otherwise.[22]

Each year, an executive agency is obliged to make payments to the state budget, into the current account of the state budgetary unit providing services to the minister supervising this agency and any surplus of financial assets determined at the end of the year after settling its tax obligations. Such a surplus of this executive agency is transferred immediately after settling its due and payable obligations within a reporting period, yet not later than 30 June of the following year in which the surplus originated. Particularly in substantiated cases resulting from the necessity for providing an efficient and complete performance of the tasks of an executive agency, the Council of Ministers may, at the request of the minister supervising the said executive agency, grant consent, in the form of a resolution, not to pay the surplus. The minister supervising the executive agency in agreement with the Minister of Finance specifies, by an ordinance, the manner of establishing a surplus.[23]

Public legal persons are established under separate acts. The basis of their financial management is a financial plan prepared pursuant to their establishment acts, as adjusted by the stipulations of the APF. The drafts of financial plans of other public legal persons established under separate acts in order to perform public tasks are conveyed to the Minister of Finance under the procedures and deadlines determined by the laws applicable to the elaboration of a draft of a budgetary act.[24] It needs to be emphasized that executive agencies and public legal persons established under separate acts elaborate their task-based financial plans for the financial year and two subsequent years.[25]

All the aforementioned entities from the sector of research and from the sector of state universities possess legal personalities. The term "legal person" has not been defined in the regulations on research and state universities. Therefore one needs to refer to its definition pursuant to Article 33 of the Civil Code (acknowledging it as effective within the entire legal system).[26] Pursuant to the stipulations of the Civil Code, legal persons are the State Treasurer and organizational units which have been granted legal personalities.[27] The establishment, the structure, and the termination of legal persons are governed by proper regulations; the organization and the manner of operation of a legal person is also governed by its statute.[28] The term "legal person" is a basic legal term. An organizational unit which has been granted a legal regulation and in connection with this may act as a subject of legal-civil relationships, is recognized to be such a person.[29]

The relevant sources indicate three typical models of establishing a legal person: a model of government acts, a concessionary model, and a normative model. In the first model, the establishment of a legal person depends only on the decision of the state (through a normative act or through the decision of a state administration body), e.g., the National Bank of Poland.[30] In the second model, a legal person is established on the initiative of so-called founders, yet the state reserves the right to supervise the establishment procedures of such legal persons, making their establishment dependent on the consent (concession) of a proper state body. A cooperative bank constitutes an example of this type of legal person. Pursuant to the Banking Law, it may be established after it has been granted permission by the Polish Financial Supervision Authority.[31] The third model indicates that a proper act is sufficient for the establishment of a legal person, which applies to establishing, e.g., incorporated companies (limited partnerships) and the like. In this model the initiative for establishing a legal person is taken by its founders, and the state only supervises whether all the conditions are fulfilled.[32] As a consequence, it is very important to enter the legal person into the proper register.[33] In numerous cases such registration has a constitutive nature, which means that an organization obtains its legal personality only after it has been registered.[34]

In relation to the variety and complexity of such entities, they may be categorized according to various criteria. A basic division—on account of the state's approach to a given person—is the division into public and private legal persons. Three types may be distinguished among public legal persons: the first being the State Treasury in Warsaw; the second being state organizational units granted legal personalities (e.g., state-owned enterprises, local government units); and the third being all the remaining persons established under normative acts. However, private legal persons may be divided into only two types. In order for the first to be established, permission from an administrative body is required (e.g., a bank in the form of a stock corporation). The second type is established only under their founders' declaration of intent, or after being registered (e.g., a limited corporation).[35] Apart from this, legal persons may be categorized as state-owned companies, and also strictly individualized legal persons, such as the Polish Academy of Sciences.[36]

It results from the above presentations and analyses of the acts constituting the basis for the establishment of particular entities operating within the area of research and state universities that certain characteristic features of their legal forms may be pointed out, as well as the principles for their financial management. Such units operate as legal persons and consequently they act in their own name and of their own account. The State Treasury may not be held responsible for their liabilities, and vice versa. They perform public tasks in the form of services, which may be chargeable or free of charge. Thus they receive income, the amount of which depends on the type of services rendered by them. This influences the manner and extent of their financing by the state budget. Therefore research and higher education are principally financed from state budget subsidies. Besides their statutory activities, the above entities may conduct separate business activities and in this way obtain additional financial resources. Such activities are liable to the same legal regime as business activities conducted by other entrepreneurs.[37]

The Finances of a University

The issues related to financing universities are inherently connected with the tasks which they are supposed to perform.[38] In the Act "Law on Higher Education" (LHE) a number of such basic tasks have been indicated. They involve, first of all, educating students in order for them to acquire and broaden their knowledge as well as the skills necessary for professional activities. Moreover, they teach students to act responsibly for Poland, to reinforce democratic principles, and respect human rights. Additionally, universities conduct research and development work; they also provide research services as well as the education and promotion of the research faculty (vocational colleges offering only first-degree courses do not have this obligation). The tasks of a higher educational institution are also to popularize and increase the achievements of scholarship, national culture, and technology through accumulating library and information resources and rendering them available. Yet another group of tasks involves organizing post-graduate courses and training sessions in order to develop the skills necessary for operating in the employment market in the system of lifelong learning, creating the conditions necessary for the development of physical education, acting for the benefit of local and regional communities and enabling the disabled to participate in the process of education and scholarly research. Apart from this, the tasks of a medical school or the basic organizational unit of a school operating within medical or veterinary sciences may also involve providing medical or veterinary care within the scope and forms determined by the regulations on healthcare institutions and the regulations on veterinary establishments. Universities may also run student dormitories and cafeterias.[39]

Public universities receive financial assets for the fulfillment of their tasks from the state authorities under the principles stipulated by the Law on Higher Education. These assets also support nonpublic universities within the scope and forms stipulated by this law.[40]

The activity of a nonpublic university is financed from a subsidy granted by the state budget for the statutorily defined tasks; it may be financed from its own resources as well. Nonpublic universities are obliged to keep their own financial assets in separate bank accounts.[41] The state budget provides nonpublic universities with subsidies for:

1. tasks related to educating students who attend full-time courses (excluding students attending more than one full-time course), and related to educating full-time doctoral students and the academic faculty as well as the maintenance of university buildings, including their renovation,
2. tasks of a military academy related to national defense,
3. tasks of a public service school related to the safety of the citizens,
4. tasks of an art school related to cultural activity as specified by the regulations on cultural activity,
5. tasks of a naval academy related to the maintenance of training ships and specialist training institutions for naval personnel,
6. tasks of a school training aviation personnel for civil aviation connected with the maintenance of training aircraft and specialist training institutions for aviation staff,
7. tasks related to non-repayable financial assistance for students in the form of maintenance grants, special grants for the disabled, president's grants for the best students, minister's scholarships for outstanding achievements, and subsistence allowances,
8. research related to non-repayable material assistance for doctoral students in the form of maintenance grants, subsistence allowances, scholarships for the best PhD students, maintenance grants for the disabled, minister's scholarships for outstanding achievement. One needs to emphasize that a public university, within the subsidies for the financial assistance for undergraduate and graduate students, may also finance the renovation of its buildings as well as its student canteens,
9. tasks related to medical care performed within the education process of full-time students in the basic organizational unit of a medical school or another public university where teaching in the field of medical studies is supervised directly by academic teachers qualified to perform the medical profession relevant to the contents of the course.
10. tasks related to post-graduate education aimed at obtaining specializations by doctors, dental surgeons, veterinary surgeons, pharmacists, nurses, and midwives, as well as laboratory diagnosticians,
11. subsidizing or financing investment costs, including those aimed at educating undergraduate and graduate students who are handicapped—particularly those conducted with the participation of the state budget, state earmarked funds or developmental resources from EU funds or other foreign sources,
12. tasks related to providing handicapped undergraduate and graduate students with the conditions allowing them to fully participate in the education process.[42]

The aforementioned subsidies are granted by the state budget in the form of a specified-user subsidy (apart from the resources for financing the investment costs, which are granted in the form of a designated subsidy), from the part of the state budget which remains at the disposal of the Minister of Science and Higher Education. However, they are granted on the following conditions:

- Military academies are granted suitable subsidies from the part of the state budget which remains at the disposal of the Minister of National Defense,
- Public service schools are granted suitable subsidies from the part of the state budget which remains at the disposal of the minister responsible for internal affairs,
- Art schools are granted suitable subsidies from the part of the state budget which remains at the disposal of the minister responsible for cultural issues and national heritage preservation,
- Naval academies are granted suitable subsidies from the part of the state budget which remains at the disposal of the minister responsible for maritime economy,
- Schools training aviation personnel are granted suitable subsidies from the part of the state budget which remains at the disposal of the minister responsible for transportation,
- Medical schools or other nonpublic schools established by a university hospital conducting didactic and research activities in the field of medical sciences are granted subsidies from the part of the state budget which remains at the disposal of the minister responsible for health care.

Nonpublic universities receive subsidies for the tasks related to non-repayable material assistance for undergraduate and graduate students within the same scope as public universities. Furthermore, nonpublic universities receive subsidies for the tasks related to providing handicapped undergraduate and graduate students with conditions allowing them to fully participate in the education process. Apart from this, a nonpublic university may also receive a grant for covering part of the fees paid by full-time undergraduate and graduate students, as well as for subsidizing the completion costs of certain tasks, provided the task meets the applicable statutory conditions.

The Minister of Science and Higher Education defines, by way of an ordinance, the conditions and procedures for nonpublic universities which apply for the aforementioned grants, as well as the manner by which the use of such grants is supervised, taking into consideration the quality of teaching, the number of academic teachers for whom a given university is the primary place of employment, the number of full-time undergraduate and graduate students, the use of the university's own assets for infrastructure development, as well as the university's educational achievements.[43]

Universities may also receive other financial resources from the state budget as well as from other local government units or their affiliates; moreover, universities may receive designated subsidies if the subsidized tasks fall within the tasks of such units of local government.[44]

The subsidies for tasks connected with non-repayable financial assistance for undergraduate and graduate students, as well as for doctoral students in research units, are granted from the part of the budget which remains at the disposal of the minister responsible for higher education.[45]

Apart from the subsidies discussed above, the state budget also includes a specified-user subsidy for professional-quality tasks, which may be allotted to the following areas:

1. subsidizing organizational units which have the status of a KNOW, including remuneration bonuses for employees as well as special scholarships for full-time doctoral students, and special scholarships for undergraduate students,[46]
2. subsidizing basic organizational units of universities, whose evaluation, based on the opinion of the Polish Accreditation Commission, has been above average,
3. subsidizing basic organizational units of universities within the implementation of teaching quality improvement systems as well as the National Framework of Qualifications. This subsidy is awarded by way of a competition,
4. financing tasks connected with teaching full-time PhD students at nonpublic universities,
5. financing the increase in the amount of doctoral scholarships for the best 30 percent of doctoral students, both at public and nonpublic universities.

A specified-user subsidy for financing quality tasks is granted from the state budget from the part of the state budget which remains at the disposal of the minister for higher education issues.[47]

Summing up the issue of subsidies it needs to be added that the expenditure of the state budget for financing the activity of public universities from the part allocated to salaries is indexed annually, at least by the annual average growth rate of salaries in the state public sector determined by the budgetary act for any given fiscal year. The expenditure of the state budget for financing the activities of public universities from the part which is not allocated to salaries is indexed annually, at least by the annual average consumer price index, determined by the budgetary act for any given fiscal year.[48]

Apart from the subsidies indicated in the budgetary act, public universities also have other sources of income. These are, among others:

- resources obtained from the state budget for teaching according to the stipulations of the act on the principles of financing education,
- fees for educational services rendered by them as well as for conducting extramural PhD courses and also for artistic services rendered by universities,
- fees for school admission procedures, and one-time fees for issuing diplomas, certificates, and other documents connected with a course of studies,
- fees for specialist and research services, specialist and highly-spe-

cialist diagnostic, rehabilitation, or medical services, and also license fees and cultural activity revenues,
- revenues from business activity, and shares and interest from the sales of the components of their own properties as well as fees for using these components by third parties under rent, lease, or other contracts,
- revenues on account of endowments, inheritances, bequests, and public donations,
- non-returnable funds coming from foreign sources,
- other funds from the state budget or local government units.

Two other significant issues also need to be emphasized, namely the fact that a public university covers the costs of its activities, its obligations, and its expenditure on development and other needs resulting from the aforementioned revenues, and that unused financial funds in any given year remain at the disposal of the university.[49]

Moreover, the fact that a university is engaged in teaching, scholarly research, experimental, artistic, sports, diagnostic, rehabilitation, or medical activities does not constitute business activity within the meaning of the regulations on freedom to conduct business activities.[50] In relation to this, the activity of a university connected with the performance of its statutory tasks involves exemption from income tax, VAT, property tax, farm tax, forest tax, and from tax on civil law transactions under principles defined by separate acts. Universities are also exempt from fees for the perpetual usufruct of state-owned properties, except for the fees determined in the regulations on the management of agricultural properties of the State Treasury.[51]

Public universities conduct independent financial management that is based on financial and factual plans accepted by each university's senate, according to the regulations on public finance and accounting. Nonpublic universities conduct independent financial management based on financial and factual plans, accepted by the collective body indicated in a university's statute, according to the regulations on accounting and within the scope of the management of state budget resources, also pursuant to the stipulations of the Act on Public Finance. Universities submit their financial and factual plans to the minister that supervises them within fourteen days of their acceptance as well as to the Minister of Finance, while nonpublic universities submit them to the Minister of Science and Higher Education.[52]

The principles and the financing procedure for research and development activities conducted by universities which have qualified for financing with the resources planned within the state budget for education are defined in the Act on Principles of Financing Scholarship.[53]

The Financing of Research

The financing of research involves financing activities conducted for the benefit of the implementation of the scholarly, technical, and innovative policy of the state, particularly for carrying out research and development work as well as performing other tasks of great importance to the civilizational, economic, and cultural development of the country.[54] Financial resources for education are alloted to the following areas:

1. strategic programs for scientific research and development works as well as other tasks financed by the National Center for Research and Development (NCRD),
2. scientific research or development works for the state's defense and security, conducted within strategic programs for scientific research and development works as well as other aforementioned tasks. The Minister of Science and Higher Education transfers financial assets to the NCRD in these forms:

    a. a designated subsidy for implementing strategic programs for scientific research and development works as well as the other aforementioned tasks of the NCRD, in addition to conducting scientific research or development works for the country's defense and security, determined above at the request of the Director of NCRD,
    b. a specified-user subsidy for covering the current expenditure on the management of the tasks performed by NCRDs determined above,
    c. a designated subsidy for financing or subsidizing investment costs related to the performance of the aforementioned tasks.[55]

3. basic research and other tasks financed by the National Science Center (NSC); the Minister of Science and Higher Education transfers financial assets to the NSC in the following forms:

    a. a designated subsidy for the performance of the tasks of the Science Center, determined in this item at the request of the Director of the NSC,
    b. a specified-user subsidy for covering the current expenditure for the management of the tasks performed by NCRDs determined in this item,
    c. a designated subsidy for financing or subsidizing investment costs related to the performance of the tasks defined in this item.

4. statutory activities of research units,
5. the activities of the research units of a university, research units of the Polish Academy of Sciences, research institutes, and international science institutes involve conducting scholarly research or development work, as well as all the tasks related to them that are aimed at the development of young researchers and PhD students, financed within an internal competition,
6. investment in an extensive research infrastructure as well as investment in construction works related to scholarly research or development work,
7. scholarly cooperation with other countries,
8. the tasks co-financed with EU structural funds, or with non-repayable funds from aid funds granted by the member states of the European Free Trade Association (EFTA),
9. activities popularizing science,
10. programs and undertakings established by the Minister of Science and Higher Education,
11. prizes for outstanding scientific or technical achievements or scholarships for young outstanding scholars,

financing the activities of the Committee for the Evaluation of Research Units and
12. the Scientific Policy Committee, teams, reviewers, and experts as well as controlling activities,

financing scientific libraries which are not part of research units, within the scien-
13. tific activities being conducted as well as the activities promoting science.[56]

The financing of statutory activities involves the following:

1. the maintenance of the research potential of research units, including the following:

    a. activities necessary for the development of scientific specializations or research areas as well as the development of the academic faculty, encompassing scientific research or development works included in the financial plans of research units (a specified-user subsidy),
    b. the maintenance of research infrastructure, including libraries and archives (a specified-user subsidy),
    c. expenses connected with the employment of necessary academic, engineering, and technical personnel (a specified-user subsidy),
    d. the purchase or development of scientific research equipment, constituting an extensive research infrastructure (a specified-user subsidy),
    e. scientific cooperation in Poland and abroad, necessary for the performance of [statutory] tasks (a specified-user subsidy),
    f. activities of a research unit within the popularization of science (a specified-user subsidy),
    g. the restructuring costs of research units (a designated subsidy);

2. the maintenance of specialist research equipment for research units, and within the IT infrastructure for learning, including at a university (a specified-user subsidy),
3. the activities of the academic units of a university, the research units of the Polish Academy of Sciences, research institutes, and international science institutes involving conducting scientific research or development work, as well as all the tasks related to them that are aimed at the development of young researchers and PhD students, financed from an internal competition (a designated subsidy),
4. the activities of research units, universities or other authorized entities, connected with the maintenance and development of scientific databases, including the functioning and maintenance of the Virtual Library of Science—a system allowing scientific databases and publications to be available in electronic versions (a designated subsidy).

In the case of universities, the maintenance costs of their research infrastructure, including libraries and archives, as well as the expenses connected with the employment of the necessary academic, engineering, and technical personnel, do not include the maintenance costs of their research potential connected with their teaching, and the costs related to the employment of academic teachers.

The amount of the subsidy for maintenance of the research potential of a research unit depends on the category of said research unit. At this point it needs to be explained that research units are categorized on the basis of a comprehensive evaluation of the quality of scholarly or research and development activities:

- A+—outstanding level;
- A—very good level;
- B—satisfactory level, with the recommendation that scientific activity, research and development activity as well as activities stimulating the economy should be strengthened;
- C—unsatisfactory level.

The evaluation parameters and criteria for research units depend on their size, type, and scholarly profile, and they are adapted to the specificity of each of the four groups of the fields of scholarship, separately for research institutes of the Polish Academy of Sciences, the Polish Academy of Learning, basic organizational units of universities, research institutes, and research units.[57]

A scholarly unit which has been given a category-C ranking is granted a subsidy for the maintenance of research potential, including financing of restructuring costs, only for a period of six months from the date on which the category has been designated. A scholarly unit which has been given a category-C rankling may submit a re-evaluation application not earlier than twelve months after the date on which the category-C rank has been designated. Financial assets obtained in relation to the category-C rank being designated are allotted by the minister to the tasks performed by the NCRD and the NSC.

A grant application for financing the statutory activities involves obtaining reviews from the following:

- the president of a university, in the case of basic organizational units of said university; in the case of military schools, an additional review is required from the Minister of National Defense;
- the president of the Polish Academy of Sciences, in the case of research units of the Polish Academy of Sciences;
- the minister supervising a research institute, in the case of a research institute;
- the minister of internal affairs, in the case of public service schools.

Any unused financial resources alloted to the financing of statutory activities in any given calendar year remain at the disposal of said scholarly units for the subsequent year; however, their intended use must remain the same.[58]

The financing of investments within an extensive research infrastructure used for scholarly or development purposes involves financing the costs of the following:

- the purchase or development of scientific research equipment, constituting an extensive research infrastructure,

- an extension of the IT infrastructure for learning,
- participation in an investment project within an extensive research infrastructure, performed under international agreement,
- investments within an extensive research infrastructure, co-financed with structural funds.

Financial resources for education alloted to the financing of investments within an extensive research infrastructur, used for the needs of scientific research or development work are transferred to research units, universities, or research units in the form of a designated subsidy.[59]

The financing of construction investments used for the needs of research or development work involves financing the costs of the following:

- the development of new construction entities,
- the remodeling, extension, or renovation of construction entities,
- the purchase of properties,
- participation in a construction project carried out under an international agreement,
- construction projects co-financed with structural funds.

Grant applications for a construction project co-financed from a different part of the state budget are submitted along with a review by that part's administrator. In the case where a construction project is supposed to be used for performing tasks other than research or development work, the resources for financing education may only be used for financing that part of the said investment which is needed for conducting research or development work. Financial resources for education alloted to the financing of construction projects used for the needs of research or development work are transferred in the form of a designated subsidy.[60]

The financing of international scholarly cooperation involves carrying out projects jointly with a foreign partner, involving research, development work, or activities popularizing science conducted within international programs, initiatives, or scientific undertakings, co-financed with non-repayable foreign financial resources. Additionally, this also involves supporting the participation of research units and other entities in scholarly programs, initiatives, or undertakings. This also applies to the membership fees required for international organizations, under binding international agreements, excluding contributions from natural persons. And finally, this involves contributing to the benefit of a joint international program or undertaking, within which, scientific research or development works are financed.[61]

The financing of activities popularizing science involves the following:

- promoting innovative undertakings making use of the results of research or development work,

71

- popularizing and promoting scholarly or scientific and technical achievements,
- developing, processing, and popularizing scientific and technical information,
- elaborating expert opinions, assessments, and scholarly evaluations,
- taking part in other activities which are particularly important to the development of scholarship.

The aforementioned resources are granted to the Polish Academy of Learning, acting for the benefit of scholarship as well as schoarly libraries which are not part of research units. They are granted for the maintenance and expansion of library assets, for publishing activities, and also for cataloging the assets of scholarly libraries and library records. A grant application for financing scholarly libraries is submitted by the library manager.[62]

The financing of programs or enterprises established by the Minister of Science and Higher Education involves activities related to the performance of specific tasks resulting from the state's policy on science and technology. The Minister issues announcements in the Official Journal of the Republic of Poland, *Polish Monitor*, about the establishment of programs and enterprises. Financial resources allotted to financing such programs or enterprises are transferred to the scientific unit or other entity authorized under an agreement. The Minister may grant financial resources for the organization and financing of a program of an enterprise to an entity acting for the benefit of scholarly development, which is selected by way of a competition. The announcement of such a competition is placed in at least one weekly magazine and three Polish national dailies, on the website supporting the minister's activities in the Public Information Bulletin, and also at the seat of the Ministry of Science and Higher Education.[63]

On the basis of the submitted applications, the minister grants not more than three prizes a year for outstanding scientific or technical achievement. The amount of such prizes may not exceed the total of fifteen minimal basic monthly salaries for a full professor employed at a public university. Each year, on the basis of submitted applications, the minister also grants scholarships for outstanding young researchers employed in research units who conduct scholarly activities. The scholarships are granted for the maximum period of three years, in the amount which may not exceed the total of fifteen minimal basic monthly salaries for a full professor employed at a public university. The candidates for prizes for outstanding scientific or technical achievements may be proposed by academic councils, department councils, or bodies representing other research units or non-governmental agencies whose statutory objective is to operate for the benefit of scholarly development, by the president of the Polish Academy of Sciences as well as its committees. Candidates for scholarships for outstanding young researchers may be proposed by academic councils, department councils, or bodies representing other research units which employ these persons.[64]

The Minister of Science and Higher Education makes announcements in the Official Journal of the Minister about the subsidies granted from the resources for financing education. The minister also issues a bulletin in which he places important research-related information, as well as reports on his activity and the activity of the Committee for the Evaluation of Research Units. Apart from this, the minister issues communications in the Public Information Bulletin related to financial resources for education granted in the form of subsidies or under agreements, including the names of research units or other organizational units which receive financial resources for education; the names of tasks, programs, and enterprises; and the first and last name of their managers as well as the amount of the financial resources being granted.[65]

The Polish Academy of Sciences (Polish initials, PAN)

As of 1 October 2010 new regulations of the new Act on the Polish Academy of Sciences, constituting part of the package of six acts establishing the new system of education, became effective. The Polish Academy of Sciences is a leading national research institution; it is a corporation embracing 350 of the most highly regarded Polish researchers who are full members of the Polish Academy of Sciences as well as corresponding members.

The academy contributes to the development, promotion, integration, and popularization of scholarship, thus developing education and enriching national culture. The principal tasks of the academy are as follows:

- conducting scientific research and development work,
- supporting the development of individuals who are at the beginning of their scholarly careers, organizing PhD courses, postgraduate courses, and other courses,
- formulating the principles of ethics in scholarship,
- presenting opinions and programs related to scholarly issues as well as using the results of scholarly research and development work in practice,
- elaborating assessments, expert opinions, and forecasts concerning the issues significant for planning and implementing state policy that occur at the request of the president of the Republic of Poland, the Speaker of the Sejm, ministers, central governmental bodies, or on its own initiative,
- commenting on drafts of normative acts applicable to scholarship, its applications, and education,
- cooperating with other universities, research institutes, and learned societies, particularly within the scope of conducting scholarly research and development work as well as cooperation with the eco-

nomic and social environment within scholarly research and development work so as to implement them,

- promoting international scholarly cooperation through establishing scholarly consortiums and implementing research projects jointly with its foreign partners,
- participating in international scholarly organizations and research programs and collaborating with foreign scholarly institutions, as well as concluding agreements on scholarly cooperation with international scholarly organizations and research institutions.[66]

The supervision of the academy, including its research units and other organizational units, within its conformity to the stipulations of the Act on the Polish Academy of Sciences, the academy's statutes or the statutes of its research units—excluding its financial management—is performed by the Prime Minister. The president of the academy submits an annual activity report to the Prime Minister and an annual financial report to the Minister of Science and Higher Education.[67]

The academy's operation is financed with state budget resources and other assets. State budget resources are classified in the "Education" section and included in a separate part of the state budget, "the Polish Academy of Sciences," which remains at the disposal of the Minister of Science and Higher Education. The president of the academy performs his tasks and has the authorization to manage the academy's budget. Regarding the resources from the state budget, the president of the academy is accountable to the minister responsible for educational issues.[68]

Pursuant to the act, the academy possesses several sources of income. The first is a specified-user subsidy for covering the running costs of the academy's operation. This applies to the operation of the academy's bodies and corporations of scholars (including per-diem allowances and reimbursement of traveling and accommodation expenses); to scholarly international cooperation conducted under contracts and agreements signed by the academy (including the membership fees for international organizations); to the activity of the academy's office, auxiliary research units, and other organizational units operating within the academy's structure; and to the operation of international institutes, partly including the current maintenance of buildings used as the seats of these institutes and the maintenance costs of administration and technical support, unless international contracts or agreements provide otherwise, in addition to activities popularizing scholarship.

The second important source is designated subsidies. The first one involves the tasks within the scope of PhD courses, postgraduate courses, and other forms of education. The second one involves financing investments realized by the academy's office, auxiliary research units, and other organizational units operating within the academy's structure. The third one is a designated subsidy for its own contribution to the programs being implemented by the Academy, with the use of resources from the EU budget as well as non-repayable foreign resources, including the aid provided by the member states of the European Free Trade Association (EFTA).

Yet another important source are the resources obtained by the academy from he structural funds according to separate regulations, or from non-repayable aid funds granted by member states of the European Free Trade Association (EFTA), EU framework programs, and other foreign sources.

The next source of income is of a collective nature, and it combines income from business activities, selling, letting the academy's properties and property rights, allowances, inheritances and bequests, and finally, financial assets from other sources.

The academy's income may also comprise designated subsidies for financing or subsidizing transformations or the restructuring of auxiliary research units as well as other organizational units operating within the academy's structure.[69]

The aforementioned sources of income, due to their collective nature, are alloted by the academy for the performance of its statutory tasks, i.e., the development of scholarship, including the promotion of innovative research, the partial funding of investments supporting scholarly activities, promoting young researchers by awarding scholarships from the president of the academy, and also for the maintenance of the academy's properties, including renovations, remodeling, or extensions and other investments, as well as financing public and civil law obligations. Those resources unexpended in any given year are transferred to the following year.[70]

Moreover, the academy and its institutes may, in order to commercialize the results of scholarly research and development work as well as those connected with the transfer of technology and promotion of science, with the consent of the Minister of Science and Higher Education, establish companies or acquire and possess shares and stocks of business corporations. The proceeds on account of the dividends as well as from the disposal of shares of business corporations constitute income for the academy and its institutes.[71]

The academy conducts its own independent financial management. The basis for the management of resources is a financial plan accepted by the Presidium of the Academy at the request of its president and is subject to confirmation within twenty-one days by the minister responsible for scholarly issues. It involves, among other budget items:

- income from conducted activities;
- grants from the state budget or from the budgets of local government units;
- costs
- resources for asset-related spending and resources granted to other entities,
- receivables and accounts payable at the beginning and at the end of the year.

Until the plan is approved on the basis of the amounts indicated in the statutory act, a draft of the plan constitutes the basis for financial management. A financial report on the plan's performance is prepared by the president of the academy by 31 March of the following fiscal year, and is submitted for acceptance to the Minister of Science and Higher Education.[72]

Notes

1. See W. Mendys in *Higher Education in Poland: Political System—Law—Organization*, ed. S. Waltoś and A. Rozmus (Rzeszów, 2009), p. 149.

2. See J. Wilkin in *The Economic and Financial Conditioning of the Development of Higher Education in Poland*, a report elaborated by J. Wilkin with the use of expert analyses conducted by the following persons: A. Janiszewska, W. Kulczycki, J. Siwińska-Gorzelak, P. Strawiński, J. Wilkin (Warsaw, 2009), p. 81.

3. See the website of the Ministry of Science and Higher Education, "Strategic documents: The Place of Science and Higher Education in the System of Strategic Documents."

4. Cf. Communication no. 22 of the Minister of Science and Higher Education of 30 October 2008, on the National Program for Scientific Research and Development Activities, p. 3.

5. Cf. Act of 30 April 2010. Regulations Introducing Acts Reforming the System of Scholarship (*Journal of Laws*, no. 96, Item 620).

6. Cf. Act of 30 April 2010 on Principles for Financing Scholarship (*Journal of Laws*, no. 96, Item 615), further referred to as APFS.

7. Cf. APFS (*Journal of Laws*, no. 96, Item 619).

8. Cf. Act of 30 April 2010 on the National Science Center (*Journal of Laws*, no. 96, Item 617), further referred to as ANSC.

9. Cf. Act of 30 April 2010 on the National Center for Research and Development (*Journal of Laws*, no. 96, Item 616), further referred to as ANCRD.

10. Cf. Act of 30 April 2010 on Research Institutes (*Journal of Laws*, no. 96, Item 618), further referred to as ARI.

11. See the website of the Ministry of Science and Higher Education, "Scholarship, Reform of Scholarship, Reform of Scholarship Accepted!"

12. Cf. Act of 29 August 2009 on Public Finance (*Journal of Laws*, no. 157, Item 1240), further referred to as APF.

13. Cf. Art. 3 of the APF.

14. See W. Wójtowicz in *The Outline of...* ed. W. Wójtowicz , p. 17.

15. See ibid., pp. 18 and 19; see also C. Kosikowski in *Public Finance and Financial Law*, no. 3, ed. C. Kosikowski and E. Ruśkowski (Warsaw: Wolters Kluwer Polska, 2008), p. 25.

16. See W. Wójtowicz in Wójtowicz), *Outline of...*, p. 20.

17. See ibid., p. 20.

18. Cf. art. 9 of APF.

19. See A. Gorgol in Wójtowicz, *Outline of...*, p. 41.

20. Cf. Art. 1, sec. 2 ANCRD and Art. 1, sec. 2 ANSC.

21. Cf. Art. 18 and Art. 19, sec. 1 of the APF.

22. Cf. Arts. 20 and 21 of the APF.

23. Cf. Art. 22 of APF.

24. Cf. Art. 30 of APF.

25. Cf. Art. 32 of APF.

26. Cf. Act of 23 April 1964 on the Civil Code (*Journal of Laws*, no. 16, Item 93 as amended), further referred to as CC; see also A. Mariański in *A Commentary on the Act on Corporate Income Tax 2008*, ed. W. Nykiel and A. Mariański (Gdańsk: Wyd. ODDK, 2008), p. 20.

27. Cf. Art. 33 of the CC.

28. Cf. Art. 35 of the CC.

29. See A. Wolter, J. Ignatowicz, and K. Stefaniuk, *The Civil Code: General outline, Issue no. II amended* (Warsaw: Wydawnictwa Prawnicze PWN, 2000), p. 204.

30. Cf. Art. 2, sec. 1 of the Act of 29 August 1997 on the National Bank of Poland (i.e., *Journal of Laws*, no. 1 [2005], Item 2 as amended).

31. Cf. Art. 30a of the Act of 29 August 1997 on the Banking Law (i.e., *Journal of Laws*, no. 72 [2002], Item 665, as amended), further referred to as the Banking Law.

32. See J. Frąckowiak in *The Private Law System.* Vol. 1, *The Civil Code—General Part*, ed. M. Safjan, Institute of Law Studies of the Polish Academy of Sciences (Warsaw: Wydawnictwo C.H. Beck, 2007), pp. 1051–52.

33. Cf. the Act of 20 August 1997 on the National Court Register (i.e., *Journal of Laws*, no. 168 [2007], Item 1186 as amended), further referred to as the Act on the NCR.

34. See Wolter, Ignatowicz, and Stefaniuk, *Civil Code*, pp. 205–6.

35. See J. Frąckowiak in Safjan, *Private Law System*, pp. 1056–57.

36. For more, see Wolter, Ignatowicz, and Stefaniuk, *Civil Code*, pp. 212–27 and J. Frąckowiak in Safjan, Private Law System, pp. 1058–74.

37. See K. Sawicka in *The Financial Law System: The Financial Law of the Public Finance Sector*, ed. E. Ruśkowski (Warsaw: Wolters Kluwer, 2010), pp. 77–79.

38. The above issues will be presented only after amendments to the Law on Higher Education Act, which will be implemented as of 1 October 2011. Cf. the Act of 27 July 2005 on the Law on Higher Education (*Journal of Laws*, no. 164, Item 1365), further referred to as LHE as amended by the Act of 18 March 2011 on an Amendment to the Law on Higher Education Act, the Acts on Scholarly Degrees and Titles, as well as Degrees and Titles in the Arts and Amendments to Other Acts (*Journal of Laws*, no. 84, Item 455).

39. Cf. Art. 13 and 14 of the LHE.
40. Cf. Art. 15 of the LHE
41. Cf. Art. 92 of the LHE
42. Cf. art. 94, sec. 1 and 2 of the LHE.
43. Cf. Art. 95 of the LHE
44. Cf. Art. 94, sec. 3–6 of the LHE.
45. Cf. Art. 94a of the LHE
46. The status of a Leading National Research Center, further referred to as LNRC (Polish initials, KNOW) may be granted to a basic organizational unit of a university or a research center operating within a university, which conducts scholarly research at the highest level in a specific field of scholarship, related to PhD courses of the highest quality which are offered by such a university. The status of an LNRC is granted by a decision of the minister for higher education issues for a five-year period. An LNRC is selected by means of a competition conducted within field-specific areas of knowledge and education held by the minister for higher education issues and the minister for science. The competition is held by a commission appointed by the minister for higher education issues from among the experts in specific fields of scholarship, including foreign experts. The number of LNRCs within any one field of knowledge and education may not exceed three. The minister for higher education issues will determine, by way of an ordinance, the criteria, the conditions, and the application procedure for the status of an LNRC, particularly taking into consideration the quality of scholarly research, the quality of teaching, and cooperation with the social and economic environment. The status of an LNRC involves applying for funds from the state budget and from EU structural funds for financing investments in research equipment as well as investment in teaching. The commission evaluates the effects of the activities of LNRCs on the basis of final reports presenting the results of the research being conducted, its connections with the scholarly achievements of employees and doctoral students, its connections with the teaching process and the social and economic environment, as well as on the basis of final financial reports. Cf. Art. 84a and 84b of the LHE.
47. Cf. Art. 94 of the LHE
48. Cf. Art. 93 of the LHE
49. Cf. Art. 98, sec. 1 and 3 as well as Art. 100, sec. 1 of the LHE.
50. Cf. the Act of 2 July 2004 on the Freedom to Conduct Business Activities (i.e., *Journal of Laws*, no. 220 [2010], Item 1447 as amended).
51. Cf. Art. 106 and Art. 91 of LHE.
52. Cf. Art. 100, sec. 2–3 of the LHE.
53. Cf. Art. 97 of the LHE
54. Cf. Art. 3 of the APFS.
55. Cf. Art. 7 of the APFS.
56. Cf. Art. 5 of the APFS.
57. Cf. Art. 42, sec. 3 and 4 of the APFS. The basic criteria for a compre-

hensive evaluation of the quality of scholarly activity or research and development activity of research units involve, on the one hand, the evaluation of the scholarly level of the research conducted and the development work, and on the other hand, the evaluation of the effects of the scholarly activity in relation to international standards—including the publications of work by the employees of a a scholarly unit in reputable publishing houses as well as their scholarly monographs, ideas for new technologies, materials, products, systems, and services, as well as patents, licenses, and protective rights for usable formulas, in addition to evaluation of the international importance of the activity of said scholarly unit. Also evaluated is the increase in inventiveness on a national level and within artistic fields, the active participation in international exhibitions and festivals, including performing and fine arts, theatrical, and cinematic events. The minister responsible for scholarly issues makes announcements in the Official Journal of the Minister about categories attributed to research units as well as subsidies granted from educational funds. Cf. Art. 43, sec. 5 and 6 of the APFS.

58. Cf. Art. 18 and Art. 19, sec. 1–6 of the APFS.
59. Cf. Art. 20, sec. 1 and 5 of the APFS.
60. Cf. Art. 22, sec. 1 and 1–4 of the APFS.
61. Cf. Art. 23, sec. 1 of the APFS.
62. Cf. Art. 25, sec. 1 and 1–4 of the APFS.
63. Cf. Art. 26 and Art. 27, sec. 1–2 of the APFS.
64. Cf. Art. 28, sec. 1 and 1–5 of the APFS.
65. Cf. Art. 30 of the APFS.
66. Cf. Art. 2 of the APAS.
67. Cf. Art. 5, sec. 1 of the APAS.
68. Cf. Art. 78 of the APAS.
69. Cf. Art. 79, sec. 1 and 3 of the APAS.
70. Cf. Art. 81 of the APAS.
71. Cf. Art. 83 of the APAS.
72. Cf. Art. 84, sec. 1 and 3–5 APAS.

The Legal Personality of an Institution of Higher Education: A Few Remarks Related to Ongoing Legal Changes

AGATA SKOREK

The ongoing reform of the system of higher education in Poland is of a multi-level character. Adopted on 4 February 2011 by the Sejm (the lower house of the Polish parliament) and recently signed by the president of the Republic of Poland, entering into force on 1 October 2011, the Act of 18 March 2011 on the change to the Law on Higher Education, the Act on Academic Degrees and Titles and on Degrees and Titles in the Arts. and the change to a number of acts,[1] implies a change in the educational system, an introduction of a funding model for higher educational institutions which depends on the quality of education, a simplification of scholarly career paths, and the creation of stronger links between the academic world and the job market. Furthermore, the new change, at least as planned by its creator, expands the autonomy of higher educational institutions. This fundamental reform is being carried out under conditions in connection with implementation of the Bologna Process in Poland. Finally, the change to the Civil Code under preparation will also be significant in relation to the legal status of higher educational institutions.

Only a very few regulations in the Civil Code relate to the status of higher educational institutions; their importance is immense, however, as they concern the very foundations for the functioning of these entities in legal transactions. This article discusses the issue of the legal personality of a tertiary-level school, a strictly civil issue. Yet this is not an in-depth study of the matter, as evidenced by the very form of this article, but rather a voice in the debate raised in reaction to the restructuring of the system of higher education. Thus, in addition to regulations of the Civil Code—both current and proposed—the article also refers to those provisions of the Act on Higher Education which relate to various aspects of legal capacity and the capacity of higher educational institutions to perform legal actions, and particularly those regulations which introduce a *novum* in comparison to the current legal status.

The Meaning of the Concept of Legal Personality

The construction of a legal personality is a specific legal structure that applies only to legal persons.[2] The Civil Code uses a number of concepts relating to the civil legal status of persons: legal entitative character, legal personality, legal capacity, and the capacity to perform legal acts.

Legal entitative character is of fundamental importance in terms of civil-legal relations. The attribute of a legal entitative character implies being subject to civil law, and to the rights and obligations of a civil-legal nature. The civil-legal relationship consists of three elements: the entities, the subject, and the content. Entitative character is obviously related to entities. It is a normative feature, as the law decides whether to declare a person or organizational unit an entity under civil law.[3] In relation to natural persons, legal entitative character is granted to everyone in the above mentioned act (Art. 8 CC).[4] In relation to legal persons, their entitative character also results from the decision of the legislature, but it is not granted to any organizational unit.[5]

A concept almost identical in its coverage to the scope of "legal entitative character" is "legal capacity."[6] Legal entitative character is a status, whereas legal capacity is a feature necessary to acquire that status. Each legal entity has legal capacity, i.e., the ability to be a legal entity subject to rights and obligations in civil law. We say that such a feature is imminent. However, if someone is able to be an entity subject to rights and obligations, or has such an ability, it does not mean s/he uses that capacity. Thus, the legal capacity is of a passive nature, that is—in relation to the actual ownership of rights and obligations—it is potential. It is only a property of that entity, not a power.[7]

An active correlate of legal capacity is the ability to perform legal acts. This is a higher-level qualification that allows personal participation in civil-legal relations.[8] This means having the ability to acquire rights and obligations within civil law as a result of one's own actions. Unlike legal capacity, capacity to perform legal acts is an inseparable feature of an entity subject to civil law. For example, completely incapacitated persons have legal capacity (and therefore, as indicated above, legal entitative character), i.e., they may be the subject of a law within civil law; however, they do not have a capacity to perform legal acts, i.e., on their own; they cannot acquire that right by their own actions (they can do so through their statutory representative) (Art. 12 CC).[9]

Finally, a legal personality in relation to the concept of entitative legal character is a superior concept. It is used in relation to legal persons. The term "legal personality" also refers to natural persons, although there is a dispute about this. Certainly the concept, as its name implies, does not refer to the third category of entities in civil law, i.e., organizational units without a legal personality (Art. 33[1] § 1 CC) sometimes also called "incomplete" or "imperfect legal persons."

It is worth mentioning that in the new Civil Code under preparation the latter category of entities is to be removed;[10] the division of natural and legal persons is to remain, with a broader definition of the concept of a legal person. A legal person shall be an entity of a specific organizational structure, to which the law grants legal capacity.[11]

Legal personality includes both legal capacity and the capacity to perform legal acts.[12] Obviously the essence of a legal person to a certain extent determines the extent of its abilities. As to the legal capacity, a legal person whose nature is strictly associated with human psychophysical nature may not be subject to those rights and responsibilities. Moreover, the scope of legal capacity of a legal person may be restricted by a statute or by acts. However, there are no other systemic limitations of that ability, which means that a legal person may be (except for the aforementioned departures) subject to all rights and obligations of a civil nature.[13] The capacity to perform legal acts by legal persons is always full. A legal person shall, through its authorities, perform legal acts in the manner described by the act and a statute based on it (Art. 38 CC). Competencies or the authorities in performing legal acts determine, as suggested above, both the regulations and provisions of the statute.

Only the legislature may grant legal personality (i.e., consider an organizational unit as a legal person). This is described in Art. 35, sentence 1 CC ("The establishment, organization, and termination of legal entities shall be determined by relevant provisions"). At the same time, according to Art. 37 CC, an organizational unit acquires legal personality upon its entry into a relevant register, unless special provisions provide otherwise (e.g., a normative act appointing a legal person may relate to its obtaining legal personality with the act's entry into force, as in the case of the creation of a tertiary-level school).[14]

In conclusion, it should be mentioned that the provision of Art. 43 of the proposed new Civil Code makes legal personality equal with entitative legal character.[15] Legal personality is a normative feature, and its essence is the legal capacity of an entity. Thus, if the act recognizes an organizational unit as having a legal capacity, it recognizes that unit as an entity capable of independent actions. A direct granting of personality is not necessary. The authors of the draft point out that such a regulation does not constitute a departure from the normative system that exists in Polish law of appointing a circle of legal persons. The rule that there are only such types of legal persons that have been provided for by the legislature will remain in force. "Without an act entrusting a particular type of organizational unit with entitative legal character, no social organization (partnership, family, marriage) or volume of an estate (inherited property, joint assets of a married couple) would be provided with legal personality. The difference, in comparison with the law in force, lies in the fact that, while it is still required that the act regulating a specific type of organizational unit should contain the words 'shall acquire legal personality' and 'is a legal person' according to the draft, it is enough for the act to point to a defined scope of legal capacity (e.g., the entity may acquire rights and assume liabilities, file a suit, and be sued)."[16]

This solution restores the classic identity of the concepts of legal capacity, entitative legal character, and personality (namely, a legal person or a natural person), which in the current normalization is not quite clear.

Tertiary-Level School: The Concept and Types

The basic legal act defining the status of higher educational institutions is the Act of 27 July 2005 Law on Higher Education (hereinafter referred to as

PSW).[17] According to Art. 1, sec. 1 of the PSW, the entitative scope of the act includes two groups of entities: public and private higher educational institutions. The former are created by the state represented by a competent official authority or public administration. Nonpublic institutions are created by a natural or legal person (the founder of a nonpublic higher educational institution) rather than legal persons that are the state or local government.

Since the regulations of the PSW relate to the whole higher education system (both public and nonpublic), as based on this very act, one should look for a semantic meaning and the juridical meaning of the concept of a "tertiary-level school" or a "higher educational institution" and indicate to which specific entities these terms can be ascribed. In accordance with the statutory definition, a higher educational institution is a school offering studies of higher education, established in a manner prescribed in the act (Art. 2 PSW). The legislature has used a functional perspective that allows assigning the attribute of a higher educational institution only to an organizational unit dealing with education which meets the following two conditions:

- First, it offers higher educational studies, where higher education studies are defined in the act as studies of the first or second degree or uniform MA-equivalent studies, conducted by a higher educational institution authorized to do so (Art. 2, sec. 2 PSW); and
- Second, it was created in accordance with the Law on Higher Education.

Therefore the unit's name, which can often be misleading, is not of decisive importance.[18]

However, this does not mean that the act does not refer in any way to the names used by tertiary-level schools. On the contrary, the legislature explicitly determines the requirements to be met by a higher educational institution in order to include specific terms in its name. Permission to use words explicitly associated with tertiary-level schools requires strict compliance with the minimum threshold criteria for being entitled to award doctoral (PhD-equivalent) degrees. The word "university" (*uniwersytet*) can be used in the name of an institution whose organizational units have the authority to award doctoral degrees in at least ten disciplines, including at least two powers in each of the following disciplines: 1) the humanities, law, economy, or theology; 2) mathematics, physics, earth sciences, or technical science; 3) biological, medical, chemical, pharmaceutical, agricultural, or veterinary science (Art. 3, sec. 1 PSW). The word "technical university" (*uniwersytet techniczny*) can be used in the name of an institution whose organizational units have the authority to award doctoral degrees in at least ten disciplines, including at least six powers in technical science (Art. 3, sec. 2 PSW). The word "university" (*uniwersytet*) complemented with an adjective defining the profile of that institution (e.g., of medical, technical, and agricultural or natural science) can be used only in the name of a tertiary-level school whose organizational units have at least six powers to award doctoral degrees, including at least four in the science being a part of the institution's profile (Art. 3, sec. 3 PSW). A higher educational institution whose organizational units have the authority to award doctoral degrees in at least six disciplines, including at least four powers in technical science, may be called a "polytechnic" (*politechnika*) (Art. 3, sec. 4 PSW). "Academy" (*akademia*) may be included in the name of a higher educational institution whose organizational units have at least two powers to award doctoral degrees (Art. 3, sec. 5 PSW).

The act also uses the following terms:

- "academic institution" (*uczelnia akademicka*) is a higher educational institution with at least one organizational unit having the authority to award doctoral degrees;
- "vocational school of higher education" (*uczelnia zawodowa*), includes any institution that offers first- or second-degree studies or uniform MA studies but is not entitled to award doctoral degrees;
- "military academy" (*uczelnia wojskowa*) is understood as a public institution supervised by the minister in charge of national defense;
- "school of public service" (*uczelnia służb państwowych*) is a public institution supervised by the minister in charge of Internal Affairs;
- "arts school" (*uczelnia artystyczna*) is a public institution supervised by the minister in charge of culture and National Heritage Protection;
- "medical school" (*uczelnia medyczna*) is a public institution supervised by the minister in charge of health;
- "naval academy" (*uczelnia morska*) is a public institution subject to supervision by the minister in charge of maritime economy;

The reason the legislature has to determine the abovementioned requirements concerning naming conventions is undoubtedly to maintain quality in higher education (it performs the function of standardization) and to make it easier for the recipients of this type of education to understand the rank and profile of an educational institution (it performs an informational function). By the way, the legislature has created a kind of hierarchy for tertiary-level schools. "The statutory rigorism, which must be met by a higher educational institution to use in its name one of the words or terms mentioned, in conjunction with the prestige enjoyed by academic employees in public opinion, especially the ones with the title of professor, regardless of any other conditions, makes recognizable elements for the reputation of a university, polytechnic, or academy."[19]

The Tertiary-Level School as a Legal Person

As noted in the discussion on the condition of higher education, problems in the functioning of public tertiary-level schools may have their source in the absence of a clear determination of their legal nature, which implies the entirety of rights and obligations of a specific entity.

Tertiary-level schools are legal persons. This is stated explicitly in Art. 12 of the PSW. Traditionally, there are three systems of appointment of legal persons: a system of acts by state authorities, a normative system, and a system of licensing. The system of acts covers the creation of state higher educational institutions, state vocational schools of higher education, and others. It comes down to the issuance of an act by a competent public authority stating an entity to be a legal person, and that may be both a normative act (an act or regulation), or an administrative act. The distinguishing feature of the normative system, which occurs most frequently, is the creation of general provisions defining the conditions to be met in order to create a legal person. The licensing system, in turn, requires a prior authorization from a competent state body granted to the founders of a legal person.

Public tertiary-level schools are a type of legal person created by the state, which are organizational units (other than the Treasury) with legal personality, whose property is wholly state property (Art. 1a, quotation from the Act of 8 August 1996 on the rules of execution of the rights granted to the Treasury).[20]

The source of the legal personality of a higher educational institution is to grant it by an appropriate normative act. The creation of a public academic institution, its liquidation, a change in its name, or a merger with another public higher educational institution shall follow the act (Art. 18, sec. 1 PSW). The creation of a public vocational school of higher education, its liquidation, a change in its name, or a merger with another public higher educational institution shall follow a regulation by the minister in charge of higher education, at the request of a provincial assembly or the president of that particular educational institution (Art. 18, sec. 2, 4 PSW).[21] The president of a higher educational institution has acquired this privilege as a result of the said amendment of 18 March 2011.

The creation of a nonpublic higher educational institution and the obtainment of the power to organize higher education in a specific domain and at a certain level of education, requires permission from the minister in charge of higher education. A request for permission to establish a nonpublic higher educational institution made to a minister in charge of higher education may be submitted by a natural or a legal person as long as they are not a legal person of the state or local government (Art. 20, sec. 1, 2 PSW).[22] Permission shall be in the form of an administrative decision (Art. 20, sec. 7, Art. 30 PSW). The next steps to be taken after obtaining permission are the following: the founder of the nonpublic higher educational institution submits a declaration of intent to found a nonpublic higher educational institution in the form of a notarized deed (memorandum) where the statute shall be granted to the higher educational institution (Art. 23, 24 PSW). In the current legal status, i.e., until the date when the act on the change in the Law on Higher Education comes into force, the Act on Academic Degrees and Titles and on Degrees and Titles in Arts, and on the change of some other acts (1 October 2011), the statute of a higher educational institution has been subject to confirmation by the decision of the minister in charge of higher education. The new regulation does not provide for such a requirement, which is certainly an element of the strategy to extend the autonomy of higher educational institutions (Art. 30 PSW). The moment when a nonpublic higher educational institution obtains its legal personality is the moment that institution enters the register of nonpublic institutions and associations of nonpublic higher educational institutions run by the minister in charge of higher education, at the request of its founder (Art. 29 PSW).

When discussing the establishment of a legal person, it is worth mentioning the proposed amendment to the Civil Code, whereby a legal person is both an organizational unit, explicitly recognized by the act as a legal person, and one which is granted legal capacity by that act. In the latter case, the scope of legal capacity shall be determined by the provisions granting it to the organizational unit.[23] So the emphasis has been transferred to the existence of an entity with an organized structure equipped with legal capacity. An explicit entry in the act saying that a legal personality is granted to such an entity by the act will no longer be necessary.[24] At present, the creation of a legal person means 1) organizing a specific structure (with its personal or property substrate) and 2) equipping it with a legal personality. After the proposed changes enter into force, the "creation" of legal personalities will become more automatic, consistent with the principles of normative theory. Art. 44 of the draft confirms that the establishment, organization, and termination of legal persons shall be determined by relevant provisions. In addition, by these provisions the draft enables the transfer of certain issues concerning the organization and functioning of a legal person into a statutory regulation.

Although the status of the higher educational institution as a legal person should not be in doubt, detailed provisions of the PSW Act are not exhaustive in this respect and include some contradictions. The doctrine suggests that the inclusion of public tertiary-level schools to the group of state legal persons evokes many doubts. The term "public" is clearly a broader concept, not identical with the concept of "state" (here used as an adjective).[25] The public sector now covers state and local government entities. At this point, we should note that the funds of a higher educational institution are derived from state property and municipal (community) property, as stated in Art. 90, sec. 5 of the PSW: "In the case of liquidation of a public higher educational institution, its property, after redeeming its liabilities, becomes, as appropriate to the source of that property, the property of the Treasury or of a local government unit."

Legal regulations concerning the organization and functioning of higher educational institutions and internal solutions used in them show, in relation to other legal persons, many significant differences, which justifies the assertion of their special character. Particularly important is the requirement that their teaching, scientific, research, experimental, artistic, sporting, diagnostic, rehabilitation, or treatment activities not be business activities, as defined in the Act of 2 July 2004 on freedom of business activity.[26] However, they may charge fees for teaching services rendered (Art. 99 PSW), and their incomes may also include some other fees for research and specialist services, specialized and highly specialized diagnostic services, rehabilitation or treatment activities, licensing fees, and revenues from business and cultural activities (Art. 98, point 6 and 7, PSW). In the amendment to the PSW Act, the entry of Art. 7 remains in force, namely, that the university may conduct business activity, but organizationally and financially separate from the core business. A particular type of activity also has a distinctive effect on the institution's catalog of personal rights under protection. The doctrine identifies four spheres related to the functioning of a legal person as a manifestation and realization of its personality, which are useful for the division into individual personal properties, namely, the spheres of identity, freedom, confidence, and good reputation.[27]

The Autonomy of a Higher Educational Institution as an Important Aspect of Its Legal Personality

A characteristic feature of a higher educational institution is its autonomy, granted by Art. 4 of the PSW in all areas of its operation. The autonomy of tertiary-level schools should be understood as a constitutionally protected sphere of freedom for the conducting of scholarly research and education within the existing legal order.[28] It means in practice that the authorities of a tertiary-level school must be allowed to decide on matters of research and teaching, and this autonomy of decision making extends to matters of internal organization and the makeup of authorities, deciding on the admission of students, and identifying some of their rights and responsibilities. "The interference of the legislature in the sphere of autonomy in higher education should be the *ultimum remedium*."[29]

Autonomy is closely linked to the entitative character (not only in terms of legal relations).[30] Autonomy is also a feature included within the entitative character. As already mentioned, tertiary-level schools have a legal personality which differentiates them structurally and legally from other units, including their constituent entities. This is confirmed by Art. 12 of the PSW. This personality is a condition necessary to execute the granted autonomy, independence, and self-governance. Autonomy applies to both nonpublic and public schools that are the remaining state legal persons, which implies that in terms of organization, structure, and property they are separate entities distinct from the Treasury.[31] Governmental administrative bodies and local government bodies may make decisions about higher educational institutions only in the cases provided for in the acts (Art. 4, sec. 5 PSW).

The granting of autonomy to higher educational institutions is related to the roles the play in the state and for society and is there to enable them to perform their tasks efficiently. This matter gained constitutional importance (Art. 70, sec. 5 of the Constitution of the Republic of Poland). Some of the functions of tertiary-level schools are discussed in detail in Art. 4 of the PSW. Higher educational institutions shall be guided by the principles of freedom of instruction, freedom of scholarly research, and freedom of artistic expression. In fulfilling the mission of discovery and transmission of truth through scholarly research and the education of students, higher educational institutions are an integral part of the national system of education and research. They work together with other entities in the socioeconomic milieu, in particular in the field of scientific research and development for business entities, in separate forms of activity, and also may include representatives of employers in designing curricula and the teaching process. In turn, the basic tasks of a higher educational institution include these: the education of students in order for them to gain and supplement the knowledge and skills necessary for professional work and raising the students' sense of responsibility for Poland, strengthening the rules of democracy and respect for human rights; conducting research and development and providing research services; educating and promoting academic staff; the dissemination and multiplication of the achievements of scholarship, national culture, and technology, including through storage and the sharing of library collections and data sets; offering post-graduate studies, courses, and training in order to teach new skills needed for the labor market as a system of lifelong learning; providing conditions for the development of students' physical education and acting in favor of local and regional communities; and creating conditions for people with disabilities to participate fully in the process of education and research (Art. 13, sec. 1 PSW).

The autonomy of higher educational institutions is obviously not complete in terms of their independence, since the autonomy is granted "subject to the conditions specified in the act." It manifests itself in many of its powers relating primarily to the education the institution offers. A higher educational institution has in particular the right to:

1. conduct scholarly research and development and to determine the direction of this R&D;
2. cooperate with other academic and scholarly entities, including foreign ones, in the implementation of research and development, on the basis of agreements, in order to raise funds from the implementation of research proposals, including their commercialization, and to promote mobility of researchers;
3. support research conducted by young researchers, in particular through competitions funded from the institution's funds, referred to in Art. 18, sec. 1, point 3 of the Act of 30 April 2010 on the principles of financing education;[32]
4. offer higher education studies as first- or second-degree studies or uniform MA-equivalent or PhD-equivalent studies, in accordance with the powers granted to the institution, including the following actions to:

   a. determine the conditions for admission of students, including the number of vacancies for specific courses and types of studies;[33]

b. determine plans of studies and curricula,[34] considering the effects of education,[35] according to the National Qualifications Framework for Higher Education (National Qualifications Framework) for the fields of study established by a regulation by the minister in charge of higher education;[36]

5. offer postgraduate studies, supplementary courses, and training;
6. issue diplomas of graduation certifying the professional title obtained and certificates of graduation from postgraduate studies and supplementary courses (Art. 6, sec. 1 PSW).

Eligible organizational units of higher educational institutions may grant doctoral and post-doctoral degrees, and apply to grant the title of professor.[37]

With regard to decision making about an educational offer, the amendment to the PSW significantly broadens the autonomy of higher educational institutions having the power to grant postdoctoral degrees and meeting the requirements for organizational units to offer certain majors and at a certain level of education, as defined in a regulation by the minister in charge of higher education. Such an institution can offer a major and at a level of education defined by the institution's senate, by resolution, within the areas of education and fields corresponding to the powers to award postdoctoral degrees. The resolution of the senate determines the teaching effects, to which study plans and curricula are adjusted, as appropriate, to the level and profile of education (Art. 11, sec. 1 PSW).

However, these powers of a higher educational institution, which are a manifestation of its autonomy, are (as already noted) subject to certain restrictions.

Art. 33 Sec. 1 limits the autonomy of a higher educational institution in this respect: the minister in charge of higher education supervises the compliance of higher educational institutions with the provisions of the law, the statute, and the content of permission granted to create a nonpublic university, as well as the appropriateness of the expenditure of public funds.[38] The minister in charge of higher education may request some information and explanations from the authorities of the higher educational institution and from the founder of a nonpublic higher educational institution. He/she may also inspect the activities of these institutions. According to Art. 34 of the PSW, the supervision shall include the verification of the compliance of school authorities with laws, the statute, and the powers granted, and in the case of nonpublic higher educational institutions, with the content of the permission given to the institution for its establishment as well. The supervision also refers to the inspection of the expenditure of public funds. An inspection may also be performed of the conditions of implementation of the educational process.

In exercising his/her supervisory function, the minister in charge of higher education also has the power to annul the resolution of the collective body representing a higher educational institution or the decision of its president, except for administrative decisions, if it is found to be in conflict with the law or the statute of that institution (Art. 36, sec. 1 PSW); s/he may appeal to the senate to dismiss the president if s/he is guilty of serious breaches of law or of the statute, and by the time of examination of that application, s/he may suspend the president from performing his/her function (Art. 38, sec. 1 and 3 PSW), while in the case of a gross violation of law by the president, the minister may even dismiss the president upon consulting the Central Council of Science and Higher Education and the Conference of Presidents of Polish Academic Institutions or the Conference of Presidents of Polish Vocational Schools of Higher Education, and set a deadline for the appointment of a new president in the manner prescribed in the institution's statute (Art. 38, sec. 5 PSW).

If a higher educational institution or the founder of a nonpublic higher educational institution performs an activity contrary to law, the statute, or permit, or does not respond to requests or does not comply with recommendations made as a result of an inspection of the institution's activity, the minister in charge of higher education shall call on the authorities of the institution or the founder of a nonpublic institution to cease that activity and remove its effects, setting an appropriate deadline to do so. If the violation is serious, the minister in charge of higher education shall initiate proceedings for the liquidation of a public higher educational institution or revoke his/her authorization to establish that institution and also order the founder to liquidate it within a set deadline (Art. 37 PSW).

Moreover, in accordance with Art. 40 of the PSW, the minister in charge of higher education has some powers of an extraordinary nature. He or she may, upon consultation with the institution's senate, commission a specific task to be performed by the institution in the field of teaching or training of academic staff, providing adequate resources for its implementation. The amendment to the PSW also allows an obligation to be imposed on a higher educational institution to perform other tasks, providing a means for their implementation in the event of a natural calamity, or to comply with international obligations.

An important limitation on the autonomy of tertiary-level schools is the possibility of suspension or even revocation of the permission to offer a specific major and at a certain level of education. It arises when an organizational unit fails to meet the statutory standards which regulate 1) the quality of education, 2) the minimum number of staff members, 3) conditions to be met by organizational units to offer a certain major and at a certain level of education, and 4) educational standards for certain selected fields of study specified in the Act (Art. 11a—11c PSW).

In addition to its core activity, that is, the wide-ranging teaching activity, another aspect which reveals the autonomy of higher educational institutions is their ability to run business activitiesin the areas and forms specified in the statute separately from activity associated with its basic tasks (Art. 7 PSW), and also the ability to run canteens and dormitories (Art. 14 PSW).

The self-governance and self-organization of a higher educational institution is also reflected in the fact that all issues not regulated in the act relating to the institution's internal organization and functioning shall be set out in the institution's own statute (Art. 17 PSW). The act amending the PSW has introduced a modification relating to the issue of the statute entering into force and so, evidently, also the scope of inspection powers regarding the internal organization of a higher educational institution. The statute of a public higher educational institution shall enter into force on the date specified in the resolution of its senate (Art. 56, sec. 2 PSW) and independently from the powers granted to that institution; it will no longer require the authorization of the minister in charge of higher education (Art. 1, sec. of the Law on Higher Education, the Act on Academic Degrees and Titles and on Degrees and Titles in Arts, and on the change of some other acts, hereinafter referred to as UOZM PSW).[39] Also for a nonpublic higher educational institution, the requirement to obtain a decision issued by the minister in charge of higher education authorizing the statute has been cancelled (point 47 UOZM PSW). The statute of a nonpublic higher educational institution shall enter into force on the date specified in the resolution of a collective body (representing the institution) referred to in the statute or a decision of the founder (Art. 58, sec. 4 PSW). Internal regulations remaining within the competence of the higher educational institution, without interference from a supervising body, are a factor that favors the institution's autonomy.

As noted by the Constitutional Tribunal, the constitutional guarantee of autonomy of higher educational institutions implies that the legislature assumes the existence of internal acts of these universities, with which they may regulate the rights and obligations of students. Thus, they are entitled to delete from the list of students those who do not meet the requirements set out by these acts. The right to such internal regulations shall be granted to all tertiary-level schools, so that they could pursue the public objective of educating students and conducting research (including artistic and creative work).[40]

A further step toward expanding the autonomy of higher educational institutions is the transfer of powers to create, restructure, and liquidate basic organizational units of that institution, including non-local units, from the minister in charge of higher education to the (discretion of) the president (of the institution), who may do so upon consultation with the senate. So far, only those institutions which have at least four powers to award doctoral degrees have been able to do so, and in the case of arts schools, only those with two such powers (Art. 84 PSW). It has already been mentioned that as a result of the amendment of 18 March 2011, the president of an institution has also gained the right to apply for the creation of a public vocational school of higher education, its liquidation, a change of its name, or a merger with another public vocational school of higher education (Art. 18, sec. 2, 4 PSW).

The autonomy of a higher educational institution should be manifested through its financial independence. The institution has its own assets, which include property and other financial rights (Art. 89 PSW). Because of the sources of funding, an institution's financial self-governance will be more complete in the case of nonpublic higher educational institutions. Public authorities, under the terms of the act, provide public educational institutions with financial resources necessary to carry out their tasks and they provide assistance to nonpublic institutions in the scope and forms defined in the act (Art. 15 PSW).[41] The amendment, however, also facilitates the management of property by a public higher educational institution. Managing the elements of fixed assets under accounting regulations, to the extent specified in the Act of 8 August 1996 on the principles of exercising the powers granted to the Treasury (OJL, no. 106, Item 493, as amended) requires the consent of the minister in charge of the Treasury only if the market value of the element subject to the regulation exceeds the equivalent of PLN 250,000, calculated on the basis of an average exchange rate announced by the National Bank of Poland, as of the date of applying for permission (Art. 90, sec. 4). Before the amendment, legal acts regulating that matter drawn up by a higher educational institution were dependent on the consent of the minister even in situations where there was a fivefold lower value of assets than that referred to in the regulation. This provision was challenged as overly invasive, thus rendering some of the manifestations of an institution's legal personality deceptive. Since the institution's property is its assets separate from the Treasury (Art. 89 PSW), "the right granted to the Minister of the Treasury in Art. 90, sec. 4 of the act violates the competences of a higher educational institution resulting from the institution's legal personality and its rights of ownership."[42] The issue is particularly important, given that the law, in accordance with Art. 21 of the Constitution of the Republic of Poland, is subject to special protection, as repeatedly confirmed by the rulings of the Constitutional Tribunal, which noted that the general constitutional norm: "The Republic of Poland shall protect ownership" applies not only to personal property, and so a category of property which applies to citizens, but to all entities, i.e., also those whose both status and existence are regulated entirely by public law provisions.[43]

Despite the statement in Art. 100 of the PSW that a higher educational institution (public or private) shall manage an independent financial economy on the basis of a material and financial plan approved by its internal collective body, the independence is somewhat limited by the requirement to submit that plan to the relevant minister within fourteen days of its adoption. This requirement also applies to private higher educational institutions, which is clearly underlined in the revised PSW.

Differences in the financial autonomy of public and nonpublic higher educational institutions are usually primarily noted in the way they raise funds for their own functioning, particularly in the setting of tuition fees. The amendment to the PSW slightly compensates for these differences. It is true that a public higher educational institution may raise funds from "fees for educational services, particularly for training full-time students, if they are studying in second or subsequent courses of full-time studies, and for part-time BA/MA-equivalent or doctoral studies, and for artistic services provided by schools of arts" (Art. 98, sec. 1, point 3 PSW), but this is subject to further restrictions, even stricter than the ones for nonpublic institutions.[44] A significant change introduced by the amendment to the act relates to the principles of charging fees and the amount of fees in nonpublic higher educational institutions. They are defined by the authority specified in the statute, except that fees for educational services related to the education of students in BA/MA-equivalent studies and doctoral studies and fees associated with the repetition of certain courses of study in BA/MA-equivalent studies or doctoral studies should not exceed the costs incurred to the extent necessary to launch and run that educational institution, BA/MA-equivalent studies or doctoral studies, respectively, and courses of study at BA/MA-equivalent studies or doctoral studies, including the costs of preparing and implementing the strategy of that institution's development, in particular the training of academic staff and the development of teaching and academic infrastructure, including depreciation and repairs (Art. 99, sec. 4 PSW). Determination of the upper limit for those fees in relation to non-state entities is certainly a form of interference with their autonomy. In addition, a new limiting of financial self-governance of a higher educational institution is introduced by Art. 99a of the PSW, prohibiting the collection of fees for registration for a consecutive semester or year of study, exams, including re-sit exams, exams in front of a commission, the final diploma examination, the issue of a professional practice journal, submission and assessment of the diploma thesis, and the issue of a supplement to the diploma.

We should mention that agreements relating to the payment of fees for educational services with students are not of a defined legal nature. Doubts concern only the question of whether they are service agreements, to which commissioning provisions duly apply (Art. 750 CC) or consumer agreements (Art. 384, 385, 3851-3 CC) to which the provisions of the Act of 15 December 2000 on the Protection of Competition and Consumers apply.[45] The Office of Competition and Consumer Protection Branch in Wrocław, as a result of a preliminary investigation into models of contracts governing the terms of payment for higher education, confirmed the "consumer" nature of those contracts. This means that students who use the services of a higher educational institution for a fee have the status of consumers as defined in the Act of 15 December 2000 on the Protection of Competition and Consumers. The institution therefore has the status of an entrepreneur, and is subject to that act and to the ban on practices infringing collective consumer interests. As noted in the doctrine, this evokes difficulties in interpretation, as that institution is an "entrepreneur" in light of that law, but is not an "entrepreneur" in light of the Law on Freedom of Economic Activity, with the resulting privileges.[46]

From the standpoint of the financial autonomy of higher educational institutions, it is important that the amendment to the PSW allows the institution, in order to commercialize the results of research and development, to create a limited liability company or a joint-stock company (a "special purpose vehicle"). It is formed by the president with the consent of the senate or other collective body representing the higher educational institution. The tasks of the special purpose vehicle include in particular buying shares in companies, or creating companies formed in order to implement the results of scientific research or development work carried out at a university. Moreover, by contract, the president may entrust the SPV with the management of the institution's industrial property within the scope of its commercialization. The SPV's dividend is allocated by the institution to its statutory activities (Art. 86a PSW). The SPV can be formed by several public higher educational institutions or nonpublic higher educational institutions (Art. 86b, sec. 1 PSW).

Summary

One of the basic assumptions of the amendment to the Law on Higher Education was to achieve a greater degree of autonomy for higher educational institutions. To this end, regulations were introduced through which universities that may grant postdoctoral degrees will be able to independently decide to offer some new majors; tertiary-level schools will also be able to more easily manage their own assets and obtain funds for their activities. The new solutions further enhance the relationship between higher educational institutions and the socioeconomic environment, adapting education to the market.

While recognizing the benefits of these changes, it is clearly noticeable that not all the changes serve to enhance the autonomy of higher educational institutions. The minister responsible for higher education has a wide range of competence, which arouses concern about the illusory nature of some autonomous powers of higher educational institutions. Some regulations, such as ones concerning parity (the participation of women in certain bodies is only 30 percent)[47] and restrictions on the collection of tuition fees, limit the ability of higher educational institutions to self-organize and self-govern. The very fact that the regulation of matters relating to the activities of a higher educational institution is on a case-law basis results in the withdrawal of that institution's decision-making power, unless it is reduced to repeating or supplementing provisions of the act. As stated by the Constitutional Tribunal, "acts determining the rules of the public [and nonpublic] tertiary-level schools must, in accordance with Art. 70, sec. 5 of the Constitution, respect their autonomy, i.e., they may not cancel the essence of that autonomy through a complete normalization of all issues. . . . Otherwise, the role of state tertiary-level schools would be limited to complying with legal acts, and the bodies representing these schools would become state bodies, which would amount to abolishing their autonomy. It is . . . impossible, in light of the Constitution, to make the authorities of a public tertiary-level school, on matters concerning the substance of that school's activity, a type of authority with public power, including state administration bodies [which are characterized by hierarchical subordination]."[48]

It should also be noted that, although adapting the activity of a higher educational institution to social and economic expectations is by all means justified, subjecting these activities to the rules of supply and demand will practically affect the autonomy of higher educational institutions, e.g., in the preparation of an educational offer.

Autonomy, as indicated above, is a feature of legal personality. The scope of autonomy of an entity may, however, vary. So full independence is not an immanent element of an entitative legal character, even if understood only as legal autonomy. The sacrifice of certain aspects of the autonomy of higher educational institutions is justified by the standardization of education and raising its quality for the sake of the general public. However, whether some changes introduced in Polish law (e.g., those identified by the author) really (and not just theoretically) serve that purpose, while maintaining the principle of proportionality, is arguable. This statement made by the author should be viewed as a voice in the discussion, and certainly not as a definitive report on the matter.

Notes

1. OJL 2011, no. 84, Item 455. The text of the article takes into account the amendments introduced by this legislation.

2. It is an understanding of legal personality *sensu stricto* as an attribute of legal persons. Further, the article mentions the understanding of legal personality *sensu largo*, corresponding to the concept of legal entity.

3. See A. Wolter, J. Ignatowicz, and K. Stefaniuk, *Prawo cywilne: Zarys części ogólnej* (Warsaw, 2001), p. 109.

4. Ibid., p. 158; Z. Radwański, *Prawo cywilne—część ogólna* (Warsaaw, 2007), p. 142. There is a dispute as to whether it is an inborn feature enjoyed by a person from the mere fact of being human, although it is granted from the moment of birth. Referring to natural rights considered as human rights, one must note that among those rights the International Covenant on Civil and Political Rights states the right of everyone (the right being absolute) to recognize everywhere that person's legal entitative character (T. Jasudowicz, *Administracja wobec praw człowieka* [Toruń, 1997], pp. 21, 22, 56).

5. It is discussed further.

6. A. Bieranowski, P. Bogdalski, and M. Goettel, *Prawo cywilne: Zarys wykładu* (Cracow, 2006), p. 56.

7. Wolter, Ignatowicz, and Stefaniuk, p. 158; Radwański, pp. 143, 144, 258.

8. Bieranowski, Bogdalski, and Goettel, p. 56.

9. Radwański, p. 144. Another key feature that makes legal capacity different from the capacity to perform legal acts is that in the case of natural persons the former is always granted to the same extent (in full), while the latter may have a different scope (full, limited, i.e., partial or no capacity) (ibid., p. 259; Wolter, Ignatowicz, and Stefaniuk, p. 166).

10. A draft of the first book of the new Civil Code (hereinafter referred to as: draft CC) is available at http://bip.ms.gov.pl/pl/dzialalnosc/komisje-kodyfikacyjne/komisja-kodyfikacyjna-prawa-cywilnego/.

11. Z, Radwański, comment in "Jest już pierwsza część kodeksu cywilnego," *Gazeta Prawna*, 11 December 2008, http://prawo .gazetaprawna.pl/wywiady/100092,jest_juz_pierwsza_czesc_kod eksu_cywilnego.html.

12. Bieranowski, Bogdalski, and Goettel, p. 66.

13. Ibid., p. 70.

14. Ibid., p. 69. The proposed Civil Code (Art. 47) does not change the moment when an organizational unit obtains legal personality (draft CC, p. 54).

15. Ibid., p. 53.

16. Ibid., p. 50.

17. OJL 2005, no. 164, Item 1365, as amended. The act does not apply to tertiary-level schools or seminaries run by churches and religious associations, with the exception of the Catholic University of Lublin, unless an act or agreement between the government and the authorities of the churches or religious organizations provides otherwise (Art. 1, sec. 2 PSW).

18. For example, words such as institute, school, academy, center, department, college, or university can be found in the names of higher educational institutions, as well as other schools or even small entities doing business unrelated to education.

19. J. Piszczek, "Ochrona renomy szkoły wyższej (problematyka cywilnoprawna)," www.kancelaria-piszczek.p/upload/11.doc.

20. OJL 1996, no. 106, Item 493, as amended.

21. In the current legal status (i.e., by the date when the act on the change in the Law on Higher Education, the Act on Academic Degrees and Titles and on Degrees and Titles in the Arts, and on the change of some other acts come into force) a Resolution of the Council of Ministers issued upon request by the minister in charge of higher education or a provincial assembly in agreement with that minister is required.

22. In his authorization the minister specifies the founder of a higher educational institution, its name, official seat, the courses offered, and the level of education, a minimum size and type of property which the founder is obliged to devote to the establishment of that institution, and its operation; the amount of financial resources cannot be less than PLN 500,000 (Art. 20, sec. 4 PSW).

23. Art. 43 draft CC.

24. Radwański, comment in "Jest już."

25. U. Kalina-Prasznic, "Publiczne, rynkowe czy społeczne?," Forum akademickie, September 2008, http://www.forumakad.pl/archiwum/2008/09/41 _publiczne_rynkowe_czy_spoleczne.html.

26. OJL, no. 173, Item 1807, as amended.

27. For more on this subject, see J. Koczanowski, *Ochrona dóbr osobistych osób prawnych* (Cracow, 1999), p. 97, and others.

28. Verdict of the Constitutional Tribunal of 8 November 2000, file ref. no. SK 18/99, Constitutional Tribunal Body of Rulings Official Collection 2000, no. 7, Item 258.

29. R. Piotrowski, "Parytety niszczą autonomię uczelni," *Dziennik Gazeta Prawna*, no. 67 (7 April 2010): A17.

30. See more in A. Popławska, *Idea samorządności: Podmiotowość—autonomia—pluralizm* (Białystok, 2001).

31. Bieranowski, Bogdalski, and Goettel, p. 67.

32. OJL 2010, no. 96, Item 615 and OJL 2011, no. 84, Item 455.

33. Except for studies in the fields of medicine and dentistry.

34. In accordance with Art. 2, sec. 1, point 14b of the PSW, the curriculum is a description of consistent effects of instruction defined by the higher educational institution, consistent with the National Qualifications Framework for Higher Education, and a description of the teaching process, leading to the attainment of these effects, with ECTS points ascribed to each module of that process.

35. The effects of teaching mean the body of knowledge, skills, and social competencies acquired by the learner in the course of instruction (Art. 2, sec. 1, point 18c PSW); model effects of teaching for selected fields of study, taking into account the level and profile of education in individual areas of education, shall be determined by a regulation of the minister in charge of higher education after consultation with the Main Council for Science and Higher Education (Art. 9, sec. 2 PSW).

36. National Qualifications Framework for Higher Education—description, by determining the effects of teaching, of qualifications obtained in the Polish system of higher education (Art. 2, sec. 1, point 18a PSW), established by a regulation by the minister in charge of higher education (Art. 9, sec. 1, point 2 PSW).

37. These matters are regulated by the Act of 14 March 2003 on Academic Degrees and Titles and on Degrees and Titles in the Arts, OJL 2003, no. 65, Item 959.

38. Powers of the minister in charge of higher education in the supervision referred to in sec. 1, are held by the Minister of National Defense (in relation to military academies), the minister in charge of internal affairs (in relation to schools of public services), minister in charge of culture and national heritage protection (in relation to arts schools), the minister in charge of health (in relation to medical schools), the minister in charge of maritime

economy (in relation to the naval academies), respectively (Art. 33, sec. 2 PSW).

39. Exceptions are as follows: the statute of a military academy and civil service schools, which shall enter into force on the date when the Minister of National Defense or the minister in charge of internal affairs issues a decision approving the statute, unless the statute specifies a later date.

40. Verdict of the Constitutional Tribunal of 8 November 2000, file ref. no. SK 18/99, Constitutional Tribunal Body of Rulings Official Collection 2000, no. 7, item 258.

41. The activities of a public higher educational institution are financed with grants from the state budget for the tasks defined in the act and may be financed from the institution's own revenues (Art. 92, sec. 1 PSW).

42. Kalina-Prasznic.

43. Verdict of the Constitutional Tribunal of 20 November 1996, file ref. no. K 27/95, Constitutional Tribunal Body of Rulings Official Collection 1997, p. 264.

44. See Verdict of the Constitutional Tribunal of 8 November 2000, file ref. no. SK 18/99, Constitutional Tribunal Body of Rulings Official Collection 2000, no. 7, Item 258.

45. OJL 2005, no. 244, Item 2080, as amended.

46. Kalina-Prasznic.

47. Piotrowski, p. A17.

48. Verdict of the Constitutional Tribunal of 8 November 2000, file ref. no. SK 18/99, Constitutional Tribunal Body of Rulings Official Collection 2000, no. 7, Item 258.

THE NATIONAL FRAMEWORK OF QUALIFICATIONS IN POLISH HIGHER EDUCATION AND THE DEVELOPMENT OF CONTINUING EDUCATION

ANNA FRĄCKOWIAK

The National Framework of Qualifications for Institutions of Higher Education in Poland

The Polish National Framework of Qualifications for higher educational institutions falls into a wider qualification framework for the entire education system. It has been developed in response to the latest stages of development of the Bologna Process in which Poland has participated from the very beginning. A number of previous analyses of the Polish system of higher education demonstrated our country's backwardness within the development and implementation of the NFQ (cf. Polish Higher Education 2009). This has changed radically, particularly last year, when the Ministry of Science and Higher Education announced a survey of the NFQ, i.e., "Curriculum Autonomy of Universities: A Qualification Framework for Higher Education." Additionally, a number of educational community meetings of an informative nature have been organized alongside consultation meetings. What is the aim of implementing the NFQ? First, the principal aim is to achieve what has been emphasized in European studies—the initiation of another mechanism in order to establish a European Area of Higher Education, as well as an improvement in the understanding and transfer of qualifications achieved by university graduates in the countries constituting such an area. Second, this mechanism is supposed to result in wider acceptance of qualifications obtained in exchange programs for students, faculty, and also for graduates on the European job market. The NFQ refers to a common European structure; therefore it is meant to provide improved communication between schools, primarily in terms of administration.

The implementation of another element of the Bologna Process involves providing a basic justification for the introduction of the NFQ in higher education, yet other reasons may be found as well. These are challenges that higher educational institutions face in relation to social and economic changes, as well as a change in the perception of universities and their roles. There has been a change in the expectations of higher educational institutions and the effects of their activities, which results in the necessity for reformulating curricula, forms and methods applied, means of evaluating knowledge, and the skills and attitudes developed in universities. Thus the entire system of higher education teaching is being formulated anew under the NFQ.

A Critical Analysis of the Polish National Framework of Qualifications

The document entitled "Curriculum Autonomy of Universities: The Qualifications Framework for Higher Education" has been issued by the Ministry of Science and Higher Education using EU funds from the Operational Program—Human Capital in Higher Education called "The National Framework of Qualifications in Higher Education as a Tool for Improving the Quality of Teaching." This fact itself along with placing logos of the OP HC and the ECF (European Cohesion Fund) on the cover, as well as providing this information on the document's first page results in positive associations. This project has been co-financed with EU funds, which means it is good, reliable, and it also allows distributing the results in the form of documents describing the Polish NFQ. Yet not mentioned in this document is whether only the elaboration of the NFQ proposal for Polish higher educational institutions has been co-financed or its implementation as well.

Initially, the reader is presented with a strong justification for implementing the NFQ in Polish schools. This justification is of a specific character, although a reliable analysis concerning the positive and negative aspects of the changes in higher education under the NFQ has never been conducted. What Polish universities may gain or lose has not been mentioned, which needs particular attention so that the implementation of the NFQ will be efficient, and it will not become a parody of itself. Instead, as early as in the contents page, the following wording appears: "Why have all the countries of Europe decided to use this form of education description in their schools?" or "Why should we develop a national framework of qualifications as well?" Such expressions are based on willingness, typical of our Polish mentality, to be rightful members of the community of European countries, to follow European trends, as well as on a willingness to be accepted and make progress. Therefore this justification refers to a social perception on a macro scale—what will be our image in comparison to other countries if we fail? Thus, this is a reference to what others do, and what Poland should do in such a situation, without any internal justification of how the implementation of the NFQ will contribute to Polish universities.

Specific documents that constitute the basis for formulating the Polish NFQ were mentioned in the cover letter comprising the introduction to the entire NFQ, which is signed by the Minister of Science and Higher Education, Professor Barbara Kudrycka, PhD These are as follows: the Bergen Declaration of 2005, which resulted from the fourth conference on the Bologna Process, attended by ministers of education, as well as the Recommendation of the European Parliament of 2008, which applies to qualifications within the entire education system (Curriculum Autonomy 2010, 5). These documents are also referred to in annex no. 1, presenting the European background to the NFQ in response to the aforementioned Recommendation of 2008, as well as the Recommendation of the Parliament and Council of 2006 on key competencies for lifelong learning (Chmielecka 2010, 119).

In the introduction explaining what the NFQ is, there are certain discrepancies concerning the justification for its implementation, following the convention "if this is what everybody does, so will we." Let us examine how the NFQ is defined:

The national framework of qualifications for higher education is . . . a particular method for describing the education offered to students by Polish universities. . . . [D]escriptions have been formulated as teaching results, which means that they define the requirements that students should meet on completing studies within a given teaching period. Secondly, these descriptions, using a common European framework, will allow comparing diplomas obtained at different universities within the entire territory *of Europe* [my emphasis]. (Chmielecka, Marciniak, and Kraśniewski 2010, 7)

It is easy to explain what the NFQ is, yet preliminary information justifying its implementation includes three references to "European countries." In the above quotation the expression "within the entire territory of Europe" has been used, also on p. 9 of the justification of why we should also implement these frameworks, the expression "all the countries of Europe" occurs, and previously on p. 8, "all the countries of the European Union." It is evident that the reader has been misinformed. First, not all the countries of Europe are members of the European Union, whereas regarding frameworks of qualifications for higher education, they apply to the countries which are signatories to the Bologna Declaration. The number of such countries has now reached forty-sic; however, not all of them belong to the EU. Second, one may not conclude that all the European countries, without any exceptions, have been involved in the elaboration and implementation of the NFQ. Belarus, a country which is undoubtedly situated in Europe, remains a blank spot on the map of countries involved in the Bologna Process. Thus, such a generalization leads to an overinterpretation of the NFQ implementation process already at its very beginning.

Furthermore, other reasons are discussed briefly. These are, inter alia, mass education at the university level and the necessity for coping with an increasingly diverse group of students, which is not only typical of Polish schools, but is a phenomenon characteristic of higher educational institutions from a global perspective (cf. Altbach, Reisberg, and Rumbley 2009). As it has been emphasized, the implementation of the NFQ in Polish universities aims to "remain a basic tool for adjusting the teaching offer both to the needs of particular groups of students, and to the needs of the employment market. Presently, the National Framework of Qualifications is the most effective method for improving the efficiency of teaching in Polish universities" (Chmielecka, Marciniak, and Kraśniewski 2010, 9). Therefore, for universities, implementation of the NFQ means dealing with the diversity of students in the days of mass education, and under such circumstances its implementation is justified as the best method for maintaining the teaching quality in higher educational institutions.

The use of the words "qualifications" and "competencies" for defining particular areas which constitute the NFQ raises certain doubts. It needs to be pointed out that these terms have not been thoroughly explained, and the only definition results from the document issued by the European Parliament and the Council of Europe on the European Framework of Qualifications in a life-long perspective. The document states that "a qualification is understood as a formal competence, i.e., a title, a degree, or the like, identified with a diploma, a certificate, or another document equivalent to it, issued on completion of a given stage of education, certifying the achievement of specific educational results" (Chmielecka, Marciniak, Kraśniewski 2010, 12).

Therefore a European term has been adopted, which is different than the Polish terms "competence" and "qualification," but without conducting any comparison or analysis. According to *The Lexicon of Work Pedagogy*, these terms have been defined as follows:

> *Qualifications* are attitudes, physical environment, as well as practical and mental sensorimotor structures, allowing the solving of tasks within a certain area of activity. (Nowacki 2004, 115)
> *Competencies* are powers and entitlements vested on the basis of appropriate qualifications, as well as the right to take decisions within a specified area. A person is competent if he possesses a qualification, and the authorization to act. The term "competencies" is also used when qualifications are accompanied by complete responsibility for how they are employed by a qualified person. (Nowacki 2004, 100)

Therefore it is worth noticing that one may hold qualifications for performing a given profession, but not necessarily be competent at participating in the tasks performed.

The Polish NFQ has been elaborated with elements based on the European Framework of Qualifications, involving knowledge, abilities, personal and social competencies, whereas the latter has been described using the term "competencies." Therefore students graduating from schools need to be able to apply their knowledge in a responsible manner within their professional tasks. Yet the element of attitudes, which is also shaped in the education process at the university level, has not been emphasized. The explanation of difficulties associated with the terms used and their definitions may be found on page 139, in a study by E. Chmielecka, devoted to personal and social competencies. In the footnote added by the author there was information that the terms used had been taken from an officially accepted Polish translation of the Recommendation of the European Parliament and Council of 23 April 2008.

The National Framework of Qualifications raises serious reservations and doubts in other areas as well. This refers to examples and expressions which are aimed at preparing curricula according to principles determined by the assumptions lying at the root of the NFQ. The NFQ extensively explains its essence; the changes in the curricula of higher educational institutions have been mentioned as well. They are supposed to indicate specific educational results. Presently, it is pointed out that educational results are supposed to be guidelines for selecting teaching contents and the manner in which they are accomplished. At the same time, one might conclude that these objectives are depreciated or misconceived. It is advisable to have a closer look at the definitions used by the authors of the NFQ:

> The objective of a subject describes a change that is expected to result from the realization of the subject-related curriculum. Objectives are the teacher's intentions . . . . They display what knowledge the recipients possess, what they learn, how their abilities improve, how their life situation changes, and what possibilities emerge. . . .
>
> Teaching effects are direct and immediate results (measured on completion of a subject or its part), stemming from the provision of a product in the form of lectures, laboratories, exercises, projects, and others. . . .
>
> Teaching objectives are entry elements and they do not guarantee specific effects/results, which should be defined as those which crown the process of education. (Saryusz-Wolski 2010, 105)

In the above quotation it is easily noticeable that actual convictions have been confused with erroneous ones. It is true that objectives differ from educational effects, it is true that objectives are formulated by teachers, and it is true that they do not guarantee specific results. Yet objectives are formulated in order to realize what we *wish* to achieve during the teaching process, i.e., what knowledge and skills students should acquire and what attitudes they should demonstrate as a result of completing a given course. However, educational effects are what is in fact attained on completion of a course, i.e., what students actually know, and what attitudes they demonstrate. Generally, effects differ from objectives, meaning that objectives are not 100 percent accomplished. Yet objectives constitute a point of reference in the evaluation process of effects. For example, we may assume that we want our students to be able to name and define correctly basic teaching concepts, such as teaching, education, learning, self-teaching, and the like, and then while checking exam papers it appears that, e.g., 70 percent of students taught by us are able to perform well, which means that the formulated objective has been 70 percent accomplished. The evaluation of this fact, as well as feedback for teachers on the efficacy of their teaching methods, remains a separate issue. The authors of the document on the NFQ also neglect to mention that objectives may be formulated at different levels—starting with general objectives and finishing with operational ones. The discussion presented to date has indicated that the picture illustrating the difference between objectives and educational effects in the document on the NFQ (on p. 105), is incomplete. The correct diagram should be as shown in figure 1. The arrow between teaching effects and objectives means supervision over the achievement of objectives, without which we do not know if the education process conducted by us has been effective.

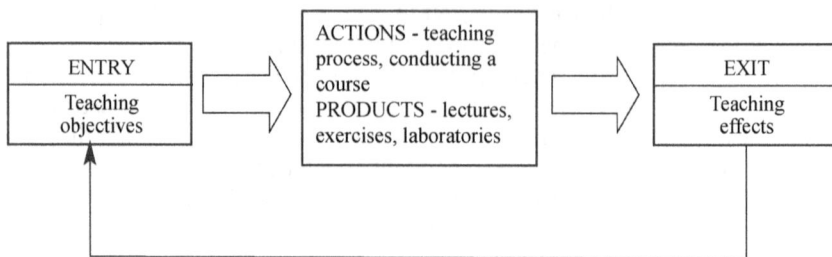

Figure 1. The difference between objectives and teaching effects.

The term "products" also raises reservations with regard to lectures, exercises, and laboratories. Wincenty Okoń states explicitly that lectures, exercises, seminars, and laboratory classes are teaching tools in higher education; however, they are also forms of education (Okoń 1971, 178).

In the document on the NFQ for higher education the reader is persuaded that, up until today, teachers conducting classes have concentrated excessively on objectives while ignoring teaching effects. This is obviously untrue, considering that the teaching process always brings specific effects, more or less advanced, and these effects are always evaluated. The alteration suggested involves perceiving teaching effects in universities not only from the teacher's perspective, but also from the perspective of students and their future situation in the employment market. The emphasis placed on teaching effects in the NFQ document is significant, and the manner in which this is described gives the impression that including these effects in the curriculum is supposed to guarantee their accomplishment. Admittedly, the NFQ included a passage devoted to the evaluation of teaching effects, yet without concrete propositions. It only mentioned the necessity for the evaluation of teaching effects, the establishment of evaluation criteria, their assessment along with the interested party, and the maintenance of quality; yet this evaluation has not been compared to the objectives being formulated. It has only been stated that within further studies it is possible to provide and promote examples of so-called good practices within the scope of the evaluation of the teaching effects being conducted. Yet the authors focused on presenting differences between teaching objectives and effects and on promoting the latter to such a significant extent that the relationship between teaching objectives and effects has completely escaped them.

Such a focus on teaching effects may be associated with what has been mentioned in the second chapter of this document. "The use of a coherent set of teaching effects as the basis for developing syllabuses results from shifting responsibility during the process of education from the teacher to the learner, and from teaching to learning" (Próchnicka, Saryusz-Wolski, and Kraśniewski 2010, 91). Hence the conviction of the authors expressed in the statement that the implementation of the NFQ in Polish universities brings about a certain type of revolution. Obviously, such an assumption may be made, although it is a mental revolution concerning the perception of the teaching process rather than a revolution causing actual and radical change in academic practices. Thus the following conclusion has emerged: "The core of modern curricula consists of teaching effects, in contrast with the curricula developed using traditional methods, based on curricular content" (Próchnicka, Saryusz-Wolski, and Kraśniewski 2010, 91).

The authors intended to emphasize that the changes introduced by the NFQ in the development of curricula involve taking into account the educational needs of students to a greater extent, as well as the professional requirements that graduates need to satisfy. Moreover, they need to focus on the actual results of the teaching process in schools. Yet presenting the NFQ as in the above quotations gives the impression that such phenomena have not been occurring in Polish universities until now, which is already a distortion, as until now it has been assumed in curricula that students, as a result of the teaching process, will need to display the knowledge, skills, and attitudes appropriate for the course studied by them. Presently these results have only been emphasized more strongly; they have been virtually placed in the foreground.

Therefore teaching effects are frequently overemphasized, pushing teachers into the background or even eliminating them. The perception of the teaching process and its organization which favors teachers and expects students to adjust to the requirements and teaching models imposed by schools has not been beneficial and does not perform well in contemporary society. Nowadays we observe that schools and their organization lean toward the opposite direction, subordinating everything to students. A school where teachers are the most important is considered to be bad or even abnormal, a school where students are the most important to be good and most desired. However, a certain balance between the teachers' and students' needs and expectations is necessary for the proper functioning of universities, which should be reflected in their curricula. Regrettably, the NFQ document seldom mentions teachers and when it does, with rather negative connotations:

> Objectives are usually formulated from the teachers' point of view, whereas teaching effects involve detailed descriptions of the results achieved by students. (Próchnicka, Saryusz-Wolski, and Kraśniewski 2010, 92)

> As it may be noticed, developing curricula based on teaching effects (according to the procedure described above) brings numerous benefits. . . . [I]t limits the possibilities of creating a curriculum dominated by a faculty's interests. (Próchnicka, Saryusz-Wolski, and Kraśniewski 2010, 99)

> In other words, evaluation and accreditation procedures should be less and less based on assessing teaching effects—"exit," and not "entry," i.e., on assessing the efficiency of "learning" instead of "teaching." (Próchnicka, Saryusz-Wolski, and Kraśniewski 2010, 101)

> Teaching effects defined for a given subject do not determine what a lecturer is supposed to teach students, but they define what knowledge, skills, personal and social competences students will be able to demonstrate on completion of a course. (Saryusz-Wolski 2010, 104)

The quotations given above constitute only the most extreme examples depreciating the role of lecturers. Yet is it actually true that concentrating on teaching effects eliminates what a lecturer wishes to say to students, e.g., about the findings of his recent study? Does a lecturer not have the right to obtain information on his own teaching efficacy? Who develops curricula if not a teacher? Do teaching effects apply solely to students? In view of the promotion of such bizarre statements in the document being analyzed, it needs to be remembered with some force that the process of education, not only at university level, is a *two-party* process.

The National Framework of Qualifications and Continuing Education

We ought to examine the NFQ in a different light. As a result of the NFQ implementation, what are the possibilities for continuing education in the environment of higher educational institutions? The first issue which needs to be explained is the essence of the question posed. Why is the problem of continuing education analyzed in relation to higher education? The explanation is complex, although Polish documents on higher education reforms explain it in a rather simplified form.

Following J. Półturzycki's explanation of the essence of continuing education it may be claimed that it encompasses the entire educational system as well as the entirety of human life, consequently leading to the development of an educated society (Półturzycki 1981, 124). Therefore, continuing education encompasses the education of children, teenagers, adults, and seniors, and it may be formal, non-formal, or informal.

Once understood properly, higher educational institutions constitute a natural element of continuing education, ensuring not only the next stage of education, but also education for personal needs of academic youths, adult students, and other age groups as well. First of all, the National Framework of Qualifications gives each person the possibility of continuing education from a formal aspect, concerning qualifications certified by a diploma. Hence it is associated with vertical continuing education according to R. Kidd's concept (cf. Półturzycki 2010, 327).

Does the document on the NFQ mention continuing education and if so, in which context? Does the NFQ allow taking advantage of the chances given by continuing education to a greater extent than previously? At the very beginning, in the passage explaining the essence of the NFQ the concept of continuing education was referred to:

> The final outcome of implementing a framework in higher education throughout the whole of Europe was supposed to be a "map" of qualifications for levels 5–8 of the European framework. This "map" is supposed to present relations between qualifications, and indicate transition paths and the possibilities of further training in higher education in the perspective of lifelong learning. (Chmielecka, Marciniak, and Kraśniewski 2010, 9)

Obviously the NFQ may give possibilities only within formal continuing education and generally apply this to academic youths as well as adult students, thus referring only to a selected range of education encompassed by this concept.

The NFQ's implementation is supposed to render curricular contents widely available to those who wish to pursue further studies, as well as to clarify them with regards to knowledge, skills, attitudes, and further education possibilities offered to students (Chmielecka, Marciniak, and Kraśniewski 2010, 11), which is undoubtedly beneficial to each person willing to enroll in a school and select his/her course. There is one more element significant for continuing education and its development mentioned in the document, but it is not connected with lifelong learning; i.e., the NFQ's implementation is supposed to result in "an increase in the availability of education and motivation for its continuation, enhancing social integration as well as allowing the inclusion of achievements from outside the formal education in a list of accomplishments" (Chmielecka, Marciniak, and Kraśniewski 2010, 11). For adults enrolling in courses, the acceptance of their knowledge and skills, including those which are not certified, is a significant factor motivating them to start or pursue further education.

The NFQ is also perceived as a way of individualizing the teaching process, as the NFQ often refers to the needs of students, including so-called non-traditional students.[1] This statement is used on page 11 of the document, and is very significant to the issue of continuing education weighed in this article. Yet the term itself has not been explained, assuming tacitly that readers are acquainted with it. However, this group of students constitutes a real challenge for teachers, as they differ widely in their level of knowledge, experience, needs, effects, motivation, and ability to learn (in certain aspects positively, in others negatively) from the group of academic youths.

In another passage of the document, where the names of qualifications obtained at particular stages of studies are analyzed, the term "continuing education" has been used without the understanding of its core. In the discussion on confirming the completion of doctoral studies it is assumed that at this stage course completion certificates should not be issued. A PhD diploma should be the only confirmation of a third-degree qualification. However, an odd comparison has been made: "Documents confirming the completion of a PhD course or its part should be of the same character as in the case of other types of studies—through implementing the concept of lifelong learning, and documenting achievements within this scope" (Chmielecka, Marciniak, and

Kraśniewski 2010, 18). However, it is not clear what the term "concept of life-long learning" means in this context or what its significance is for issuing or not issuing certificates and documents which confirm qualifications.

The next element which relates to continuing education, but only under-stood to a rather limited extent, is the influence of NFQ-based curricula on lifelong learning. Tomasz Saryusz-Wolski, the author of this passage, claims: "The remodeling of a single subject based on teaching effects is an indispen-sable stage in the process of incorporating formal education into the system of lifelong learning. . . . [F]ormal education has become only one of the life-long learning processes, and needs to be compatible with its remaining stages" (Saryusz-Wolski 2010, 103). A number of issues strike the reader in this pas-sage. First, formal education is not considered to be an element of continuing education, whereas, as early as 1960, R. Kidd formulated a famous concept of the three dimensions of continuing education. One of them is vertical edu-cation, in other words, completing particular education stages in a given coun-try, i.e., formal education. Second, the author writes about formal education as if it has just become an element of continuing education, whereas it has been an element for a long time although our awareness today of the role of higher educational institutions in lifelong learning has been increasing. The aforementioned statements are treated as if they are being elaborated now, which results from a complete lack of understanding of continuing education issues, as well as a lack of knowledge of not only Polish but also international studies within this field of interest. This results from the fact that educators have not participated in the development of the NFQ.

While defining the third component of the NFQ, continuing education was referred to as well: "Personal and social competencies—the ability to act in an autonomous and reliable manner, including the ability to cooperate with others both as a group member and leader, and also the ability to adapt to the increasingly faster changing world through lifelong learning" (Chmielecka 2010, 143). Thus continuing education has been attributed to the third element of the NFQ, but in the context of learning which is supposed to help students to find their place in the fast-changing world, instead of lagging behind it and to adjust themselves accordingly. However, one aspect of continuing education has not been taken into consideration, i.e., its creative aspect, mentioned for instance by E. Faure (1972), which concerned going beyond the present stan-dard of living, social situation, or patterns.

Annex 8 to the NFQ under analysis, devoted to recognizing knowledge and abilities acquired outside formal education especially at university level, is also of great importance. In this context principles of the European policy on continuing education have been quoted. Four of these principles have been mentioned:

1. Placing students at the center of attention (Urbanikowska and Chmielecka 2010, 157). This principle is part of an approach, according to which, each activity per-

    formed by a higher educational institution is supposed to meet the educational needs of students and to create favorable conditions so that students will be able to complete their studies and find jobs consistent with their training.

2. A better use of individuals' potential in various places, forms, and at different stages of life, as well as a better use of the potential of professional experience (lifelong and lifewide learning) (Urbanikowska and Chmielecka 2010, 157). This principle, on the other hand, relates to various dimensions of continuing education whose complete essence they constitute. This better use of students' potential is of great significance while elaborating procedures for recognizing knowledge and abilities acquired outside formal education.

3. Equal treatment of different learning paths leading through the National Framework of Qualifications based on teaching effects in which the value (level) of individuals' qualifications is determined regardless of where and when they learned them (Urbanikowska and Chmielecka 2010, 157). The value of this principle results from comparing life and/or the professional experience of individuals learning for particular levels of qualification frameworks, owing to which they do not need to repeat in formal education what they already know.

4. Changes in the level of knowledge and skills of learning individuals constitute a proper efficiency benchmark of the LLL policy, in contrast to indicators and features concerning the operation of educational institutions (Urbanikowska and Chmielecka 2010, 157). It is true that this indicator is valid, although it exposes a certain exaggeration regarding excessive confidence in the self-teaching abilities of individuals belonging to various age groups (in the case of higher educational institutions—academic youths and adults). A proper indicator providing a more accurate image of the efficiency of actions within continuing education not only consists of a combination of information on knowledge and abilities achieved by learners, but also actions taken by educational institutions (not only training, but also consulting institutions; information on the number of individuals resigning from education, reasons for such decisions and the like).

This annex does not include any concrete proposals for Polish procedures for recognizing knowledge and abilities achieved outside formal education, any guidelines concerning what may be acknowledged, or any method for evaluating such knowledge and abilities. It has only been emphasized that: "Teaching effects acknowledged through a recognition process should be explicitly included in the course of studies (year/semester credits, diploma supplement)" (Urbanikowska and Chmielecka 2010, 159). Such procedures are characteristic of Anglo-Saxon countries, and they are applied to individuals enrolling in studies in order to save their time and money allocated to education and to save them repeating what they already know.

    In the United States there is also a system for awarding points, connected with continuing education. Such points are referred to as Lifetime Learning Credits. The procedure for awarding such points involves evaluating knowledge and experience gained by adults outside schools. Such credits are counted when receiving a diploma, yet they are treated as transfer points, which means that a diploma may not be issued only on their basis (Frąckowiak 2007, 90). Lifetime Learning Credits are awarded for experience in specific categories. The Council for Adult and Experiential Learning (CAEL) has distinguished

ANNA FRĄCKOWIAK

eight categories which universities apply to their procedures: 1) work, including military service, 2) running a household, 3) voluntary service, 4) non-credit courses, e.g., seminars, workshops, in-service training, 5) travels, 6) recreation, 7) hobbies, 8) independent study, such as reading, sightseeing, or correspondence with experts (Therrien, Power, and Earning 2001, 1). The procedure for evaluating knowledge and life experience may involve an exam, an assessment of qualifications, or of a portfolio. Each of these procedures is paid for and requires consulting with an educational advisor at a university.

However, the document on the NFQ draws attention to a fairly significant fact—doubts and controversies which the introduction of such procedures might raise in Polish higher education. In Polish culture we place great emphasis on documents which are confirmed, stamped, and signed. The lack of such documents always raises doubts.

Actual Possibilities for the Development of Continuing Education in the Academic Environment

As has been already stressed, higher education has constituted one of the elements of continuing education for a long time. Thus I have analyzed the reforms of Polish universities vis-à-vis the announcement of including higher educational institutions in the structure of continuing education. But continuing education lasts from birth until death, in formal, non-formal, and informal education alike. Admittedly, while researching and analyzing continuing education one often finds that greater attention is paid to further education following compulsory education. Therefore the area of the continuing education of adults has been identified and researched to a greater extent. However, higher educational institutions themselves are one of the elements of continuing education, as a university diploma is not compulsory. Thus the education of academic youths is part of continuing education. From the point of view of university employees the following questions arise:

- To what extent are youths prepared to study independently?
- To what extent are they motivated to study?
- To what extent have such youths been prepared for further learning at their previous educational stages?

The answers to these questions are extremely significant for forecasting results at the university level, as well as the successful completion of studies and receiving a diploma. Another important example of continuing education which occurs in higher educational institutions is, by all means, studies, including post-graduate courses, usually attended by working adults. In this case universities function not only as compensation, giving the possibility of supplementing education, but also as a factor in developing adult personalities in connection with their career development. Obviously, these are not all the examples of continuing education offered by higher educational institutions. Organizing and conducting remote studies constitute other examples (also those courses which do not provide a certificate, but are attended for personal development), so-called universities of the Third Age and of Children and Youths, promoting academic knowledge in society through open lectures and publications issued by scholarly associations, as well as through festivals of science, technology, and arts. Continuing education also includes courses, workshops, and training sessions offered by universities for non-student adults, financed with EU funds and also courses on employment organized by Career Services. These examples of university activities are definitely most widely known within continuing education although often unnoticed, and they are categorized as an indicator of continuing education in an academic environment. Due to the fact that the National Framework of Qualifications includes only formal education in higher educational institutions, the main emphasis in the analysis of the possibilities for the development of continuing education has been placed on the formal aspect that is associated with attending organized studies, along with receiving a specific diploma.

First of all, it needs to be emphasized that the concept of the NFQ has been based on the greater curriculum flexibility of Polish universities. The Ministry of Education and Higher Education has stopped centrally defining syllabuses and also standards which until now have been binding guidelines for developing educational programs. Instead of this, the NFQ determines the scope of issues which should be learned by graduates in a given field, paying special attention to the effects of such teaching:

> [U]niversities should carefully consider and describe desired teaching effects. On their basis they should develop a syllabus, leading students along various paths (depending on individual predispositions) through their modules so that they achieve the desired effects in the most efficient manner. And lastly, the most difficult problem, i.e., the necessity of developing and implementing a quality control system for teaching, which will allow monitoring these effects efficiently and making necessary modifications. (Chmielecka, Marciniak, and Kraśniewski 2010, 10)

The above quotation displays a number of elements significant for the development of continuing education. It mentions leading students through education using various paths, paying attention to their individuality and predispositions—therefore capabilities, interests, educational needs as well as restrictions resulting from difficulty in obtaining specific information or skills. This is a fairly important change in the perception of syllabuses in Polish universities. Until the present times, the fact that we have been participants in the Bologna Process from the beginning has forced certain changes in our higher educational institutions, including the division of five-year courses into two stages, including in their structure PhD courses treated as a third stage, implementing the ECTS credit system, and the like. However, in the majority of universities such changes have not translated into direct modifications of curricula, or the evaluation of students' achievements. The syllabus remained the same for all the students in a given field of study at a particular university, differing only in the form of general and principal subjects (compulsory for all the students of a given class) as well as specialist subjects (attended only by these students of a given class who have selected a particular specialization). Students receiving diplomas differ in their knowledge and abilities only within an area of specialization, e.g., all of them receive higher education in pedagogy, but some of them specialize in special education, some in school counseling, some in preschool pedagogy, etc. All students complete the same course of studies, without the possibility of changing the order of subjects or building their own program apart from compulsory subjects, as all the subjects taught are compulsory. There are universities where students may choose extracurricular classes, e.g., attending monographic lectures selected by them. Thus, *nolens volens*, they automatically obtain all the ECTS credits that they need in order to receive a diploma after a successful defense of the thesis. The previous activities of Polish universities have contributed to a great extent to the standardization of the process of continuing education.

In the above quotation it has also been stated that in Polish higher education, modules are presently associated with e-learning and with organizing the contents of virtual educational platforms in the form of succinct, coherent information units, the order of which may be altered to a certain extent during the course of studies. According to a study by the Ministry of Science and Higher Education, the National Framework of Qualifications also introduces the concept of modules in the syllabuses of courses conducted in the form of direct contact with the lecturer, thus allowing the possibility of altering the order of or even omitting certain modules by students under the procedures which are supposed to be implemented for evaluating the knowledge and skills acquired outside higher education. The development of syllabuses in the form of modules actually broadens the possibilities for continuing education and may be an important incentive for students, especially adults, to enroll in a school. All this may result in more flexible and individualized courses, which would be a novelty in Polish higher educational institutions. Some in the academic environment may perceive such changes as unfavorable, or even contrary to the Polish tradition of higher education, and likely to blur the essence of such teaching. Therefore the introduction of such changes may be understood as a threat to the identity of Polish universities and to the importance of higher education, the level of which is already considered to be significantly lowered as a result of popularizing higher education, consequently leading to the devaluation of university degrees which have become common.

Greater flexibility and the individualization of university courses is one of the assumed effects of the implementation of the NFQ. However, the document devoted to the NFQ does not refer to a different organization of the teaching process. A different approach to this process is discussed, and particularly in its conclusion, it is explained how to develop curricula according to the assumptions of the NFQ, yet still organizational aspects are ignored. Therefore, theoretically, the implementation of curricula according to the NFQ gives the possibility of organizational changes in education that would be more beneficial from the perspective of continuing education development, yet in practice universities may choose not to make use of this opportunity. Thus all will depend on the decisions taken in a particular university or department.

A consequence of implementing the NFQ, as well as of decisions on liberalizing the organization of university courses, is the necessity for introducing educational advisors in Polish universities. Thus far, such a function has been redundant as students followed curricula according to the compulsory schedules of classes for consecutive semesters. However, giving students a greater possibility of selecting their own educational paths requires preparing them for making suitable decisions and for selecting classes. Therefore counseling services for students are necessary for university activities in the face of such changes.

In the case of education studies such curricular and organizational flexibility is limited, at least within the area of certain specializations, by the requirements imposed by yet another ministry, i.e., the Ministry of National Education, as the Minister of National Education defines the educational standards for teachers and students attending education studies who choose, for example, preschool or early childhood specializations, who need to complete classes according to these directives. Thus in the case of education studies in given specializations the curricular autonomy of universities, so strongly emphasized in the document describing the Polish NFQ, is limited by other requirements.

There is another important aspect explained in the document on the NFQ significant for continuing education, namely, the question of whether the implementation of the National Framework of Qualifications will not result in a lack of regulation of qualifications at other levels in higher education:

> [I]ntroducing areas of education and teaching profiles in legislation should not result in any regulations at the central level which would create a problem with the regulation of qualifications at other levels in the education system; the specific character of qualifications (area, profile) should not constitute a formal obstacle, determined in legal regulations, preventing further education in order to obtain a qualification at a higher level. (Chmielecka, Marciniak, and Kraśniewski 2010, 20–21)

This means in practice that neither the act on higher education nor any ministerial orders may include statements which would prevent graduates of BA courses from continuing education at the MA level due to the fact that the first level of studies completed by them was of a different profile (e.g., a practical course) than the course offered at the second level (e.g., a general academic course). This information is vital since imposing such restrictions would seriously limit the development of continuing education.

Unfortunately the next paragraph contradicts the idea expressed above: "Such a solution gives universities absolute freedom to decide on the qualification requirements for candidates for second and third degree studies in terms of the area and profile of such qualifications, as well as absolute freedom to impose possible restrictions within this scope" (Chmielecka, Marciniak, Kraśniewski, 2010, p. 21). Therefore the authorities at the central level remain above all suspicion of imposing restrictions, yet later, the possibility of imposing such restrictions is permissible at the level of universities. This is an obvious indication of their autonomy, yet has a negative influence on the development of continuing education. Introducing such restrictions and requirements in order for the profile of MA courses to correspond with the profile of BA courses actually limits the possibilities of continuing education, the predominant message of which is to develop education without barriers (of various types).

Yet another element, slightly controversial due to its wording, is the statement: "Each teaching effect should be defined at a level attainable for the least able student, and not at the highest possible level" (Saryusz-Wolski, 2010, p. 105). On the one hand, this may be considered a gesture toward the possibilities of continuing education as it has been assumed that curricula should not set excessively high standards to be achieved by increasingly diverse students who also differ in the quality of the education they previously received. However, it is difficult to determine the level of the least able student; moreover, such a description of teaching effects hinders the development of students' aspirations. However, the concept of continuing education assumes that not only should the lifelong learning process throughout the entire life of a human facilitate adaptation to changing social and economic conditions, but also enhance his or her personal development and contribute to a more creative attitude to the world and to his/her own actions. In the quotation above it was suggested that the standards for students be set at a low, if not very low, level. This will result in concerns over the quality of teaching at the university level and the scope of knowledge and abilities that students will attain as a consequence of effects described in such a manner.

Summary

The development of the National Framework of Qualifications for higher education is undoubtedly a significant step toward reforming Polish universities. It is not an undertaking which remains only on paper as a proposal. It will be improved shortly, and translated into the language of practice under the new act on higher education which becomes effective on 1 October 2011. The implementation of the NFQ undoubtedly requires changes in the awareness of university teachers, as well as changes in the area of developing curriculum. However, are all these changes positive in nature? What place and role is attributed to academic teachers according to the NFQ draft? First of all, it needs to be emphasized that the mere development of the NFQ and bringing it up for discussion in an academic environment is a significant step forward. However, while examining the project itself more closely one may notice fundamental shortcomings, issues raising doubts, or even actual terminological confusion, which consequently may result in practical problems, or even in the degeneration of teaching practices in higher educational institutions.

One may find terminological confusion not only over qualifications and competencies, teaching objectives, effects, their components, and mutual relations, but over pedagogical issues as well. Lectures, exercises, laboratories, and seminars are referred to in an inconsistent manner, and terms such as "teaching techniques," "products," and the like are used. Such shortcomings in the understanding and description of higher education pedagogy may translate into concrete problems when developing syllabi based on the NFQ assumptions at the university level.

The survey of the NFQ in higher educational institutions puts forward certain proposals for tools facilitating the development of syllabuses according to new assumptions and also for verifying whether the syllabuses prepared comply with the descriptors of teaching effects within a given area of studies. Meetings with members of the academic environment held by the Ministry of Science and Higher Education and particular universities do not serve only as consultations, but they also attempt to explain the significance and principles of the National Framework of Qualifications for Polish universities.

However, the rather negative image of the academic teacher presented in the document entitled "The Curricular Autonomy of Universities: A Framework of Qualifications for Higher Education" raises concerns. The student's perspective is very firmly stressed, simultaneously depreciating the lecturer's perspective. As a matter of fact, this document is aimed predominantly at lecturers conducting university classes and developing syllabuses.

How, on the one hand, may the prospects for the development of continuing education be assessed by an academic environment from the perspective of modifications introduced under the NFQ?

First, it is worth emphasizing that continuing education has been noticed in the document, as well as the fact that higher education is of great significance in the lifelong learning process. However, on the other hand, the understanding of the importance of continuing education and the role of higher educational institutions is fairly limited. Additionally, the survey of this issue in the document on the NFQ has been presented as if universities have not participated in continuing education so far.

The proposals presented in the document which offer greater possibilities for the development of continuing education in Polish higher education are associated first of all with introducing more flexible education paths, with a greater attention paid to teaching effects—including fulfilling the needs of the employment market—or with discerning the benefits resulting from the implementation of an evaluation system, as well as from recognizing knowledge and abilities acquired outside the formal system of education. All of this contributes to the successful development of continuing education and to raising interest in learning on the part of various social groups. Yet a great deal of effort and understanding is necessary on the part of university teachers. However, it is a matter of concern that the development of continuing education in the academic environment may be blocked, e.g., through differences between the profiles of the first-degree courses completed by students, and the second-degree courses offered. Obviously the restrictions which may be imposed in this respect will not be favorable.

In conclusion, it may be stated that the actual implementation of the NFQ in Polish higher educational institutions creates various possibilities, which all depend on how this will be translated into the language of practice in particular universities.

Note

---

1. The term "nontraditional students" is derived from English-language literature and contemporarily applies to those who may not be classified as academic youths. Therefore they may be adults, including senior citizens, in a difficult financial situation or who come from social groups who previously did not aspire to higher education; persons whose generation is the first one to study in their families; persons without a traditional education path—they often had long-lasting breaks between education levels, or did not obtain a high school diploma, but passed a substitute examination (e.g., GED in the United States) and the like.

Bibliography

Altbach, P. G., L. Reisberg, and L. E. Rumbley. 2009. "Trends in Global Higher Education: Tracking an Academic Revolution." A Report Prepared for the UNESCO 2009 World Conference on Higher Education. UNESCO.

Autonomia programowa uczelni: Ramy kwalifikacji dla szkolnictwa wyższego. 2010. Warsaw: MNiSW.

Chmielecka, E. 2010. "Kompetencje personalne i społeczne." In *Autonomia programowa uczelni.*

Chmielecka, E., Z. Marciniak, and A. Kraśniewski. 2010. "Krajowe Ramy Kwalifikacji dla polskiego szkolnictwa wyższego." In *Autonomia programowa uczelni.*

Faure, E., ed. 1972. *Learning to Be: The World of Education Today and Tomorrow.* Paris: UNESCO.

Frąckowiak, A. 2007. *Europejski Obszar Szkolnictwa Wyższego—konkurencja dla uczelni amerykańskich?* Płock: Novum.

Nowacki, T. W., ed. 2004. *Leksykon pedagogiki pracy.* Radom: ITE-PIB.

Okoń, W. 1971. *Elementy dydaktyki szkoły wyższej.* Warsaw: PWN.

Polskie szkolnictwo wyższe. Stan, uwarunkowania, perspektywy. 2009. Warsaw: Wyd. Uniwersytetu Warszawskiego.

Półturzycki, J. 1981. *Tendencje rozwojowe kształcenia ustawicznego.* Warsaw: PWN.

———. 2010. "Szkolnictwo wyższe a idea edukacji ustawicznej." In *Edukacja ustawiczna—idee i doświadczenia,* edited by A. Frąckowiak, Z. P. Kruszewski, J. Półturzycki, and E. A. Wesołowska. Płock: Novum.

Próchnicka, M., T. Saryusz-Wolski, and A. Kraśniewski. 2010. "Projektowanie programów studiów i zajęć dydaktycznych na bazie efektów kształcenia." In *Autonomia programowa uczelni.*

Saryusz-Wolski, T. 2010. "Projektowanie programu zajęć dydaktycznych (sylabus) z wykorzystaniem efektów kształcenia." In *Autonomia programowa uczelni.*

Therrien, C. A., M. Power, and B. Earning. 2001. *Credit for Life Learning Handbook.* Haverhill, MA: Center for Adult and Alternative Studies, Northern Essex Community College.

Urbanikowa. J., and E. Chmielecka. 2010. "Uznawanie kompetencji zdobytych poza obszarem formalnej edukacji wyższej." In *Autonomia programowa uczelni.*

The Role of Higher Education in Poland in Creating Academic Entrepreneurship and the Innovative Activities of Students

Contemporary education should be flexible. The essential role of higher education in Poland is not only to provide a proper education, but first of all to teach the ability to operate in the employment market and to develop competencies which will be decisive in finding a rewarding job, allowing students to take advantage of the knowledge they have gained and its further development. "Therefore education needs to focus on the future, on inventiveness, and on progressiveness."[1] Globalization and social and economic changes in Poland have contributed to a significant increase in the interest in education. It is not only young high school graduates that study but to a great extent adults also who want to supplement their education, as well as those who want to complete post-graduate courses in order to develop their careers with companies while holding specialist or managerial positions. Nowadays the fact that contemporary learning is valuable has already been acknowledged. Individuals study in order to gain knowledge, owing to which their competence will improve; they study in order to comprehend others, as well as to create flexible procedures, processes which will influence their own development and also the competitiveness of the organization where they are employed. Through their knowledge and the ability to use it, they become valuable links for their companies, and for the entire Polish economy. Not only is contemporary higher education responsible for high teaching quality, but for creating resourceful attitudes and innovative activities among students as well. This is essential due to the dynamism of changes, as well as the needs of the Polish economy and employment market. Resourcefulness and innovative activities do not refer to students only, but also to the teaching faculty. A very good method for combining knowledge and shaping key skills among students is through establishing spin-off or spin-out enterprises.

This essay illustrates the fact that academic entrepreneurship is heading toward changing the model of education based solely on providing knowledge for the model of shaping skills which are necessary for the development of the domestic economy. In contemporary higher education an academic should act as a mentor, as a person preparing students to understand the employment market and to perform in their acquired professions.

Entrepreneurship and Academic Entrepreneurship

Numerous concepts of entrepreneurship may be found in relevant literature. Despite this abundance of definitions, a model concept of enterprise has not been formulated yet. This is due to the fact that enterprise is multidimensional, and it may be understood as a process, a phenomenon, and a group of features determining a particular manner of human conduct. Enterprise may be found in both economic practice and science. From the economic point of view it is understood as "readiness to accept and solve new problems in a creative and innovative manner, being aware of the risk related to it, the ability to take advantage of emerging opportunities and possibilities as well as a flexible adaptation to changing conditions."[2] Entrepreneurship understood in this way clearly emphasizes the significance of developing abilities to respond to changes and to adapt to them. Each change poses a risk, yet without elaborating adequate steps in order to follow the direction of an evolving economy and research it will not be possible to achieve active innovation and a competitive advantage. The European Commission interpreted the term *entrepreneurship* as "providing young people with life management skills so that they will be able to use them efficiently afterwards."[3] Entrepreneurship has become a contemporary challenge. It is responsible for "promoting and broadening one's knowledge, for assuming innovative undertakings as well as selecting a proper development strategy within an organization."[4] One needs to bear in mind that *learning by doing* is an essential feature of entrepreneurship. The knowledge that an individual acquires during the process of education at a university is the most valuable intangible asset for a future employer. In combination with employees' skills and their motivation for further development of specialist knowledge, an organization is able to obtain a significant added value, which relates to the increase in competitiveness on the market.

Taking into consideration a process-like approach to defining entrepreneurship, it may be stated that it is understood as an activity aimed at achieving economic benefits while exploiting a new idea through taking specific business steps under risky circumstances. This is possible owing to employing a set of human features: "a shaped awareness of inventiveness, flexibility, creativity, a tendency to take risk, an ability to notice and take advantage of opportunities, a permanent search for improvement as well as sharing one's knowledge with others."[5] According to this definition, entrepreneurship is "a feature of an individual, of a group or an organization which triggers their aspirations for fulfillment through actions. It requires faith in one's own power, an ability to make innovations, accept risk, act independently as well as an effective performance."[6] In order to be able to call oneself enterprising, first of all one needs to be motivated to act, and may not be afraid of risk or change. A considerable number of individuals possessing such predispositions also work at higher educational institutions. Contemporary research and the economy should go hand in hand with each other. In order to take advantage of their already acquired knowledge, students expect to receive not only theoretical training, but also practical tools. Therefore Polish universities have started employing experienced specialists, who wish to develop as researchers as well, increasingly often. The potential brought into a university by a "practitioner" is enormously extensive. The quality of teaching increases, and students work using tools employed in the contemporary economy, which provides them with easier access to the employment market. Such employed "practitioners" develop their scholarly abilities while participating in numerous domestic and overseas conferences, publishing their articles, obtaining grants and scholarships, writing PhD dissertations, and organizing conferences. As a result of this, they convey necessary knowledge to students in a very efficient manner; knowledge which is supported by examples and exercises consistent with the present economic situation. Students become active participants in the acquisition and development of their knowledge through brainstorming and asking questions frequently, which is an indication of an emerging academic entrepreneurship in Polish universities. "At present the real academic nature of a school is determined by whether it creates conditions for taking advantage of the knowledge presented, the intellectual potential, the ideas, and the enthusiasm of young people, students, and alumni, or not. Higher educational institutions are the best, the richest, and the most abundant source of new ideas where thought is shaped, where research is conducted, and where new concepts which may be used to establish a business emerge."[7] First of all, academic entrepreneurship may be defined as the willingness to start a business by people connected with higher educational institutions, i.e., research/teaching employees, students, or alumni. In a narrower context, it is a "process related to establishing spin-off or spin-out companies/firms in order to commercialize the results of scientific research."[8] A strategic objective of academic entrepreneurship is, first, the protection of intellectual property as well as support in the scope of commercialization. Academic entrepreneurship, which is strictly connected with the world of research and the economy, challenges the stereotype that a university teacher is only supposed to "conduct classes and do research."[9] Thus it is possible to run a business to the benefit of a university, the students, and the research/teaching employees as well.

A spin-off company is a new enterprise which emerges during the process of becoming independent by an employee(s) of a mother company or another organization (e.g., research laboratory, higher educational institution), using, for this purpose, the intellectual assets of the parent organization). Spin-off companies are independent of their mother organizations. A spin-out type of a business activity is a new enterprise which emerges during the process of becoming independent by an employee(s) of a mother company or another organization (e.g., research laboratory, higher educational institution), using, for this purpose, intellectual and material assets of the parent organization). Spin-out companies are connected with their mother organizations operationally, or in terms of capital. Operational connections may include, among others, legal services, accounting and marketing services, and distribution channels of a parent institution. Establishing enterprises of this type in relation to innovative projects is a form of "taking advantage of the enterprising potential of a founding team by a parent company, while still holding partial control over the development of such projects."[10] In the United States, academic entrepreneurship is expressed through establishing knowledge-based companies. In Europe it is definitely understood more widely, predominantly in the form of the pre-incubation and incubation of enterprises originating from universities. An excellent activation form of enterprising students, or university graduates, is the possibility of establishing a company within an Academic Business Incubator (ABI).

The Academic Business Incubator

Academic entrepreneurship, including Academic Business Incubators, falls under applicable legal regulations stipulated by the Law on Higher Education.[11] Article 4, section 4 of this act defines academic entrepreneurship as the cooperation of higher educational institutions with "the economic environment, in particular by selling or providing, on a free-of-charge basis, results of their research and development work to entrepreneurs and by promoting the idea of entrepreneurship in the academic community, within the framework of economic activity to be pursued as organizationally and financially separate" from the essential tasks of universities, i.e., teaching and educating students, or conducting scientific research and promoting the academic faculty. Article 86 of this act is very significant as well; it allows the creation of new university instruments for the transfer of technology.

1. In order to ensure better use of the intellectual and technological potential of higher educational institutions and the transfer of research findings to the economy, higher educational institutions may operate academic business incubators and technology transfer centers.
2. An academic business incubator shall be established in order to support the economic activity of the academic community or staff and students of a higher educational institution who are entrepreneurs.
3. An academic business incubator established as:

   a. an institutional-level unit shall operate on the basis of its regulations to be approved by the senate of the higher educational institution concerned;
   b. a commercial partnership or a foundation shall operate on the basis of the relevant documents regulating its status.

4. A technology transfer center shall be established in order to sell or transfer, free of charge, research and development findings to the economy.
5. A technology transfer center established as:

   a. an institutional-level unit shall operate on the basis of its regulations to be approved by the senate of the higher educational institution concerned;
   b. a commercial partnership or a foundation shall operate on the basis of the relevant documents regulating its status.

6. An academic business incubator or a technology transfer center established as institutional-level organizational units shall have supervisory boards whose composition and powers shall be defined in their regulations.

7. The director of an academic business incubator or a technology transfer center operating as an institutional-level organizational unit shall be appointed by the rector after consultation with the senate from among candidates proposed by the supervisory boards of such units.In the Polish reality three types of academic incubators may be distinguished, i.e.,

   a. incubators, which operate within an all-Poland initiative, e.g., the Foundation of Academic Business Incubators, where the company being incubated operates within an incubator as a department of the Foundation with its own sub-account, which results in its using the Foundation's legal personality and cost-cutting.
   b. Academic Incubators, which operate within higher educational institutions. Generally, they function as an individual project, and are established under the Law on Higher Education.
   c. Pre-incubators which operate within technological parks and incubators, as well as student organizations. They have all the hallmarks of a public-private partnership.[12]

The establishment and operation of business incubators at universities and colleges in Poland contribute to the activation of students' entrepreneurship, and also provide them with an opportunity to develop their practical skills and acquire business qualifications indispensable for surviving in the domestic market. The possibility of using their knowledge, interests, and skills constitutes an excellent method for testing themselves as entrepreneurs, and it also stimulates creativity, business experience, and innovative talents (inspiring activeness, accepting responsibility for changes, involving and observing existing functioning conditions, following change, and adapting to the market situation, responding to change, and using it for innovative activities).

Students are supposed to aspire to be independent in the area of economic life. Universities do not provide practical knowledge relating to running an enterprise; neither do they stress the value of individualism and inventiveness. Students receive extensive factual knowledge, they are aware of the essence of business, yet they lack the ability to perform in practice as self-employed entrepreneurs. Due to this fact and a lack of self-confidence, they often choose to be unemployed or find jobs significantly below their abilities. Good business ideas, participation in numerous contests, or the presentation of interesting projects during classes do not translate into their practical application. Using knowledge and abilities, and not the idea itself, is the formula for success. The knowledge acquired during academic studies is not sufficient for an individual to function well in a constantly changing economic reality. However, it constitutes a good basis for developing entrepreneurship. Thus it is necessary to improve students' practical abilities and qualifications, for which ideal instruments are the ABIs.

The activities of ABIs contribute to developing an enterprising attitude among students; it also influences their creativity and involvement, thus resulting in the shaping of innovative talents. An incubator is an organization aimed at supporting new enterprises through establishing conditions for their development and their efficient operation on the market. It helps focus on building a business and allows the entrepreneur to minimize costs and risks typical in the first year of business activity, thus increasing the business's chances of survival. Such risks are related to the establishment and development of an enterprise. Not only does an entrepreneur acting without support need to deal with his business, but also with organizational and administrative matters (accounting, maintenance of an office and other facilities, legal advice). A student within an ABI definitely has greater chances of remaining on the market independently. The student has the time and possibilities which facilitate making the decision to establish a company and operate on the market without the ABI's help. Such a form of enterprising activity combines learning and practice. The possibility of operating in such an organization is a great supplement to the factual knowledge acquired during studies and is a factor which increases the number of companies established by university graduates. This is because the participation in an incubator allows developing practical skills influencing entrepreneurship, i.e., creative thinking, inventiveness, independence, negotiating skills, interpersonal skills, adaptation to the changing environment, the ability to manage resources, an active attitude to obtaining information, and a more thorough understanding of clients' expectations. The emphasis should be placed on providing students with as much practical knowledge as possible, creating opportunities to use and test them under existing conditions. Creating conditions for the development of entrepreneurship and inventiveness for the commercialization of new ideas based on knowledge and new technology, as well as strengthening the potential of young entrepreneurs, are the most important objectives of academic business incubators in Poland. The opportunity to combine theory with practice proves that it is an ideal solution for young entrepreneurs. A significant number of students wish to try their hands at becoming entrepreneurs during their studies or directly after graduation."Individual initiative and an innovative idea combined with passion and the thorough knowledge acquired during studies constitute an ideal combination of factors in order for young entrepreneurs to be successful."[13] Openness to business as well as enhancing entrepreneurship among students is a way toward the country's development.

In the contemporary world the basic factor for creating progress and economic development is the entrepreneurship of young people and their inventiveness, understood as the ability to acquire and take advantage of new knowledge. An ABI gives young people the opportunity to establish their own business through creating workplaces for graduates and students, as well as inspiring cooperation between academic research environments and entrepreneurs. An ABI allows the realization of public actions related to the promotion of entrepreneurship, self-employment, and the prevention of unemployment.

Student Organizations and Mentoring in an Institution of Higher Education

Young people are often aware of the fact that, the contemporary employment market places great demands on them. Apart from the requirements such as a university diploma and knowledge in a certain field, professional experience is required as well. Where is it possible to acquire it? Student organizations provide students with a solution. The possibility of young students' participation in academic clubs and in organizing student conferences, as well as their participation in research and in numerous contests, constitutes very rewarding practice for them; when displayed in a CV, this indicates commitment and motivation to gain experience, which is greatly appreciated by employers. Student organizations are a suitable place for those who wish to acquire interpersonal competencies and develop teamwork and group work skills, which prospective employers expect from young people. They are also great places to evaluate one's organizational and leadership skills. Each of the acquired competencies influences an individual's involvement and creativity and facilitates performing a task within its deadline while maintaining high quality. Competence consists of the following elements: knowledge, skills, personal features, and attitude. Students who actively participate in the activities of academic clubs not only acquire knowledge, but also the motivation for expanding it. Consequently their personalities and attitudes change. They start to notice the future priorities of professional life. Owing to their work, which benefits the university, a student also has access to internships as well as numerous training sessions organized by Academic Career Services. Therefore it may be confidently stated that there are many organizations open to students, so that each of them could find something for themselves. All such organizations have very different structures, from small to greatly developed ones; therefore a student may gain rewarding professional experience there, "to see one's performance in different roles and situations, but also to meet interesting people all over the world who have similar passions and problems."[14]

Academic clubs operating in higher educational institutions also prove that they are a great treasure trove of innovative projects. Student activists are interested in research activity as they find it interesting to evaluate their knowledge potential and economic realities. Inventiveness and unconventional approaches to the subjects under examination may often be found in their studies. This is how innovative students' projects are developed, examples of which may be, for instance:

- *Hybrid vehicle drive with a disc motor*—a design prepared by Student Club SEP from Szczecin University of Technology—an innovative attempt to combine two popular concepts of vehicle drives, particularly up-to-date in the era of developing economical and ecological means of transportation;
- *Remote-controlled video head*—a project of the Student Scientific

Club of Robotics at Łódź University of Technology—developed and implemented software allowing the operator to expand the range of movement of a remote-controlled camera;

- *Unmanned aerial systems*—the structure of a lifter—a design by the Student Scientific Club "SAE" from Warsaw University of Technology—another success from Polish students who belong to the leading designers of unmanned aerial vehicles with the most favorable proportion of weight and load capacity, aerial vehicles built for many years by the club's members have received the highest scores at the international contest AERODESIGN, held every year in the United States.[15]

Research supervisors, who are often mentors for students, play a very important role in the activity of student academic clubs. "First, they are people who, through their own work and actions, frequently help others to use their actual potential."[16] A mentor associates with a knowledgeable advisor, whose strategic role is to provide their charge with development possibilities. This is the case with a university teacher; he or she should be a mentor in a contemporary higher educational institution.

A student wishes to perceive an academic as a person who treats others as equals. They are able to transfer knowledge efficiently and clearly, channel students into acquiring practical skills, and always give advice to those who need it. The communication between a university mentor and student is a very important process. First of all, it is a bilateral communication process aimed at enabling each of the parties involved to comment on a given subject. "A mentor is an authority, a person who helps as they are genuinely willing to do so. Thus one may acknowledge without superfluous grandiloquence that the help of a mentor is invaluable and impossible to purchase."[17] A mentor at a university may also be a thesis supervisor, who indicates to a seminar student the proper way of thinking. Among the numerous studies on university mentoring, the one conducted in March 2011 among students in the first year of undergraduate courses in management as well as students in the first year of master's degree courses in economics at the University of Warmia and Mazury in Olsztyn, has been of great importance. The question, "Would you be interested in participating in a mentoring program at the university?" was answered "yes" or "probably yes" by as many as 90 percent of master's degree students and 60 percent of undergraduate students respectively. Approximately 80 percent of students would expect assistance with planning their career paths, over 55 percent with meeting new challenges, and approximately 36 percent with developing their interpersonal skills.[18]

Thus it may be noticed that students are interested in this form of development, and this is also a signal to universities that they should implement mentoring programs, which are already popular in other countries. The activity of students in the form of taking part in student organizations or academic clubs, or using the training services offered by academic career services provides a young person with the opportunity to acquire useful professional competencies in the form of knowledge, personality attributes, and a proper attitude, as well as skills in time, project, and group work management.

Knowledge and Inventiveness in the Teaching Process

Knowledge is an intangible asset, which does not wear out and is within the reach of those who wish to use it. Its basis consists of information and data, yet knowledge, in contrast to them, always relates to a specific person. "It is the result of work performed by individuals and it represents their opinions on cause and effect relationships."[19] According to the results of the study "Employer Friendly University 2010" conducted by the Institute for Employment and Social Matters, the company e-Dialog in cooperation with the Polish Confederation of Private Employers Lewiatan (PKPP Lewiatan), it may be noticed that employers greatly appreciate the knowledge which students acquire at university.The study indicated that over 80 percent of employers claimed that knowledge and skills were the most significant when employing young people, over 60 percent emphasized the importance of experience. From the employers' point of view, psychosocial competencies, the ability to work as a team, meeting deadlines, and discipline are also very important. Practical skills and so-called soft qualifications, which are hardly ever taught at Polish universities, are poorly assessed in comparison to theoretical ones.[20] Knowledge is each person's individual asset. As thinking beings, humans are capable of gathering and processing information in practical activities. Knowledge is a very valuable asset as it expands when developed and used. It is, first of all, a unique asset; therefore Polish students realize that they need to develop it internally and invest in it.

In Poland, studies on the identification and analysis of the needs related to the management of students' and graduates' professional careers are scarce. A significant number of universities are simply uninterested in the rate of unemployment among students, where graduates find employment, whether they work in accordance with their education, how their professional careers develop, and how they assess the quality and usefulness of education. Without these data it is impossible to assess whether a given university educates students according to the needs of the economy, to what extent it produces specialists who are in demand on the market, and to what extent its graduates become unemployed. The Ministry of Science and Higher Education would like universities to monitor their graduates' professional careers, starting in September 2011. These studies are supposed to be obligatory. Such monitoring will allow Polish universities to modify their educational and professional offer and the research results may also become an important indicator for high school graduates concerning the choice of a university in order to find employment consistent with their training. Despite a considerable improvement in the situation in the employment market in recent years, the unemployment rate among students and graduates still constitutes one of the major problems in the Polish employment market, both because of its scale and the significance of their status in the employment market for these young people's lives. The ability to use knowledge and competencies becomes and is essential to make progress. The demand for workers with low qualifications has decreased, while the demand for new specializations related to the current shape of the Polish economy within, e.g., finance, marketing, information technology, trade, telecommunication, public relations, and human resources management has increased. Skills such as foreign languages, creativity, the ability to work in teams, or the capacity for permanent improvement and development have become important. The lack of coherent syllabuses which are consistent with the needs of the economy results in educating, in our country, potentially unemployed alumni. A university diploma itself no longer guarantees a safe and confident entry into the employment market in a knowledge-based economy. Students and university graduates—regardless of the type and prestige of their school—despite searching for many months, fail to find employment. If they find a job, it frequently does not correspond with their studied profession or does not require specialist knowledge. This gives rise to undesirable social and economic effects, such as the partial or complete loss of professional qualifications acquired during the course of learning and the feeling of injustice, frustration, marginalization, and the like. Therefore higher educational institutions should not only be places where students acquire knowledge, but also places which prepare them for work and give them the opportunity to find it fast.

Above all, it is important for each of the students and graduates to realize the current situation in the employment market and also to think about their prospective professions in advance and plan their careers in accordance with the knowledge, skills, and education acquired. The beginning of a professional career as well as the first job generally determine its further course. When entering the employment market we do not realize our own trump cards, or our own plans. Sometimes graduates do not consider such problems at all. Thus on completion of studies, they enter a completely unfamiliar area. At the time they are accompanied by the feeling of uncertainty, serious doubts, and a lack of confidence in their own actions. The aforementioned dilemmas result firstly from insufficient experience or knowledge of the employment market as well as a lack of information on the risks and chances of job seeking. One of the limitations on the employment market is a lack of self-promotional skills (e.g., poor communication, lack of motivation, improper body language, lack of negotiating skills, lack of assertiveness). Yet another problem involves limited access to training sessions and workshops (high costs of this form of education), which may be referred to in the applications submitted and during interviews, or the lack of information on up-to-date job offers. Therefore, professional assistance for students and graduates is needed to increase their activity and job-seeking abilities under the conditions of progressive globalization.

The employment market allocates the most important asset—human resources—and the feature determining their chances on the employment market should be their level of education, which has influence, not only on their efficient job seeking, but also on their ability to adapt to change. Therefore, there is a need for continuous further training of students and graduates in order to adjust their qualifications to market needs; this would contribute to the development of the Polish knowledge-based economy. The role of contemporary higher education is to provide students with knowledge and skills that will allow them to take risks and introduce innovations into an economic market. The academic environment is a treasure trove of numerous concepts and values. Their efficient use shows higher educational institutions as creators of entrepreneurship and inventiveness.

J. Schumpeter is believed to have developed the inventiveness theory. He made an assumption that inventiveness is an occurrence of introducing a new solution—an invention for the operation of an enterprise. He also created a classification of five categories of inventiveness:

1. the introduction of a new product of a considerable quality improvement to an existing product.
2. the introduction of a new or substantially modernized manufacturing method.
3. the development of a new market segment or an efficient entry into a geographically new market.
4. the acquisition of a new source of supply of raw materials or intermediate goods.
5. the development of a new organizational type of enterprise.[21]

It may be stated that Schumpeter perceived inventiveness as a very broad concept. He did not confine his theories to one specific process. His considerations display the fact that inventiveness may take place in diverse fields, processes, and market segments. Humans create innovations and the opportunity for implementing modern solutions depends on their knowledge, abilities, involvement, and openness. Inventiveness from Schumpeter's perspective may be summarized as the translation of "inventiveness into a material reality."[22] A similar approach is presented by Robbins and DeCenzo, for whom inventiveness is "a process of transforming a creative idea into a useful product, service, or mode of operation."[23] The ability to transform the possessed and newly acquired knowledge into practice is undoubtedly a significant factor determining the shaping of inner entrepreneurship and inventiveness.

A number of other definitions of invention are also worth mentioning:

- by Rogers, according to whom invention is what an individual perceives as new, regardless of the objective novelty of a given idea or object;
- by Freeman, who associates invention with the first business application of a new product;

- by Mansfield, who treats invention in a similar way, as the first application of an invention; and
- by Kotler, for whom invention relates to any product, service, or idea considered by an individual to be new.[24]

A highly significant element of invention, stressed by Kwiatkowski in his considerations, is first of all, the fact that it is not "an accidental and separate occurrence so much as it is a process which may be managed."[25] It is possible to be managed.

An important issue in the process of defining innovation was also presented by Drucker, who emphasized that change constitutes the basis of innovation as it provides the opportunity to develop new products or services. In his opinion "systematic innovation involves a deliberate and organized search for change as well as a systematic analysis of possibilities which such change might offer to the benefit of economic or social innovation."[26] Monitoring, mentioned by Drucker, first of all relates to seven innovative sources:

1. something unexpected;
2. a discrepancy between what exists and what should exist;
3. the need for success;
4. a change in the structure of a line of business or in the market structure;
5. demography;
6. a change in perception, tendency, meaning;
7. recent scientific and non-scientific knowledge.[27]

Drucker stressed the fact that scientific and non-scientific knowledge are sources of innovation for a reason. It is worth taking into consideration.

Scientific knowledge acquired in the form of research studies by academics at higher educational institutions is then transferred to other entities, among others, to students. It is a new type of knowledge as research studies present the realities of a contemporary economy, business, or employment market. They are an excellent compendium for establishing at universities new majors compatible with the requirements of the employment market. The higher educational institutions that wish to be both modern and innovative should educate prospective entrepreneurs, managers, specialists, computer scientists, and office workers as they are indispensable to the Polish economy; the economy will continue to undergo dynamic changes , therefore the economy needs students who are trained and supplied with new knowledge and technological skills. Owing to the ability to transfer scientific knowledge as well as the ability to acquire and use it in the future, it may be expected that the Polish economy will head toward innovation. It also needs to be remembered that apart from scientific knowledge a university is also responsible for providing non-scientific knowledge in the form of acquiring practical skills and developing personality features which students need to possess in order to become acquainted with the contemporary employment market. A contemporary university should also emphasize to students the priorities for a modern economy as future graduates will become its creators. The greater the number of universities educating innovation-oriented young people who are not afraid of change and risk and who are creative and motivated as well as willing to expand their knowledge and share it with others, the more competitive and innovative the Polish economy will become in comparison to other European countries. The ever-progressing development of technology is aimed at innovation. This is also stressed by Brilman, who claims that innovation is "the application of a creative idea."[28]

Creativity may lead to discovering a new solution, process, method, or manner which has not been discovered yet, thus standing a chance of becoming competitive. Innovation means new, developed, improved; therefore in order to achieve such "novelty" one needs to possess vast reserves of knowledge, be aware of economic conditions, and be creative; these are the most significant elements when attempting to obtain innovative results.

Conclusion

Nowadays the Polish economy is undergoing a considerable metamorphosis and needs to adapt to numerous changes accompanying this process, which undoubtedly contributes to a significant revolution in higher education as well. Universities also need to change and create new majors, following the realities of the domestic economy. First, this is important to the extent that universities should educate innovation- and entrepreneurship-oriented students, and not only young people who join the ranks of the unemployed. Second, owing to an education consistent with the requirements of the employment market the number of applicants who wish to study at a modern university, training the future personnel of a knowledge-based economy, will increase. Third, the Polish economy requires young, competent scientists, engineers, specialists, and managers who will focus on innovative solutions, not on a stagnant economy. Nearly 50 percent of young high school graduates enter university. First of all, higher educational institutions in Poland need to consider themselves to be strategists whose primary aim is not to educate the largest number of students, but to provide young people with high-quality teaching, which may be achieved through the introduction of practitioners into the education process; they deal with economic issues on an everyday basis, thus enabling students to acquire the necessary practical skills. The role of a contemporary higher educational institution is to observe economic changes and through curricular autonomy, adapt the education process to such changes as well as act as a creator of entrepreneurship and inventiveness in its students.

Notes

---

1. J. Zieliński, "Conditioning and assumptions of educational changes in the 21st century," in *Education compared with the employment market and European integration*, ed. K. Szczepańska-Woszczyna and Z. Dacko-Pikiewicz (Dąbrowa Górnicza: Academy of Business, 2007), p. 21.

2. S. Sudoł, *Enterprise* (Toruń: Wyd. Dom Organzatora, 2002), p. 33.

3. Joint publication, *Toward more resourceful generations*—European Commission Communication, http://ec.europe.eu/enterprise.

4. B. Bojewska, "The significance of education in triggering entrepreneurship," in *Economic instruments for supporting the economic boom in Poland* (Warsaw: Warsaw School of Economics, 2003), p. 272.

5. J. Kortan, *Essentials of economics and enterprise management* (Warsaw: C.H. Beck, 1997), p. 77.

6. K. Sanatarek, *Transfer of technology from university to business* (Warsaw: PARP, 2008), p. 135.

7. Z. Kruszewski, "Innovations for the economy in the education process of students," in *Higher educational institutions as creators* of innovation in economy, ed. R. Marcinkowski (Warsaw: Publishing House of Warsaw Technical University, 2009), pp. 57–58.

8. P. Tamowicz, *Academic entrepreneurship: Spin off companies in Poland* (Warsaw: PARP, 2006).

9. T. Cichocki, *Academic entrepreneurship: Spinnaker of knowledge* (Lublin: Innpuls, 2010), p. 12.

10. http://www.pokl.wrotapodlasia.pl/index.php?Faq#faq25 (accessed 26 April 2011).

11. The Act of 27 July 2005 Law on Higher Education (*Journal of Laws*, no. 164, Item 1365 as amended).

12. L. Kwieciński, "Institutions and instruments of the commercialization process of the knowledge of students and university graduates," in *Academic entrepreneurship: Intellectual property*, ed. P. Kubiński, L. Kwieciński, and L. Żurawowicz (Wrocław: DPPPA—Lower Silesia Portal of Academic Entrepreneurship Promotion, 2010), pp. 12–13.

13. P. Majewski and P. Żywicki, *Academic entrepreneurship in Toruń: Good practices of an Academic Business Incubator* (Toruń: Toruń School of Banking, 2009), p. 7.

14. J. Stawska, "Student organizations as a path to a career," in Szczepańska-Woszczyna and Dacko-Pikiewicz, *Education compared with employment market*, p. 169.

15. A. Jakubiak, "Student academic clubs as incubators of innovation," in Marcinkowski, *Higher educational institutions as creators of innovation*, p. 146.

16. R. Luecke, *Coaching and mentoring: How to develop greatest talents and achieve better results* (Warsaw: MT Biznes Sp. z o.o., 2004), p.125.

17. R. Molenda, "The role of a mentor as the person preparing for professional tasks" in Szczepańska-Woszczyna and Dacko-Pikiewicz, *Education compared with employment market*, p. 104.

18. M. Gruszczyńska and M. Szul, "The use of mentoring in knowledge management at a university," in *Social and organizational aspects of change management*, ed. J. Lendzion and M. Szczepanik (Łódź: Wydawnictwo Media Press, 2011), p. 73.

19. G. Probst, S. Raub, and K. Romhardt, *Knowledge management in an organization* (Cracow: Oficyna Ekonomiczna, 2004), p. 35.

20. http://praca.gazetaprawna.pl/artykuly/508660,lewiatan_szkoly_wyzsze_nie_ przygotowuja _absolwentow_do_pracy.html (accessed 27 April 2011).

21. J. Schumpeter, *Theory of economic development* (Warsaw: PWN, 1960), p. 104.

22. J. Bogdanienko, M. Haffer, and W. Popławski, *The innovative nature of enterprises* (Toruń: Nicolaus Copernicus University Press, 2004), p. 8.

23. D. A. DeCenzo and S. P. Robbins, *Essentials of management* (Warsaw: PWE, 2002), p. 347.

24. R. Nowacki and M. W. Staniewski, *Innovative approach to enterprise development* (Warsaw: Difin, 2010), p. 16.

25. S. Kwiatkowski, *Intellectual resourcefulness* (Warsaw: PWN, 2000), p. 84.

26. P. Drucker, *Inspiration and luck*, that is, innovation and entrepreneurship (Warsaw: Studio Emka, 2004), p. 39.

27. Ibid., p. 40.

28. J. Brilman, *Modern concepts and management methods* (Warsaw: PWE, 2002), p. 168.

The Quality of Teaching at the University Level in Light of the Bologna Process

JOANNA KOPROWICZ AND KAZIMIERZ WALUCH

Changing realities force us to reflect on the function, place, and role of higher education in the contemporary world. The new challenges that European societies must face require new solutions, which would allow them to adjust to the ever-changing conditions of our lives. Demographic problems, including migrations or aging societies, are one of the most important issues.[1] This should be accompanied by information technologies, which are tools supporting the development of economies and societies, yet providing that the skills necessary to employ them at work and in everyday life are acquired. Moreover, this should be combined with the need for increasing the competitiveness of European higher education, particularly in the context of the globalization of education, thus leading to an increase in the role of continuing education, while also influencing the European labor market. These assumptions result from a permanent concern over qualitative changes in education, particularly at the tertiary level.

The involvement and willingness to contribute to these changes were reflected in the Sorbonne Declaration, adopted in 1998, whose signatories (France, Germany, Italy, and Great Britain) emphasized that European higher education showed greater potential for establishing new employment opportunities and the continent's general development.

The Bologna Declaration, signed by twenty-nine countries (including Poland) in 1999 constituted a reply to the aforementioned issues. It set two goals, i.e., strengthening the international competitiveness of higher education in Europe, and establishing a European Higher Education Area (EHEA). Their essence stems from changes to the system of higher education. Objectives defined in this way do not lead to the unification of higher education in Europe; however, they are supposed to strengthen and enhance it while maintaining its diversity. The achievement of the latter was announced by the representatives of the countries participating in the Bologna Process during meetings in both Vienna and Budapest during the first half of 2010. Yet it seems that it is a premature declaration, as even if notable effects had been attained, certainly not all the changes and reforms of higher education in particular countries were brought to a successful conclusion. Moreover, in the same declaration the ministers stated that it was necessary to continue these reforms in parallel with mutual relations between European higher educational institutions.

According to the ministers, the establishment of the EHEA allowed the countries to increase the role of higher education in the international arena.

The Bologna Process also has a number of academic targets, which should be achieved in consequence of the changes initiated within the scope of higher education. These targets include increasing the employability of university graduates (thus preparing them more efficiently to function in the labor market), activating graduates, raising the number of graduates actively contributing to the development of civic society, and also contributing to their societies' sustainable development in various areas, including knowledge. These objectives were extended and the methods for achieving them were determined as well, including:

- the introduction of *two- and three-cycle courses*;
- the adaptation of *easily readable and comparable degrees* (diplomas);
- the establishment of a *European system of credits*, allowing a student or graduate to transfer achievements (ECTS);
- the promotion of *mobility* of students and employees of European higher educational institutions;
- cooperation in *education quality assurance*;
- the promotion of the European dimensions of higher education—establishment of *departments or modules related to European issues*;
- the propagation and establishment of structures for *lifelong learning* (implemented through *LLP—the Lifelong Learning Program*);
- the improvement in *cooperation between schools and students*;
- the promotion of the *European Higher Education Area* throughout the world;
- strengthening cooperation between the sectors of education, research and innovation; the synergy of the European Higher Education Area and the European Research Area;
- an emphasis on the *social dimension of education*: establishment of *equal access to higher education*—including study opportunities—for all persons, regardless of their socioeconomic status, through ensuring proper financial support, as well as vocational and personal counseling;
- an increase in the *employability of graduates*, i.e., their capability to find and maintain employment as well as mobility in the labor market;
- implementation of the *Diploma Supplement* issued free of charge for all university graduates;
- a change in the approach to the teaching process—transition to *student-oriented education* (instead of teacher-oriented).[2]

A great number of the aforementioned issues overlap, thus blurring the lines between one another. They remain interdependent, particularly due to the fact that study programs constitute a common element aimed at improving the quality of a great many of these areas. The suggested method of describing and developing study programs, called the National Framework for Qualifications, predominantly focuses on the efficiency and effectiveness of education. The said efficiency can be measured by the obtained document, which certifies the acquisition of these qualifications. This system ensures that programming starts with the identification of the desired effects (knowledge, skills, personal and social competencies), in order to be able to determine the curriculum in particular faculties or teaching methods for the teaching process. Yet another significant element of this system is the assessment of the extent to which the assumed teaching effects have been fulfilled. Such an approach enables one to compare the qualifications acquired by the graduates of higher educational institutions in different European countries. This system considerably increases the independence of universities, providing the opportunity to individualize the teaching process in order for graduates to obtain proper qualifications in any given field. This state of affairs also allows one to diversify the range of university courses, thus adjusting the educational offer to students' interests and reacting to the actual needs of the labor market.

The extent to which the assumptions adopted in the Bologna Declaration have been implemented has been discussed during ministerial conferences on higher education, which are held every other year and are concluded with a communiqué summarizing the achievements to date. This document also includes guidelines, which determine actions for the subsequent years. These meetings allow one to widen the scope of cooperation in new areas, to extend the measures already being implemented, or to initiate new ones (see table 1).

TABLE 1
The Decisions of the Conference of Participants in the Bologna Process

Year	Document	Main points
2001	Prague Communiqué	Lifelong learning as a condition to improve social cohesion, equal opportunities, and quality of life; Lifelong learning as a condition to use new technologiesand to face the challenges of competitiveness; Building a knowledge-based society and economy; The importance of cooperation between institutions of higher education and students.
2003	Berlin Communiqué	Introducing the third cycle in the system of studies; Enhancing cooperation within the European Higher Education Area and European Research Area.
2005	Bergen Communiqué	Development of doctoral courses; Stronger connections between the research sector and higher education; Access to higher education for students in difficult situations (including financial problems); Promotion of the mobility of students and staff.
2007	London Communiqué	Building national strategies for the social dimension of higher education; Developing databases related to mobility and the social dimension; Promoting graduate employability; Promoting the Bologna Process throughout the world.
2009	Leuven/Louvain-la-Neuve Communiqué	Promoting multilateral partnerships for lifelong learning (public authorities, institutions of higher education, students, employers, employees); Developing qualifications frameworks; Internationalizing studies; Increasing mobility; Monitoring the tools used for classifying and comparing higher educational institutions in Europe.
2010	Vienna Communiqué	Enhancing the effectiveness of the actions taken toward the implementation of the Bologna Process.

Sources: The conference communiqués.

The first conference of the signatories of the Bologna Declaration was held in Prague on 19 May 2001. Apart from confirming the assumptions adopted in Bologna, it set new tasks for European higher education. During the following conference (Berlin, 18–19 September 2003) the need to strengthen the connection between higher education and research was discussed, as was the issue of doctoral courses. On 19–20 May 2005 in Bergen a subsequent conference was held, during which forty-five representatives of countries participating in the process adopted two documents, significant from the perspective of national higher education systems, i.e.,

1. the Standards and Guidelines for Quality Assurance in the European Higher Education Area—the document was prepared by ENQA;
2. the framework of qualifications and skills for the European Higher Education Area.

The next Ministerial Conference on higher education was held in London on 17–18 May 2007. In the London communiqué it was stressed that the National Framework of Qualifications ought to be based on the Framework of Qualifications for the European Higher Education Area.

The meeting's participants agreed on the establishment of an independent Register of Quality Assurance Agencies, as well as "The European Higher Education Area in a Global Setting." The next conference was held in Leuven / Louvain-la-Neuve, Belgium, on 28–29 April 2009. Among its numerous decisions was the one on enhancing mobility of students by 2020 to the level of 20 percent of graduates participating in a study or training period abroad. After this conference the meeting called "Bologna Policy Forum" with the participation of fifteen countries from outside Europe took place.[3] The last conference was held in Budapest and Vienna on 12–13 March 2010. The meeting took on the nature of a jubilee event; therefore the achievements to date were discussed, and the official establishment of the European Higher Education Area was announced.

The efforts to have the highest possible quality of higher education are not only typical of Europe; universities all over the world strive to raise their teaching standards, which is connected with gaining a particular competitive advantage within the economy of the entire region or part of a region. This trend is also being pursued through a European initiative related to the Bologna Process. Reflecting on the diversity of education systems, languages, traditions, political systems and the like, this task appears to be difficult. In this case there occurs a certain discord: on the one hand, the diversity that Europeans pride themselves on, and on the other hand, an attempt to standardize a given area, which involves uniformity and similar procedures.

During the first conference, the ministers already acknowledged that the quality of education might support the process of the recognition of qualifications throughout Europe. In consequence of this standpoint, there appeared incentives to strengthen cooperation between all the European higher educational institutions and between the networks which deal with recognition and quality assurance in order "to disseminate examples of best practice and to design scenarios for the mutual acceptance of evaluation and accreditation/certification mechanisms."[4]

The communiqué after the conference in Berlin expressed very clearly the standpoint of the signatories to the Bologna Declaration on educational quality issues. Admittedly, according to the principle of the autonomy of universities, quality depends on the higher educational institutions themselves; however, it is necessary to support actions toward improving the quality of education at the national and European level as well. Hence the conclusion that national quality assurance systems should include the following:

- a definition of the responsibilities of the bodies and institutions involved;
- the evaluation of programs or institutions, including internal assessment, external review, the participation of students, and the publication of results;
- a system of accreditation, certification, or comparable procedures;
- international participation, cooperation, and networking.[5]

Simultaneously, the participants of the meeting called upon the European Network of Quality Assurance in Higher Education (ENQA)[6] "to develop an agreed set of standards, procedures and guidelines on quality assurance, to explore ways of ensuring an adequate peer review system for quality assurance and/or accreditation agencies or bodies."[7]

Hence the meeting in Bergen, held on 19–20 May 2005, was particularly significant for the development of cooperation on the quality of education in European higher educational institutions. Yet it should be noticed that in this case the efforts made toward the quality of education actually relate only to one education level, determined by the Bologna Process. However, a number of difficulties appeared. One of them resulted from problems connected with numerous terms associated with quality standards at the European level; due to their ambiguous nature it was necessary to define certain terminology items, e.g., "standard" and "quality." Another arguable issue was the conditioning as well as the regional or national context of the way these terms were understood. If we combine these doubts with the diversity of relations between higher educational institutions and external quality control institutions, it may appear that building a uniform standard of higher educational quality in Europe is an exceptionally complex task.

In such a case it seems that the only proper direction of a common undertaking within this scope is to respect this diversity, in parallel with an attempt to improve the transparency of educational quality systems.[8] These actions are accompanied by the principles which are clearly presented in the document "Standards and Guidelines for Quality Assurance in the European Higher Education Area," elaborated by the European Association for Quality Assurance in Higher Education:

- providers of higher education have the primary responsibility for the quality of their provision and its assurance;
- the interests of society in the quality and standards of higher education need to be safeguarded;
- the quality of academic programs needs to be developed and improved for students and other beneficiaries of higher education across the EHEA;
- there need to be efficient and effective organizational structures within which those academic programs can be provided and supported;
- transparency and the use of external expertise in quality assurance processes are important;
- there should be encouragement of a culture of quality within higher educational institutions;
- processes should be developed through which higher educational institutions can demonstrate their accountability, including accountability for the investment of public and private money;
- quality assurance for accountability purposes is fully compatible with quality assurance for enhancement purposes;
- institutions should be able to demonstrate their quality domestically and internationally;
- processes used should not stifle diversity and innovation.[9]

In consequence of the undertaken actions, a document on education quality assurance[10] was agreed upon and adopted; its primary conclusions include the following:

- there will be European standards for internal and external quality assurance and for external quality assurance agencies;
- European quality assurance agencies will be expected to submit themselves to a cyclical review within five years;
- there will be an emphasis on subsidiarity, with reviews being undertaken nationally where possible;
- a European register of quality assurance agencies will be produced;
- a European Register Committee will act as a gatekeeper for the inclusion of agencies in the register;
- a European Consultative Forum for Quality Assurance in Higher Education will be established.[11]

The work on this document allowed one to draw a number of significant conclusions. One of them relates to a multilevel and a "dynamic" approach to the quality evaluation procedure, which is connected, inter alia, with the constant pursuit of educational improvement. The structure of the acquired qualifications is subject to evaluation, due to which the cohesion of measures, obtained results, and achieved teaching objectives are the most important. Therefore universities should possess determined-upon mechanisms for approving programs and their periodic review; they should also have internal control systems in order to respond to the question on the teaching effects achieved in the didactic process formulated for a particular study program. It is worth remembering that the evaluation of teaching effects does not determine the evaluation of, for example, conducting the process of education, particularly from the students' point of view, e.g., counseling (career services), financial assistance, or accommodations. Apart from this, it should also be noticed that internal quality assurance procedures often go beyond the teaching process, also encompassing other aspects of activities conducted by universities, e.g., research and the nonteaching activities of their staff. This has become an inherent part of the so-called quality culture, which is a defined idea of the functioning of an entity as a whole.

External entities, accreditation agencies, and bodies dealing with the supervision of quality assurance guarantee the quality of higher education in Europe. The document presented in Bergen recommended establishing a register of quality assurance and/or accreditation agencies which are recognized in Europe in addition to a body managing the said register. This solution allows universities to be accredited by any agency entered in this register. In the case of this accreditation, it is particularly important to evaluate the efficiency of an internal quality assurance system, paying special attention to assessing the assumed teaching effects which were agreed upon for any given study program in relation to the actual results achieved. An interesting phenomenon would be to employ persons from outside higher education to perform these procedures, e.g., representatives of industry, although such a situation occurs very rarely.

Actually, the legitimacy of establishing such agencies does not pose a problem (none of the participants of the Bologna Process question this legitimacy, as the agencies are supposed to promote trust in higher educational institutions through enhancing the transparency of quality assurance systems in higher education), but there were questions regarding the criteria qualifying these entities for this register and also the possibilities of limiting the accreditation recognition of these agencies in particular countries. Finally, the parties reached an agreement, and since 2008 the European Quality Assurance Register for Higher Education (EQAR) has been functioning. It is led by a board comprised of the following representatives of the academic environment: the European Association for Quality Assurance in Higher Education (ENQA), the European University Association (EUA), the European Association of Institutions in Higher Education (EURASHE), and the European Students Union (ESU). Significant decisions related to the register are made by an assembly, comprised of, in addition to the aforementioned entities, representatives of Business Europe and Education International.

It needs to be emphasized that EQAR is only one of a number of important European initiatives toward quality assurance;[12] actions on a global scale have been taken as well.[13]

JOANNA KOPROWICZ AND KAZIMIERZ WALUCH

TABLE 2
List of European Standards for Quality Assurance in Higher Education

Internal quality assurance in higher educational institutions	
Policy and procedures for quality assurance	Institutions should have a policy for quality assurance. They should have standards for their programs and their outcomes. They should develop and implement a strategy for the continuous enhancement of quality. The strategy, policy, and procedures should have a formal status and be widely available.
Approval, monitoring, and periodic review of programs and outcomes	Institutions should have official mechanisms for the approval, periodic review, and monitoring of their programs and results.
Assessment of students	Students should be assessed using published and consistently applied criteria, regulations, and procedures.
Quality assurance of teaching staff	Institutions should have methods ensuring that staff members involved with the teaching of students are appropriately qualified and competent to do so. The methods should be available to those conducting external reviews and commented upon in their reports.
Learning resources and student support	Institutions should ensure that the resources for supporting student learning are adequate and appropriate for each of the programs offered.
Information systems	Institutions should gather, analyze, and use relevant information for the efficient management of the study programs and other activities.
Publishing information	Institutions should regularly publish current, impartial and objective information, both quantitative and qualitative, on the programs and awards offered.

External quality assurance in higher education	
Use of external procedures for quality assurance in higher education	The efficiency of external procedures for quality assurance should be taken into account.
Development of external quality assurance processes	The objectives and goals of quality assurance processes should be published with a description of the procedures to be applied.
Criteria for decisions	Formal decisions taken in consequence of external quality assurance activities should be based on explicit criteria, published and used consistently.
Processes fit for purpose	The external quality assurance processes should be developed in a way ensuring their fitness to achieve the aims and goals determined for them.
Reporting	Reports that are comprehensible for their intended readership should be published. Readers should be able to easily find any decisions, commendations, or recommendations.
Follow-up procedures	Quality assurance processes containing recommendations for actions or requiring a subsequent action plan should have a predetermined follow-up procedure, which is implemented consistently.
Periodic reviews	External quality assurance of institutions and/or their programs should follow a cyclical pattern. The length of these cycle and review procedures should be clearly de fined and published in advance.
System-wide analyses	Quality assurance agencies should issue time summary reports which discuss and analyze the general findings of their reviews, evaluations, etc.

Continued on next page

European standards for external quality assurance agencies	
Use of external procedures for quality assurance in higher education	External quality assurance agencies should take into consideration the presence and efficiency of the external quality assurance processes.
Official status	Competent public authorities in the European Higher Education Area should formally recognize these agencies as external quality assurance bodies. Agencies should comply with any requirements of the legislative jurisdictions in which they operate.
Activity	Agencies should regularly undertake external quality assurance actions (at the institutional and program level).
Resources	Agencies should have adequate and proportional resources, both human and financial, enabling them to organize and conduct their external quality assurance processes effectively and efficiently, in conjunction with providing appropriate conditions for the development of their processes and procedures.
Mission statement	Agencies should operate on the basis of explicit and clear objectives and goals, contained in a statement which is publicly available.
Independence	Agencies should be independent to the extent that they have autonomous responsibility for their operations and that the conclusions and recommendations produced in their reports cannot be influenced by third parties such as higher educational institutions, ministries, or other stakeholders.
External quality assurance criteria and processes used by the agencies	The processes, criteria, and procedures employed by the agencies should be defined in advance and publicly available. Generally, these processes should include: • a self-assessment or equivalent procedure conducted by the entity of the quality assurance process; • an external assessment performed by a group of experts, including, as appropriate, student member(s), and site visits (at the agency's discretion); • publication of a report, including any decisions, recommendations or other formal outcomes; • a follow-up procedure to review the actions taken by the entity of the quality assurance process in light of any recommendations included in the report.
Accountability procedures	Agencies should have their own accountability procedures.

Source: The European Association of Quality Assurance in Higher Education, *The Standards and Guidelines for Quality Assurance in the European Higher Education Area* (Helsinki: Director General for Education and Culture, 2005), pp. 6–8.

All the countries participating in the Bologna Process make every effort to ensure the quality of higher education,[14] in compliance with the criteria adopted during the conference in Berlin. However, it must be emphasized that in spite of the contribution toward cooperation (from both institutions and persons dealing with higher education), particularly at the international level, a great many issues still remain unresolved. It also appears that the announcement of the establishment of the European Higher Education Area, which took place in 2010, is a political declaration rather than an assessment of the actual state of affairs. Although the involvement of the parties to the Bologna Declaration in the establishment of this area is undeniable, the opinion of Christian Thune, the president of ENQA, expressed in 2005, that the road to the development of common values, assessment criteria, or expectations of teaching quality still remains long and laborious.

Notes

1. For example, Z. Długosz and S. Kurek, "The aging population in Poland compared to EU regions," *Synopsis*, no. 4 (2005): 24.

2. http://ekspercibolonscy.org.pl (accessed 14 June 2011).

3. Australia, Brazil, Canada, China, Egypt, Ethiopia, Israel, Japan, Kazakhstan, Kyrghistan, Mexico, Morocco, New Zealand, Tunisia, and the United States.

4. Towards the European Higher Education Area Communiqué on the meeting of European Ministers in charge of Higher Education, which was held in Prague on 19 May 2001, p. 3.

5. "Realizing the European Higher Education Area," Communiqué of the Conference of Ministers responsible for Higher Education, held in Berlin on 19 September 2003, p. 3

6. De facto since 2004, the European Association of Quality Assurance in Higher Education.

7. "Realizing the European Higher Education Area," p. 3.

8. "The Code of Good Practices" 2004—the European Consortium for Accreditation in Higher Education (ECA); "Statement on the agreed set of standards, procedures and guidelines at a. European level" 2004—ESIB; "Statement on peer review of quality assurance and accreditation agencies" 2004—ESIB; "Quality assurance policy position in the context of the Berlin Communiqué" 2004—EUA; "Policy Statement on the Bologna Process" 2004—EURASHE; "Guidelines for good practice"—INQAAHE.

9. *Standards and Guidelines for Quality Assurance in the European Higher Education Area* (Helsinki: European Association of Quality Assurance in Higher Education, Director General for Education and Culture, 2005), p. 13.

10. Ibid.

11. Ibid., p. 5.

12. For example, in June 2003 the European Consortium for Accreditation (ECA) was established; it comprises fifteen accreditation institutions from ten European countries.

13. For example, the comparison of quality assurance evaluation in different countries on the initiative of the Organization for Economic Cooperation and Development (OECD), which is currently conducting preparatory works aimed at evaluating the teaching results in higher educational institutions—Assessing Higher Education Learning Outcomes (AHELO).

14. Presently, forty-seven countries participate in the Bologna Process: Albania, Andorra, Armenia, Austria, Azerbaijan, Belgium, Bosnia and Herze-

govina, Bulgaria, Croatia, Cyprus, the Czech Republic, Estonia, Finland, France, Georgia, Germany, Great Britain, Greece, Hungary, Iceland, Ireland, Italy, Kazakhstan, Latvia, Lichtenstein, Lithuania, Luxembourg, Macedonia, Malta, Moldavia, Montenegro, the Netherlands, Norway, Poland, Portugal, Romania, Russia, Serbia, Slovakia, Slovenia, Spain, Sweden, Switzerland, Turkey, Ukraine, and Vatican City.

The Learned Society within the Framework of Permanent Education

ZBIGNIEW KRUSZEWSKI

The Genesis of Relevant Issues

In Poland, there is a need for developing various areas of social life. A number of social relationships, the basic function of which would be social activation and the realization of various projects—cultural, educational, scientific, regional, and the like—are linked by common functions. These common functions are developed in a grass-roots fashion outside the formal public and administrative structures.

Sociology includes social relationships in so-called target groups, within which compulsory and voluntary target groups are separated. Common grounds are necessary for creating target groups, also referred to as societies or associations. Human needs and attempts to satisfy them constitute the mechanisms for establishing such societies. Autonomy and independence are the essence of each and every activation trend. A great Polish educator, Aleksander Kamiński, emphasized that "social associations exist owing to people and through people—i.e., thanks to their professional and voluntary personnel, as well as active organization members."[1]

At the beginning of the twentieth-first century we consider issues of Polish culture, education, and higher education in our country from a different perspective than in the second half of the twentieth century, particularly in the declining years of the previous system and at the beginning of the political transformations. While examining the reforms of science, culture, and education, one also needs to consider a reform of social scientific and sociocultural movements, which should involve providing increasingly improved conditions for grass-roots initiatives and unhampered development of various areas of social life. It may be assumed that different social functions involve creating active social attitudes, local patriotism, and a readiness to cooperate with others. Such actions are aimed at sustaining long-lasting humanistic values and also at establishing new values within the political, social, and economic structures being currently developed.

In Poland, learned societies are structures and organizations arising from bottom-up initiatives; they introduce specific social objectives, including educational ones. Such societies, since their establishment at the beginning of the nineteenth century, have been strengthening Polish national identity, enhancing pro-independence trends, accelerating civilizational transformations, and promoting education. As early as 1800, the Royal Society of Friends of Learning was founded in Warsaw. This society, after the defeat of the Novem-

ber Uprising, was disbanded in 1832. On establishing the autonomous Kingdom of Poland under Russian rule during the period of the Partitions, a period
of extensive economic, cultural, scientific, and educational development occurred. The development of education was in great demand. This provided a
stimulus for creating other societies. The Płock Learned Society came to the
fore, founded at the Voivoidship School in Płock in 1820, on the initiative of
then Minister of Education Stanisław Kostka Potocki.

The Necessity for Permanent Education

In the contemporary world, the development level of a country and its innovativeness stems, to a great extent, from the qualifications of its human resources. Rapid technological development, the introduction of increasingly
modern work methods, and enterprises operating beyond the borders of one
country necessitate constant professional training, as well as the acquisition
of new qualifications. This is particularly significant in the case of the European Community, constituted by member states at different levels of economic
development, which are also diverse culturally. One of the fundamental assumptions underlying the process of economic integration is the free movement of workers. There is a need for the constant development of skills,
competencies, and understanding cultures of other countries in order to follow
the pace of constant change. One may increasingly often observe learning
communities, cities, and regions. We observe the cooperation between industry, schools, and universities, as well as professional organizations, learned
societies, and local authorities. Interesting initiatives arise which are aimed at
establishing new, dynamic, cultural and educational communities shaped by
the aspirations and incentives of their potential recipients.

Education and lifelong learning—aptly referred to as permanent education—are essential to transforming a contemporary society into a knowledge-
based society. It needs to be noticed that nowadays it is impossible to acquire
sufficient knowledge for one's entire life at any university. There has been an
exponential growth in knowledge; the world has become complex, diversified,
and interdependent to such an extent that it is necessary for an individual to
continue learning throughout his/her entire life.

The end of the dominance of physical work and laborers is rooted in the
twentieth-century technological revolution. Peter F. Drucker noticed that in
the United States at the turn of the nineteenth and twentieth centuries the number of educated workers (professionals with university degrees) exceeded the
number of laborers.[2] Thus, technologically advanced societies of the world
intensively move from an economy based on processing information, to an
economy based on processing and creating knowledge.

It seems justified to draw the conclusion from the above discussion that
continuing education is consistent with the needs of a knowledge-based society; it takes into consideration time changes and market values as well as the

rhythm of the individual. The concept of lifelong learning, otherwise describing the idea of continuing education, becomes an indispensable element for contemporary man's life. In a world of constant change and abundant information, an educated and constantly developing person is able to adapt to existing professional and environmental needs.

A knowledge-based society requires a new type of education. First, modern education needs to be based on the assumption that each student has instant access to enormous information resources and knowledge available online, and may, or even should, take full advantage of this fact, however, not through copying information without understanding it but through transforming it into useful knowledge. Second, the individual should not be confronted with the Internet knowledge on his own—he needs to cooperate with other individuals on creating useful knowledge. The main objective of education should involve instructing individuals of various professions, businesses, cultures, nationalities, experiences, and the like on how to cooperate, particularly on how to cooperate through the Internet along with the use of knowledge gathered by institutions available to the general public (e.g., public libraries, open societies, and learned societies).

The future of Poland will depend on how fast such an education system is developed, and which part of society will benefit from it. An increasingly significant role in non-school education will be played by social institutions providing education and in-service training.

In light of this new situation in a modern knowledge-based society, continuing education assumes growing importance. Various views on the issues related to continuing education in educational theory and practice have been expressed.

According to Robert Kid, the process of continuing education consists of three dimensions: a) vertical education; b) horizontal education; c) inner education (self-teaching). This process becomes curricular education in schools and universities as a result of educational activities being realized in three dimensions, supported by participation in various forms of activity (e.g., social, cultural, scientific, etc.) of non-school education and self-teaching (e.g., lifestyle). Paul Legrand from France has introduced a new important element into continuing education—creativity and creation. He has recognized the continuity and regularity of the learning process as the basic principle of continuing education which guarantees constant development, and prevents previously acquired knowledge from becoming outdated.

In a report entitled "Learn in order to exist" by E. Faure, issued by order of the UNESCO Committee for the Development of Education, great emphasis was laid on the importance of developing a learning society, that promotes self-teaching and continuing education. The report contains twenty one proposals—principles concerning the system of education, including lifelong learning. Consequently, a conference in Nairobi gave rise to a number of significant objectives and tasks related to the process of globalization and the integration of Europe with the specificity of an information society. These include, among other things, creating the possibility of comprehending essential contemporary issues, striving for active participation in social life, popularizing various communication and solidarity forms, developing abilities to use different sources of knowledge, learning how to acquire knowledge of various types, and developing learning and self-teaching skills. The development of continuing education has been greatly influenced by Jacques Delors's report, entitled: "Education—a Hidden Treasure Within," in which new functions and principles of education resulting from social transformations were indicated. Education, as it was stated in the report, leads to global activity through democratic participation in a learning and information society. Education should be based on four pillars: a) to learn in order to know—in order to acquire knowledge necessary for communicating with the surrounding world; b) to learn in order to act—to be able to influence one's own environment; c) to learn in order to exist; d) to learn in order to co-exist with others.

Continuous education and training receives a great deal of attention in the social policy of the European Union. A learning society is both a priority and an important challenge that education needs to confront. Young people and adult individuals acquire knowledge and improve their skills through continuing education in order to participate actively in scientific and technical transformations, in the globalization process of economics, and in the development of an information society. This was proven in the White Paper of 1995 "Teaching and Learning: On the Road to a Learning Society." This document deals with issues of the significance of education for social and cross-cultural relations in the European Union. The scientific and technical revolution, the early days of an information society, globalization—these are important factors which undoubtedly influence the education system through setting new objectives. The White Paper makes demands within this scope, promoting directives for EU member states. It indicates the necessity of adapting educational targets and contents to the complex situation of contemporary man.

In the subsequent years, particularly in 1996, which was the Year of Continuing Education in Western Europe, numerous initiatives, ideas, and programs related to continuing education were conceived, indicating diverse educational paths. A certain number of them presently constitute part of functioning programs, e.g., the SOCRATES program.

In the year 2000, while determining tasks for education in the twenty-first century, the Council of Europe assigned continuing education the role of the most significant path allowing the acquisition of extensive knowledge and the most important abilities necessary for active participation in the life and development of a contemporary knowledge-based society.

The issues of continuing education find expression both in Polish pedagogical thought and in programs developed by educational institutions. The foundations of permanent education in Polish pedagogical theory were created by prominent educators Ryszard Wroczyński[3] and Bogdan Suchodolski.[4] Professor Suchodolski imparted new dimensions, new values, and a new approach to continuing education. Simultaneously, he stressed that one of the most significant tasks of continuing education were innovative and creative tasks that help to achieve educational objectives in a new system of education. The greatest significance of permanent education in today's complicated world, according to Professor Suchodolski, is that it helps the individual to become a human being.

The need for identifying continuing education, as a necessary axiom, was emphasized by prominent Polish educationalists and sociologists, among others Jan Szczepański, Tadeusz Nowacki, Józef Półturzycki, Stanisław Kaczor, and a number of others. The need for permanent education was also emphasized by John Paul II in his teaching.

The document "The Strategy for the Development of Continuing Education until 2010" is of great significance in Poland as well. This document, although imperfect, stresses the importance of lifelong learning. It admits that continuing education allows individuals to develop abilities, increases knowledge, improves qualifications, and alters attitudes and behavior. "The Strategy" provides five continuing education priorities: increasing access to continuing education, raising the quality of continuing education, cooperation and partnership, increasing human capital investments, explaining the role and significance of continuing education.

As may be inferred from this brief review of the issues related to the topic, the concept of permanent dissemination of information in Poland, already has its traditions and experiences. Not only does it refer to educational and teaching practices, but also to research work. The concept of permanent education accelerated considerably in the previous decade of this century. New concepts and a number of valuable studies appeared. The institutions supporting the Lisbon Strategy, such as the Polish Lisbon Strategy Forum, along with the Institute for Market Economics, published the study by A. Matysiak entitled *Continuing Education in Poland: Benefits and Development Barriers,*[5] and a joint publication entitled *Continuous Education and Training in the Development of a Civil Society,*[6] issued by the Institute for Educational Studies in 2006. The monograph by Stefan Kwiatkowski entitled *Continuous Education and Training: Theoretical and Practical Dimensions* constitutes an important study on continuing education and training.[7] Permanent education has been penetrating the practices of universities with difficulty for the last two decades. These issues were examined by the authors of the joint publication entitled *Continuous Education and Training in Universities—from the Concept to Practice.*[8] The review of studies on continuing education and training (permanent education) in Poland indicates that these issues have been prominent in the area of research studies.

Continuing education and training should be conducted, in practice, by the entire system of integrated educational and care-providing institutions such as pre-schools, junior and senior high schools, universities, non-school institutions, cultural and educational institutions, mass media, workplaces, and social associations, including learned societies.

Societies in the context of continuing education have been increasingly mobile, using their own scholarly libraries, which have been digitized to a considerable extent, for this purpose and also offering a wide range of publications broadening the offer of continuing education, such as talks and scholarly lectures, meetings with scholars and scientists, exhibitions, and the like. Thus, they contribute, outside the formal system of education, to the development of knowledge among young people and adults. Paradoxically, not a great many studies on the history of societies may be found, particularly on their activities within permanent education. It is generally known that learned societies in Poland have played a significant role in continuing education and in the development of a knowledge-based society during each period of their activities over the centuries.

The objective of this study is a thesis that general learned societies, including the Płock Learned Society in particular, by their nature as social movements, various forms of work, and a wide educational offer, have played a vital part in the popularization of continuing education and training, thus, ambitiously and successfully promoting a knowledge-based society in Poland.

Learned Societies for the Benefit of Education

The development of scholarship, strengthening the role of learning and its position as an element of social and economic development, as well as a desire for exploring and comprehending the rules governing the surrounding world, are indicators of establishing learned societies as well as scientific and professional associations and also indicators of an increase in their number and diverse forms of activity. It should not be disregarded that scholarship, constituting the basis for social scientific activity, precedes the general knowledge of society in any given field. Therefore scholars belonging to various groups wish to discuss their research activities and to transmit their achievements to society. These issues have also been an important factor in establishing learned societies. The significance of societies in scholarship and society depends on the pace of civilizational changes.

The development of this scholarly social movement was different in the various countries of Europe, as the political, economic, social, and cultural conditions differed as well.

Social and economic changes as well as the political environment in Poland have resulted in the evaluation of views on the scope of the statutory activities of learned societies. Their organizational structures, directions, and activity, as well as their significance, form the way the education system in our country has been transformed.

The infrastructural development of public educational institutions as well as the creation and revival of the learning movement in traditional, non-academic regional centers has also greatly influenced the implementation of the objectives of societies.

During the process of historical development, societies gradually became a mass form of organized participation for their members in the life of knowledge, constituting an organizational network which is diverse both in terms of structure and quantity. After the political transformation of 1989, the place and role of learned societies in the country's scholarly life underwent substantial changes. A significant number of politicians at the national level consider learned societies to be relics of socialism and therefore believe they should not be supported by the state and should function according to market rules. However, social activists and local politicians emphasize the role that the societies play in molding social awareness as well as fulfilling social conditions for the development of knowledge both in regional and national terms. Presently, learned societies are an inherent part of the Polish education system. Operating as scholarly social organizations, they fulfill their objectives and tasks through research as well as through educational functions which also promote, provide expert opinions on, and preserve cultural assets and national heritage. Societies conduct research, including research on regions, continuing education, promotion, and the popularization of science. They also run libraries (including research libraries), museums, archives, and the like, as well as carrying out publishing, auditing, and expert activities and, last but not least, they support the mobility of faculty.

It should also be noticed that learned societies have operated based on the potential of social activists—their members being willing to take various actions for the benefit of broadly defined knowledge, thus becoming involved in the concept of civiil society. A certain number of learned societies are engaged in multidisciplinary activities, uniting individuals of various local scholarly circles. As a rule, these are regional (local) general associations. Several of them act trans-locally, representing a scholarly environment connected with a specific scholarly field or discipline. These are generally specialist societies, representing sometimes very narrow fields, most frequently found within medical and technical sciences.

It is not always discerned that the activities of learned societies positively influence economic competitiveness and entrepreneurship, and this trend will increase. An active civil society and the dynamism of its actions, an innovative economy, and efficient institutions are pillars of business activity, particularly in periods of crisis. Learned societies within all these areas, through their structures and socially active members, play a specific, positive role. The activation of civic initiatives of highly qualified individuals will bring notable benefits to the competitiveness of the economy's innovative character and entrepreneurship.

Taking into account the connections of the members of learned societies, both originating from scholarly and economic circles, societies gradually become a bridge for transferring knowledge from academia to the economy, as personal contacts create a possibility of learning modern technological solutions and of their implementation. All the more so, because learned societies are a forum for a constant exchange of ideas and experiences among their members and the society where they operate. Societies are a bridge for transferring knowledge from academia to the economy, regardless of the times in which they function, and regardless of whether they deal with the humanities, social sciences, or technical sciences.

While evaluating learned societies during different periods of their functioning, certain common features may be noticed: "1) all learned societies are independent (statutory responsibility), 2) decisions have been and are taken democratically, 3) learned societies are characterized by the significant initiative of their members, 4) [they have been] established in the past, and cultivated respect for their members, 5) affiliation to societies is considered to be an honor, 6) the activities of their members are diversified in terms of worldview and the ancillary activity for the development of societies, 7) [there is] shared responsibility for decisions and financial assets."[9] At present, it may be noticed that the activity of learned societies evolves toward providing scientific, advisory, and expert opinions as well as toward the popularization of science and education at a high level using publications and IT techniques—including the Internet. Social and humanistic issues constitute the greatest field of interest for learned societies (around 60 percent), natural science, hard science, and technical science (15–20 percent), and other sciences (20 percent). These programs include social, regional, national, and global issues of the present day and of tomorrow.

During the twenty-first century, learned societies have become, along with their considerable achievements, the fourth pillar of Polish scholarship. However, the present times issue new challenges that societies should respond to. Within the European Union, governed by its specific regulations, complex laws, and principles, it is necessary to teach how to obtain knowledge in a competent manner, how to broaden knowledge using new development opportunities, but also how to make an original political and cultural contribution.[10] The entire scholarly social movement, particularly learned societies, may find its place in initiating important research—e.g., on regional problems in the EU states, on the patriotic tradition, on civic activities where contemporary patriotism is expressed—through an immediate response to the needs of social communities, which would be a contribution to the promotion of knowledge and the development of educational culture in Polish society.

Other problems raised by learned societies are sustainable development, ecology, nature conservation, providing food for individuals, improving farming techniques, new biotechnologies, power engineering, water resources, and the health of the population.

Continuing education and training aimed at developing a knowledge-based civil society play a significant role in the statutory activity of learned societies, i.e., education based on the interdependence of the education level and quality, essential pro-democratic attitudes, civilizational progress, the efficiency of the democratic system, and developing professional ethics, as well as work ethics in general.

Professor Janusz Tazbi, a noted historian, assigns learned societies in the twenty-first century the following tasks and roles: a) the struggle for leveling standards, for obliterating the division into Poland A, Poland B, and Poland C; b) directing interests toward regional history, as a distinct decrease in the interest in our national history may be noticed. According to this scholar, individuals who are unaware of the roots of the present times will not be able to comprehend them.[11] It should be acknowledged that contemporary learned societies perform these tasks to a considerable extent.

The historical continuity of this scholarly social movement in Poland is manifested through its organizational forms. The history of learned societies has been a complex process of perfecting and isolating organizational forms which meet the needs for developing and practicing scholarship, for locating the movement within a broader system of scholarship as well as for various conditionings—social, economic, and political ones. Two lines of development are clearly visible in this process: the first one, leading to general societies in terms of fields of interest and in terms of their territorial scope, and to regional societies limiting their territorial scope to regional borders; and the other one, leading to isolating (frequently from a general society) general professional associations and also to creating, along with the specialization and the development of new fields of economics and scholarship, specialist associations of nationwide scope.

The analysis of the achievements of general, specialist, and regional associations indicates that holding conferences, sessions, scholarly, and academic lectures are the most common forms of their activity, thus contributing to educating the general public. The recipients of such events are most frequently the members themselves, students, and schoolchildren, as well as interested representatives of local communities. The scale of these undertakings is diverse, encompassing such great and widely known scholarly events as, for example, the Alicja Karłowska-Kamzowa Medieval Seminar, which is periodically organized by the Poznań Society of Friends of Learning (in 2009 it was organized for the thirtieth time), yet it also involves small events promoting books frequently concerning local history and tradition, such as the book launch of *The National Democratic Party in North Masovia versus the Catholic Church 1898–1939* by Andrzej Dwojnych, which was held in 2008 by the Płock Learned Society.

Scholarly festivals, scholarly picnics, and scholarly cafés are new, increasingly popular forms of promoting research developed through education, which are increasingly popular with the general public, particularly with young people, in addition to sightseeing research expeditions; linguistic, folk, and entomological studies; or meetings with authors providing materials for organized conferences.

THE LEARNED SOCIETY AND PERMANENT EDUCATION

Learned societies employ yet another very important form of activity, i.e., they are publishing houses. Societies raise financial assets and release continuing, substantial, and occasional publications. Several thousand pages are issued by learned societies annually.

Learned societies also have a rich tradition of holding exhibitions. The cognitive and educational functions of such undertakings are undeniable. Furthermore, exhibitions, due to their nature, enjoy popularity not only with school-age youths, but also with adults. Frequently, it is the only opportunity to see an interesting incunabulum, document, or exhibit. It should also be stressed that such direct and easy contact with artifacts displayed on exhibition arouses interest for a great many years, and sometimes triggers a scholarly career.

The libraries that are run by learned societies constitute yet another aspect of their activity within both continuing education and training and building a knowledge-based society. The largest two are the Library of the Poznań Society of Friends of Learning, and the Zielinski Library of the Płock Learned Society. The Poznań institution was established in 1857, and at the end of 2007 it possessed 323,739 volumes, including over fifteen thousand early editions.[12]

The Zieliński Library dates back to 1820. In 2007 it possessed over 370,000 volumes, including thirteen thousand early editions and ninety-three incunabula.[13] Among its early editions, the library possesses the first edition of *De revolutionibus orbium coelestium* by Nicholas Copernicus published in 1543. Additionally, its collection of prints includes the complete cycle of *Caprichos* prints created by Francisco Goya—eighty prints from the first edition printed in 1799. For a number of years, the Zieliński Library has been developing a program of digital services, adjusted to the needs of contemporary readers and audience of cultural assets. Building electronic databases has been conducted through a digitization process, i.e., scanning and processing printed or handwritten materials, which allows the publishing of collections in the form of digital libraries.

The role of libraries has always been to collect books and render them available to the general public and also to secure and conserve them for subsequent generations. In this matter there have occurred no significant changes. However, the forms of library tasks related to civilizational development have changed according to the resultant needs of readers. In the area of security and availability, we are even dealing with revolutionary changes. Both of these tasks are connected to the digitization of library resources. The possibility of rendering available digital forms results in using originals less frequently, which in turn favors their preservation. However, the pleasure of using a book in its traditional form is undisputed. One needs to become accustomed to the fact that powerful servers are the future of libraries, thus allowing users to download necessary materials.

The increasingly common availability of the Internet causes learned societies to adapt to these changes in order to fulfill their mission particularly because one of the tasks of learned societies is to promote and popularize scholarship, i.e., information, broadly defined.

A rapid increase in the amount of data has represented a considerable challenge to information technologists and also to all the recipients and providers of information in the digital world. The Internet provides an opportunity for a new form of activity for learned societies. The essential feature of the twenty-first century society is the necessity of lifelong learning. The Internet is a great tool and scholarly associations attempt to employ it competently in order to offer readers, including their own members, the possibility of self-improvement and self-education.

At present, we deal with the development of local social networks, which facilitate the daily functioning of the community. There are no reasons preventing local scholarly networks or scholarship-related networks from operating in a similar manner. This has posed a challenge, among other things, in the area of continuing education and training for local social organizations, including learned societies.

There is every indication that in the not too distant future the role of learned societies will be limited to elaborate large-scale actions for the benefit of the continuing education of society, particularly in local communities. Learned societies inspire local communities to believe that scholarship, education, and culture, as well as national identity, play a significant role in the contemporary development of the country and the world.

The tasks performed by societies prove that such organizations are able to adapt to the present reality, and to elaborate mechanisms which inspire local communities to create a bond between academia and a local community; they are also able to confront economic, social, and cultural transformations. Learned societies efficiently participate in the process of educating local communities and using the Internet in the education of the entire country.

Established in 1820, the Płock Learned Society is the oldest active society in Poland, and may be referred to as an example of such activity.

Płock is one of the oldest cities in Poland. Its tradition dates back to the Middle Ages. As early as the twelfth century, it functioned as the seat of Polish rulers; it was one of the first Polish catholic bishoprics. The castle and the cathedral impart the character of a capital city. During the rule of Władysław I Herman and Bolesław Wrymouth, Płock was an important center of intellectual life which gathered around the duke's court and the bishop's palace.

In 1180 a catholic school was established at St. Michael's Church; this was later transformed into the Płock Voivodship School and at present it is the Marshal Stanisław Małachowski High School. In 1820, Płock had a population of 6,000. The city was then a significant center of administration. At first, it was the seat of the department of so-called East Prussia, later the capital of the department in the Duchy of Warsaw, and in the Kingdom of Poland the seat of district authorities. Prussian rule was marked by new investments: new buildings were erected, such as the city hall, a tollgate, a new building of the administrative power, and a prison, as well as a great many houses. The city of Płock was, at that time, the center of judicature, and the Civil Tribunal, the Criminal Court, and the Commission of Peace were situated here. Kajetan Morykoni acted as president of the Płock Voivoidship School.

On 12 September 1818, a government commission issued a directive recommending that teachers prepare various scholarly works, which inspired Kajetan Morykoni to establish a society. The following factors contributed to establishing a learned society in Płock: a) the economic situation of the Kingdom of Poland, b) the development of the city, c) the existence of the Płock Voivodship School, d) an active group of teachers at the Płock Voivodship School.

On 19 March 1820, during a school ceremony at the Płock Voivodship School, director Kajetan Morykoni read out his brief work, entitled "Initial Thoughts with Regard to the Establishment of the Learned Society at the Płock Voivodship School," in which he proposed establishing the Learned Society at the Płock Voivodship School in order to "popularize and resume, as far as possible, the illumination of the country." Therefore he proposed taking the following actions: a) publishing studies on the history of the nation, particularly those referring to the district of Płock, presenting at the same time the needs of this region; b) allowing the general public to acquire and broaden their knowledge and abilities; c) cooperating with other societies, drawing on their experience and offering them feedback.[14]

After the defeat of the November Uprising in 1830, the activity of the Learned Society came to a standstill, as was the case with other such organizations operating within Polish territories. After seventy-seven years of nonexistence, on 2 April 1907, a new management of the society was led by President Aleksander Maciesza. The society has been unceasingly active from that date until now. The most important objectives of the society involved disseminating knowledge, promoting scholarly research, and gathering materials concerning Płock, Masovia, and adjacent territories.

The activity forms defined in the society's statute involve scholarly sessions, libraries, scientific laboratories, art exhibitions, presentations, and scientific expeditions.[15] The society has remained faithful to the ideals of its predecessors. The present rules of the functioning of the Society were defined by its statute, approved during the Extraordinary General Meeting on 28 November 2003.

The preamble of the Płock Learned Society Statute of 2003 states:

> The Płock Learned Society, established in 1820, has its root in the spirit of tolerance and enlightenment. It unites individuals who are willing to work to the benefit of the general public, particularly for the local community. The fundamental objective of its activity is to popularize knowledge as the source of all progress.
>
> The Płock Learned Society, obliged by the example of its predecessors to transmit what is valuable in the over one-thousand-year heritage of Poland and Płock, guards national values and protects cultural assets, which are a measure of human civilization.

> Faithful to the ideals of our founders, we accept this Statute of the Płock Learned Society, so as to fulfill its stipulations to the benefit of the general public.
> We appeal to all those who, for the good of the Płock Learned Society, will apply this Statute to perform their duties respecting human dignity, its freedom, and applying these rules will constitute an inviolable basis of our society.

Scholarly sessions play a significant role in the society's activity for the development of the society. Prominent Polish and foreign scholars have participated in a number of scholarly sessions. The analysis of the issues raised during these sessions indicates that the activity of the Płock Learned Society has been useful for both youths and adults—teachers, lawyers, ecologists, farmers, and representatives of other social groups interested in specific problems. The subjects of these undertakings may be classified as a) ecological education; b) cultural education; c) cross-cultural education, including regional education; d) European education, e) media education; f) historical education, etc. An analysis of the above problems indicates that a great deal of attention has been paid to anniversary sessions.

At the beginning of its functioning, the society began its popularizing activity. Reports, presentations, and prelections were delivered in various circumstances. The issues raised were very diverse. The number of presentations in particular years differed as well, ranging from one to up to twenty-five annually. The speakers were prominent professors, including members of the Polish Academy of Sciences, academic teachers, lawyers, economists, engineers, and employees of cultural institutions. The topics of the prelections delivered predominantly concerned history, law, literature, culture, arts, natural and technical sciences, and social and economic issues. Such a selection resulted from social demands. This proves that the society has striven to satisfy needs within the scope of the acquisition of diversified knowledge by the inhabitants of Płock and of the adjacent region. These meetings are intended to influence the development of man and contribute to broadening knowledge in various fields.

A significant role in the acquisition of knowledge, or in the education of man, is played by the sense of sight. Therefore it is essential to present various objects (photographs, artifacts, devices, and the like) on exhibition. On various occasions, the Płock Learned Society has held at its seat, or participated in, exhibitions organized by other institutions. Such exhibitions were treated by the management and the society's members as an important element of disseminating knowledge about the region, as well as about events significant for the entire general public. A great many exhibitions have been organized in order to present the work and artistic activity of the society's members. All these undertakings have efficiently become part of continuing education and training addressed to the inhabitants of the city and region. The subjects presented have definitely been diverse, in many instances bearing a great deal of emotional charge (e.g., anniversary exhibitions related to national, political, and cultural celebrations), as well as exhibitions related to the presentation of prominent artists from various fields (literature, music, painting, photography), and exhibitions related to the society's regular activity. Undoubtedly, these exhibitions allowed knowledge of the objects presented and of their creators to be acquired. It should be emphasized that the exhibitions are often accompanied by young people's performances, both of a poetic and artistic nature. This has been particularly visible in recent years. These performances contribute to a more extensive understanding of the contents conveyed through the exhibitions.

Concise publications as well as a publishing series play an important function in the continuing education and development of society. They offer possibilities for publishing works by authors from various scholarly circles. Simultaneously, publications are invaluable material for a wide group of readers seeking knowledge within self-education and systematic education. The society has issued several publications on diverse subjects: e.g., The *Art of Płock* by K. Askanas; *The History of Płock* edited by A. Gieysztor, M. Kallas, and M. Krajewski; *The Petrochemical Industry and the Development of Płock* by J. Chojnacki; *The Homeland and Its Regions* by J. Damrosz; *Jewish Culture in Masovia* edited by Z. Kruszewski and A. Kansy; and a great many others.

The year 1956 was a significant year for the society's activity, as the first issue of the quarterly journal *Notatki Płockie* was released, the publisher of which is the Płock Learned Society. In the period between 1956 and 2010, as many as 225 issues were released. The articles printed in *Notatki Płockie* raise primarily regional issues. They relate to the history and modern times of Płock as well as Masovia. Some of the publications relate to the Płock Learned Society and its activity. Special issues have been entirely devoted to anniversaries important for the city and region. This journal, published for more than fifty years, has been an important source of knowledge of Płock and Masovia. All the work concerning the publishing of this quarterly journal has been undertaken on a voluntary basis by the editorial board, which was led for twenty-eight years by Wiesław Koński, PhD, who acted as editor-in-chief. Koński edited a volume collecting the contents of *Notatki Płockie* issued between 1956 and 2006. The work is entitled *50 Yearbooks of Notatki Płockie*, published in 2008. The publication included all the reports, articles, reviews, communications, obituaries, and chronicle notes as well as illustrated materials printed in 208 issues of *Notatki Płockie* released during the period mentioned.[16] Starting with the first issue of 2007 (no. 210), a five-member editorial board was introduced under the supervision of Zbigniew Kruszewski, and starting with the first issue of 2008 (no. 214), the journal took on a fully modern scholarly character, with abstracts, keywords, summaries, and tables of contents in the English language. Originally, the journal *Notatki Płockie* was supposed to function as "a body promoting scholarly social activity, and as the mainspring facilitating the development of regional scholarly culture."[17] It has been successful in fulfilling this mission until now. Undoubtedly the materials published in *Notatki Płockie*, as well as their authors, require a separate study and more extensive analysis, as fifty-five years of continuous publishing of this periodical is an exception on the Polish market of popular scholarly magazines. It needs to be stressed that this quarterly journal has been published pro bono since the beginning of its activity. Neither the editorial board, nor the orientation board, nor the authors have ever been remunerated.

Since 1968, the society has also published *Reports on the Activities of the Płock Learned Society*. They include the minutes of general meetings and also detailed information on scholarly and popularizing activity in a given year. These reports inform the readers separately about the activity of the society's departments and the Zieliński Library. The information on organizational matters as well as financial statements constitute a considerable part of the reports, which apart from their factual value, also display the scale of the undertakings being realized. The reports document the entire activity of the society, thus providing an exceptionally transparent picture in the local and translocal public space.

The Zieliński Library constitutes an integral part of the Płock Learned Society. It needs to be emphasized that the activity of the Płock Learned Society would not be as extensive as it is and in numerous cases would be impossible had it not been for this most important element, developed from the very establishment of the society, its library. Initially unimpressive, it had been developed by its founders at the Płock Voivodship School. Subsequently, in 1907 the society received the so-called Skępska Library, which was later named the Zieliński Library. The book collection handed over by the owners of Skępe was abundantly rich. It included the following sections: theology, philosophy, the general history of Poland, common law, Polish law, social sciences, world literature, Polish literature, natural sciences, geography, military science, pedagogy, antiquity, fine art, agriculture, encyclopedias, and magazines. The history section was the richest.[18] Additionally, these collections included 1,486 maps, 21 atlases, and 429 volumes of family archives as well as prints and manuscripts. Special collections were of particular value—approximately 15,000 items (early editions, maps, graphics, iconography, archives), which contribute to the Polish National Library Resources. Unique works have been preserved in the library's resources regardless of the society's fate; for example, among publications referring to Poland, the library contains the following works:

- over 13,000 early editions: among others, *Jan Laski's Statute*, the first collection of Polish laws printed in Jan Haller's publishing house (parchment and two paper editions of 1506), and *Historia Polonica* by Jan Długosz of 1516;
- *De revolutionibus orbium coelestium* by Nicholas Copernicus, published in Nuremberg by Johannes Perteius in 1543 (first edition);
- *The Radziwiłł Library* published in 1563;
- 92 incunabula: among others, *The Divine Comedy* by Dante of 1487, an incunabulum illustrated with woodcuts;
- *The Pitiful and Horrible Story of Franciszek Spiera* by Stanisław

Murzynowski, printed in 1551, at present the only copy in the country;[19]

- *On Local and Overseas Herbs* by Heronim Spiczyński, printed in Krakow in 1542 with numerous woodcuts;
  Crescantyn Piotr's Books on Farmsteads, printed in Krakow in 1549;
- numerous sixteenth-century prints including those by M. Miechowita printed in Krakow in 1521;
- armorials including an armorial by B. Paprocki.

The resources of the Zieliński Library also include foreign works, such as works by Martin Luther published in Wittenberg in 1523 and 1527; works by Plato in valuable and rare editions, published in three volumes in 1517; works by Lucretius published in Venice in 1495; an atlas by Hondius (a Dutch cartographer), published in 1606; and new edition of *Mercator's Atlas*, complemented with forty new maps. The library's collection also includes a seventeenth-century collection of eternal psalms in the French language, a unique volume not found elsewhere in the world. It is the only copy that French researchers managed to identify. The library, as one of very few in the country, possesses the so-called *Bibliotheque portative du voyageur*, published in the famous publishing house of the Fouriers between 1801 and 1807. It is only one of a few relics of this type preserved until now.[20]

Apart from the antique collection of books, the library also possesses in its collections the latest interdisciplinary publications. This is because it functions as an academic library for a large number of students. The purchasing of new items results from readers' requests as well as scholarly developments. If financial assets are sufficient, incunabula and old prints are purchased as well. At the end of 2010, the library's collections amounted to 374,905 volumes, including 13,366 early editions with 93 incunabula.

The valuable collection of the Zieliński Library has been complemented with thirteen family portraits, donated by Tadeusz Zieliński in 1926, illustrating the history of the family as well as the history of Poland at the turn of the eighteenth and nineteenth centuries. Apart from its antique book collection, the library also possesses other interdisciplinary publications in order to satisfy the demand of an increasing number of students and researchers, predominantly from Płock universities. The library also possesses the largest collections related to Płock and Płock Masovia; it is an extensive source of knowledge for researchers or regionalists.

In an effort to meet the needs of a knowledge-based society and information society, the Library of the Płock Learned Society undertook the digitization process of their resources on a broad scale. The digitization process of this library's most valuable assets, started in 2002, resulting in 7,440 items being digitized by the end of 2010, including 500 archival items, several thousand photographs, several hundred books from the so-called cimelia, several hundred years of press journals, a number of incunabula, posters, and other things.

A cross-section of the library's visitors is very diverse, from high school students to academic researchers. The readership consists of the employees of libraries, museums, industrial plants, government office workers, individuals broadening their knowledge, and others. University students compose a large group of the library's visitors, among them students from Płock universities: Paweł Włodkwic University College, the Płock campus of the Warsaw University of Technology, and the Państwowa Wyższa Szkoła Zawodowa w Płocku. The number of volumes borrowed by the average reader amounts to four. The Zieliński Library of today is an institution which collects, elaborates, preserves, protects, informs, and makes available its textual, electronic, and film collections. The library is the seventh oldest library in Poland.

Educational undertakings aimed at promoting individuals, both students and adults, who are active within this area, constitute very important activities of the society. Meetings concerning substantial knowledge of local history are particularly rewarding. Contests and competitions are interesting initiatives as well, e.g., a contest of knowledge about Płock in celebration of the 150th anniversary of the Płock Learned Society (1971); the "My Little Homeland" contest for schoolchildren (2003); the "Płock and the Region of Płock in Memories" contest recently organized in Płock entitled in order to prevent significant events and social transformations taking place in the Płock region from fading into oblivion. The participation in the organization of this undertaking of the Association of the University of the Third Age in Płock proves that there is a great desire for self-education and a commitment to the educational activities of adults. The first prize was awarded to Adam Neuman-Nowicki from the United States for a memoir entitled *Struggle for Life: Memories of a Płock Citizen*. Second prize was awarded for the work *My Płock in the Years 1945–1962*. Third Prize was awarded for the work *Times of Terror, Times of Hope* as well as for *Płock Episodes*. All these works may be found in the Department of Special Colllections of the Zieliński Library where they are to be described and catalogued. Moreover, the best works have been published in a separate book, and the names of those awarded in *Notatki Płockie*.

A doctoral seminar established and run pro bono continuously for over thirty years, has been a significant initiative within continuing education. To date, thirty PhD students from the doctoral seminar at the Płock Learned Society have been awarded their doctoral degrees. Presently, approximately forty students attend seminar classes. The activity of the doctoral seminar is an important element in the development of the scholarly social movement in the Płock region. Despite the fact that it does not function within academic structures, it has been a significant part of Polish scholarship, contributing to its social and regional trends. It is also a well-organized form of education and training of scholarly faculty, necessary for the cultural, scholarly, social, and economic development of the city and region. The doctoral seminar has played a very important role during the transformation of our society and economy into an information society and knowledge-based economy.

The society has supported the development of scholarly thought and the popularization of knowledge. Its mere existence supports national education through the various forms of its activity mentioned previously, such as scholarly sessions, lectures, publications, exhibitions, contests, meetings, expeditions, workshops, library classes, and the like. The society as an institution, as well as particular members, has contributed to raising the education level of society, to its development, and to providing knowledge of the region.

Summary

Summing up, it may be stated the Płock Learned Society as an institution has had great moral significance due to its activities aimed at serving the entire regional culture of Płock Masovia. The society demonstrates the ability to revive and to endure even in the face of adversity and reluctance to participate in social activity. This contributes to elevate the value of culture, patriotism, and attachment to what is Polish, to what is ours, to what is essential for the continuity of our nation and its values.

In the future, the area of permanent education and the development of a knowledge-based society in Poland need to be supported by the so-called fourth segment of education, i.e., learned societies. In practice, continuing education in Poland, despite the stipulations included both in the Constitution of the Republic of Poland and in the education system as well as rather well-developed theoretical research, remains an area which is not used to the fullest extent. The key to the efficient realization of lifelong learning needs the collective political will (or at least the will of the majority) and acknowledgment that permanent education and the development of a knowledge-based society is not only a challenge of our times, but a necessity as well. Learned societies are capable of inspiring such undertakings.

This scholarly social movement has played a significant role in creating a knowledge-based society through conducting various statutory activities, thus contributing to permanent education. With the use of the example of specific activities performed by the Płock Learned Society, one may describe the significance of learned societies for regional development.

The Płock Learned Society has fulfilled an important function in the area of continuing education, i.e., in horizontal and inner education. In the case of inner education, the society provides information on various aspects of life, science, and culture. The individual creativity of man allows us to fully utilize this dimension of knowledge supported by, among other factors, the society. When discussing inner education, which is related to the quality of education and is predominantly manifested in motivating learning, self-teaching abilities, intellectual interests, a lifestyle complying with the concept of lifelong learning, and obtaining information on art and the sophisticated use of leisure time, the importance of the society is invaluable. The Płock Learned Society combines informal education (resulting from everyday life) with non-formal education and with formal education (e.g., library classes, with the organized involvement of students in lectures constituting the contents of courses).

In the course of violent political, economic, and cultural changes in the region of Płock in recent times, (or even throughout the entire period of the society's activity), the directions of which are difficult to evaluate, there arises the need for humanistic education, which is now fully satisfied by the society's activity. This task is understood as the necessity for educating the contemporary intelligentsia regardless of the academic and professional profile of their initial education. This occurred years ago, particularly after the eradication of the Polish intelligentsia during World War II. In our times, starting from the seventies of the previous century, the need for humanistic knowledge arose along with the development of industry, when Płock became the workplace for a great number of engineers and technical workers. The Learned Society, through its educational activities, supports humanistic thought, approaching this concept as understanding other individuals, their desires and problems, respecting their paths of development and their dignity in particular. There is great interpersonal solidarity, based on mutual understanding and respect, among the members of the Płock Learned Society.

Through permanent education, the example of the Płock Learned Society illustrates the significance of scholarly social associations in the establishment of a knowledge-based society and a civil society. Continuing education and training is conducted in various forms and relates to the diverse social needs in a given region, as well as to the types of scholarly social organizations.

Notes

1. A. Kamiński, *Functions of social pedagogy*, 2nd ed. (Warsaw: PWN, 1968).

2. P. F. Drucker, *Innovation and Entrepreneurship* [*Natchnienie i fart, czyli innowacja i przedsiębiorczość*] (Warsaw: Pub. Studia Emka, 2004), pp. 6–7.

3. R. Wroczyński, *Permanent education* (Warsaw: PWN, 1973).

4. B. Suchodolski, *Permanent education: Crossroads and hopes* (Warsaw: PWN, 2003).

5. A. Matusiak, *Continuing education in Poland: Benefits and development barriers* (Warsaw: Institute for Market Economics, 2003).

6. E. Walkiewicz, ed., *Continuous education and training in the development of a civil society* (Gdańsk Warsaw: IBE, 2006).

7 .S.M. Kwiatkowski, ed., *Continuous education and training: Theoretical and practical dimension* (Radom: IBE, ITE-PIB, 2008).

8. R. Góralska and J. Półturzycki, ed., *Continuous education and training in universities—from the concept to practice* (Radom: Wyd. ITE-PIB, 2004).

9. S. Kunikowski, *General learned societies in Poland*, quotation, p. 188.

10. Z. Kruszewski, "The role of learned societies in raising the level of knowledge of local communities," *Notatki Płockie*, no. 2 (2008): 13.

11. J. Tazbir, "Learned societies in the 21st century—chances and dangers," *Nauka*, no. 1 (2000): 141–43.

12. http://www.ptpn.poznan.pl/BIBL_zbiory.html/(accessed 5 January 2011).

13. Statement of financial activities of the Płock Learned Society for 2007, TNP Płock, 2008, p. 143.

14. St. Kostanecki, "Two anniversaries of the Płock Learned Society," in *Płock Learned Society in 1820–1830, 1907–1957, Drafts and materials* (Płock, 1957), p. 6.

15. The Statute of the Płock Learned Society, Płock, 1933.

16. W. Koński, *50 yearbooks of Notatki Płockie: A Bibliography of the contents, 1956–2006* (Płock: TNP, 2008).

17. K. Askanas, "The scholarly activity of the Płock Learned Society during 40 years of the Polish People's Republic, part I," *Notatki Płockie*, no. 3 (1984): 34.

18. A. J. Nowowiejski, *Płock: A Historical monograph*, quotation on p. 648.

19. A. Stogowska, *History and functions*, quotation, p. 80.

20. Report on activities of the Płock Learned Society for 2007, TNP Płock, 2008, p. 138.

European Union Funds for Higher Education in Poland: An Opportunity for Universities to Implement Social Programs

PIOTR NASIADKO AND MICHAŁ LUCZEWSKI

Regional Policy of the European Union: Structural Funds

The European Union is one of the richest regions in the world, yet between its individual regions one can notice significant differences in terms of their development, incomes, and opportunities. A number of measures have been taken in all countries of the EU which are aimed at reducing the differences between the regions, supporting development, and leveling chances and prospects. These objectives are achieved through a regional policy, understood as "the overall activities of public authorities (both central and territorial ones), private entities, various institutions and organizations in such regions with a view to strengthening the competitiveness of regional economies, dynamizing regional development, and reducing spatial development disproportions."[1] A primary target of the regional policy, also referred to as the regional structural policy, is the transfer of assets from richer to poorer regions, leveling chances in order to achieve the same level of development and well-being within the entire EU territory. Therefore regional policy is an instrument of financial solidarity and a driving force of economic and social integration.

Regional policy has been at the center of EU strategy since 1957, when the preamble to the Treaty of Rome establishing the European Economic Community received the following notation: "strengthen the unity of their economies and ensure their harmonious development by reducing the differences existing between the various regions and the backwardness of the less favored regions."[2] Expressways, bridges, and sewage-treatment plants have been built. Additionally, a great many "soft" projects were conducted, i.e., a considerable number of the unemployed threatened with social exclusion have been trained; they adapted to the changing circumstances in the labor market or acquired new skills in order to improve their professional situation. Solidarity and cohesion are key terms lying behind such projects and the regional policy of the European Union. Such solidarity should bring specific benefits to these regions and their inhabitants, who are in a less favorable situation compared to the EU average. Striving for cohesion aimed at reducing the differences in incomes and prosperity between the countries and regions translates into benefits for all, both those receiving support and lending support.

There are still significant differences in the level of prosperity within the member states as well as between them. The wealthiest regions (levels of well-being measured as GND per inhabitant) are even several times wealthier than the poorer and younger members of the European Union. This may result from numerous causes. Centrally planned economies or long-term difficulties caused either by geographical distance or social and economic changes that have occurred recently constitute only some of them. The effects have been the impoverishment of society, a poor condition of education at each level, a high unemployment rate, and a poor condition of the infrastructure. Currently, regional policy constitutes an element of cohesion policy, which is also focused on social, environmental, or cultural issues, broadly-defined.

The European Union, after the accession of twelve new countries since 2004, has restructured and reorganized its expenditure on regional policy. A number of new members joined the EU during that period and although they constitute only 25 percent of the overall population of the EU, as much as 50 percent of all regional expenses have been allotted to them for the seven-year financing period for the years 2007–13. Three objectives have been set, which comprise cohesion policy:

- Convergence, i.e., cohesion: the European Union supports infrastructure development as well as the economic and human potential of its poorest regions;
- Competitiveness: the European Union supports innovations, scientific research, and sustainable development as well as vocational education in its poorer developed regions;
- Territorial cooperation: the European Union promotes and conducts joint projects of a transnational character within the entire territory of the community.

Apart from the issues of regional and cohesion policy, one may also encounter the term "structural policy" in the context of EU aid. The last objective is a traditional term for the intervention of the European Communities and since 1993, of the European Union, taken from the Treaties of Rome. In practice, these terms are presently used interchangeably; thus it may be assumed that regional policy, structural policy, and cohesion policy share the same objective—to level the economic and social differences between the regions of the European Union and, with the use of financial funds which have been allotted to the regions which are in a less favorable situation, to accelerate the development of backward regions, consequently enhancing competitiveness within the entire EU territory.

Instruments of Regional Policy in Europe and in Poland: The Renewed Lisbon Strategy

The most important instruments of regional policy, also referred to as structural regional policy are structural funds. They are aimed at supporting the restructuring and modernization of EU economies and are directed to these economic sectors and regions which, without financial aid, are not able to achieve the average economic level of the European Community. During the current seven-year programming period for 2007–13 and as a result of the reform of cohesion policy, there are presently two structural funds, i.e., the European Regional Development Fund and the European Social Fund, as well as a financial instrument supporting them, i.e., the Cohesion Fund, which actually is not a structural fund but is implemented at the level of selected countries, not regions (its objective is to facilitate the integration of the poorer developed countries through building transportation networks as well as supra-regional facilities aimed at environmental protection). During the previous period falling during the years 2000–2006, there existed two others: the European Agriculture Guidance and the Guarantee Fund and Financial Instrument for Fisheries Guidance, which have been included in the Common Agricultural Policy and the Common Fisheries Policy.

The document which determines the recipients and amounts of financial aid from structural funds for conducting development objectives in Poland for the years 2007–13 is called the National Cohesion Strategy (NCS) in the National Strategic Reference Framework. It defines priorities and implementation areas of the European Regional Development Fund, the European Social Fund, and the Cohesion Fund within the EC budget. As a result of proper guidance on its activity, Poland has the opportunity to make up for developmental backwardness and to achieve a level similar to other European regions. The NCS was accepted by the decision of the European Commission, taking into consideration Polish social and economic conditions, and it is a reference instrument for drawing up operational programs complying with the stipulations of the National Development Strategy for 2007–15,[3] as well as the National Reform Program for 2005–8,[4] which is a response to the challenges posed by the Lisbon Strategy.

The Lisbon Strategy is a draft accepted in 2000 by the European Parliament, which was aimed at transforming Europe into the most dynamic and competitive economic region in the world. The strategy's objectives were defined up until 2010; they focused on research investments and scientific development, which was supposed to result in an increased GNP and a decreased unemployment rate. Yet after several years it was noticeable that its objectives were often contradictory; an excessively detailed plan for changes, insufficient coordination, and the political determination of particular EU member states contributed to the fact that Europe lagged behind the world's superpowers. The activities of the Lisbon Strategy were ineffective, inefficient, and devoid of priorities, which increased the developmental gap between the EU and, for instance, the United States. It appeared that the set objectives had been realized unequally in particular EU states; additionally, previous challenges became intensified in the face of changing economic and social conditions related to globalization processes, growing competition, restructuring processes, the growth of unemployment, labor migration, and an aging society. In 2005 the European Council, as a result of the Lisbon Strategy failure, took joint activities in order to provide new solutions aimed at coordination and a cohesive achievement of particular elements of the Lisbon Strategy in all the EU countries. Consequently, a package of so-called integrated guidelines for growth and jobs between 2005–8, which included an interpretation of the Renewed Lisbon Strategy and imposed an obligation to develop national reform programs on the EU member states. Then the Strategic Community Guidelines for 2007–13 were accepted, which constitute a guiding document of EU cohesion policy for particular National Strategic Reference Frameworks for each of the member states.

The principal trends of pro-Lisbon activities are as follows:

1. The development of knowledge and innovations through:

   a. increasing and improving investments within R&D;
   b. promoting innovations, employing ICT, and a sustainable use of resources;
   c. contribution to the development of a strong European industrial base.

2. The development of EU attractiveness as an excellent place for investments and work:

   a. extending and deepening a common market;
   b. amending European and national legislation;
   c. developing open and competitive markets within and outside of the EU
   d. expanding and improving European infrastructure.

3. The development of mechanisms allowing the creation of a greater number of jobs:

   a. engaging a larger number of people in active professional activities and modernizing social security systems;
   b. strengthening the adaptability of workers and enterprises and the flexibility of labor markets;
   c. increasing investments in human capital through improved education systems and the acquisition of skills.

Therefore the aforementioned reform of the EU cohesion policy was a consequence of the Renewed Lisbon Strategy, i.e., defining the new objectives of this policy (convergence, competitiveness, and territorial cooperation) and modifying the reach of the structural and cohesion funds. This also contributes to economic growth and an increase in employment, the development of knowledge and innovations, the greater attractiveness of the EU as a place for investments and work, and elaborating mechanisms which allow increasing the number of jobs; additionally, a direct connection with the cohesion policy is enhanced. The former objectives were limited to two predominant aspects, i.e., the achievement of sustainable economic growth and a permanent increase in employment.

Each of the member states elaborating its national reform program is supposed to establish conditions making allowances for the implementation of the Lisbon Strategy through various legislative and institutional instruments. The implementation of this strategy should be conducted through diverse financial undertakings, co-financed with cohesion policy funds, pursuant to the National Strategic Reference Frameworks, defining which operational programs will be employed to implement pro-Lisbon priorities included in the Strategic Community Guidelines. The majority of the countries which joined the EU in 2004 or later set their sights on approaching the level of economic development of the wealthier "fifteen," acknowledging that the methods for achieving this target, although varied, will be concentrated on the modernization and development of their basic infrastructure. Certainly, this may contribute to an economic reserve during the initial period, yet in the long-term perspective, territorial differentiation may even be intensified. The primary objective of the "fifteen" countries is to strengthen their role as economic partners in the era of globalization and to compete against the United States efficiently. Thus the said countries give priority to activities aimed at knowledge development and the stimulation of inventiveness. Moreover, they promote cooperation with such world powers as China and India and also modify their social security systems in order to take full advantage of existing workforce resources.

Therefore it is important to level directions and the amount of support for measures aimed at infrastructure and unemployment, as well as knowledge- and innovation-oriented measures.

It has been acknowledged in Poland that the Lisbon Strategy will be strengthened through the following measures:

- reform in the sector of public research, which will allow increased investments in knowledge and innovations;
- establishing institutional, legislative, and financial conditions which will enhance the development of entrepreneurship and the growth of competitive potential;
- developing advanced power and transportation systems, consistent with European ones;
- modernization and adapting to constant change in the labor market, education systems, and vocational training, including through the popularization of lifelong learning;
- implementing instruments of active employment policy, particularly among unemployed youths and older people.

Poland, the only country among those which joined the European Union in 2004 to do so, decided to allot 60 percent of cohesion funds to activities supporting the aforementioned areas of the Lisbon Strategy. According to the National Strategic Reference Framework, it is essential in our country to invest in areas of high-growth potential, which will provide the opportunity to make up for Poland's backwardness in comparison to the wealthiest countries of the

European Community. "The document presents an analysis of the socioeconomic situation of the country and its regions, formulates the most important challenges for the country for the next several years, defines objectives aimed at achieving socioeconomic and territorial cohesion with the Community's countries and regions, and presents the allocation of financial resources to particular programs, as well as their implementation system frameworks."[5]

Objectives of the National Strategic Reference Framework: Operational Programs

The objectives included in the National Strategic Reference Framework are implemented during the programming period for 2007–13 through operational programs co-financed by structural funds, and through the financial instrument of cohesion policy, i.e., the Cohesion Fund:

- The Operational Program "Infrastructure and Environment" (OPI&E) co-financed by the European Regional Development Fund (ERDF) and the Cohesion Fund (CF);
- The Operational Program "Innovative Economy" (OPIE) co-financed by the ERDF;
- The Operational Program "Human Capital" (OP HC) co-financed by the European Social Fund;
- The Operational Program "Development of Eastern Poland" (OP DEP) co-financed by the ERDF;
- The Operational Program "Technical Assistance" (OPTA) co-financed by the ERDF;
- The Operational Program for European Territorial Cooperation (OPETC) co-financed by the ERDF; as well as
- Sixteen Regional Operational Programs (ROP) co-financed by the ERDF.

The activities fulfilling the Lisbon Strategy objectives are implemented, within the National Strategic Reference Framework, in the following areas:

- Improving the functioning standard of public institutions and the development of partnership mechanisms; support would be granted to undertakings favorable to the modernization of the Polish institution and regulatory system and which positively affect the development of social dialogue and partnership;
- Improving the quality of human capital and enhancing social cohesion; measures would be undertaken to create a bigger number of better workplaces;
- The establishment and modernization of technical and social infrastructure crucial for an increase of Poland's competitiveness;

PIOTR NASIADKO AND MICHAŁ LUCZEWSKI

measures would be undertaken in support of making Europe a
more attractive place for investments and work;
- Improving the competitiveness and innovativeness of enterprises,
including, in particular, the manufacturing sector with high added
value and the development of the services sector; knowledge and
innovations would be promoted in favor of economic growth;
- Increasing the competitiveness of Polish regions and preventing
their social, economic, and territorial marginalization; measures
would be implemented in favor of making Europe a more attractive place for investments and work and supporting knowledge
and innovations in favor of economic growth;
- Balancing growth opportunities and supporting structural changes
in rural areas; the intervention would be aimed also at making Europe a more attractive place for investments and work.

The European Social Fund: Operational Program "Human Capital"

In the period of 2007–13 the situation of the flow of resources from structural
funds became transparent in Poland. All the undertakings connected with infrastructure, investments, and transportation are co-financed by the European
Regional Development Fund, sometimes with the participation of the Cohesion Fund, while those aimed at using the potential of human resources
through increasing employment and the adaptive potential of enterprises and
their workforce, improving the quality of the education system, and reducing
the areas of social exclusion as well as developing the country's administrative
structures are co-financed by the European Social Fund. The total amount of
ESF support has been presented in the Operational Program "Human Capital"
(OP HC).

Under the OP HC support will be given to the following areas: employment, education, social integration, the adaptative potential of employees and
entrepreneurs, issues related to the development of human resources in rural
areas, construction of efficient and effective public administration based on
partnership, and the promotion of health.

The term "Human Capital" was accepted as it best reflects the gist of comprehensive support scheduled for implementation under the operational program whose objectives are strictly connected with the development of human
resources within its individual and social contexts. It is a term embracing the
knowledge, abilities, and potential of each human being and society as a
whole, defining the capability to work, to adapt to changes, and to provide
new solutions. Social capital, meaning resources of skills, information, culture,
knowledge, and the creativity of individuals as well as relationships between
people and organizations, is directly correlated with human capital.[6]

The OP HC constitutes a response to the challenges that member states
face under the Renewed Lisbon Strategy, which involves transforming Eu-

rope into a more interesting place for investments and work, developing knowledge and innovations, and establishing a larger number of permanent workplaces.

According to the objectives of the Renewed Lisbon Strategy and the objectives of the EU cohesion policy an increase in employment through the development of human capital constitutes a vital factor contributing to a more effective use of the labor force; this also supports an increase in economic competitiveness. The employment rate, the extent of social integration, or the development of a knowledge-based society are factors influencing socioeconomic development; they have also become an inherent part of the National Strategic Reference Framework. The development of human resources is an extremely important element of cohesion policy which coincides with restructuring, as well as with technological and infrastructural development.

The OP HC measures, co-financed by the European Social Fund for 85 percent and by the state budget for 15 percent, concentrate first of all on:

- A more efficient use of human resources;
- An increasing flexibility of the labor market and the adaptability of workers;
- Increasing the level of social cohesion;
- Developing a knowledge-based society through the development of education and qualifications;
- Improving the efficiency of public administration management and the quality of public services;
- Developing healthcare systems as a factor determining the quality of the labor force;
- Ensuring the cohesion of the development level of human resources in a spatial context.

Each of the member states, considering the specificity of their own problems, may envisage corrective programs using the European Social Fund. The total allocation of the ESF in our country, implemented by the OP HC, has been divided into nine priorities implemented at national and regional levels.

The centrally implemented priorities cover the following areas:

- Priority I: Employment and social integration,
- Priority II: The development of human resources and the adaptive potential of enterprises and improvement in the health condition of working persons,
- Priority III: The high quality of the education system,
- Priority IV: Higher education and research,
- Priority V: Good governance.

Priorities implemented at the regional level cover the following areas:

- Priority VI: A labor market open for all,
- Priority VII: The promotion of social integration,
- Priority VIII: Regional human resources for the economy,
- Priority IX: The development of education and competencies in the regions.

Human Capital for Higher Education

Taking into consideration the character of this publication, the authors focused on Priority IV concerning higher education and research, to which over 8 percent of all the ESF resources for 2007–13 have been allotted to the OP HC.

The Polish economy has undergone transformations which have significantly changed the situation of the educational market over the last two decades. The aspirations of young people have been awakened, as the probability for personal and professional development has increased along with their level of education. Yet a variation in the quality of teaching at different universities, too slow a pace of the growth of the number of well-qualified academic staff, or an insufficient proposal of mathematical faculties, which are of key importance for the economy, fail to exhaust the list of problems that higher education faces at present. The achievement of the objectives of the Lisbon Strategy, which emphasizes the role of science and knowledge in economic development, is supposed to ensure a high level of education, cooperation between tertiary educational institutions, units of the R&D sector, and the economy; additionally, transnational cooperation between academic environments and the mobility of staff and students are supported. Thus a closer linkage of the academic sector to the economy needs increasing qualifications of research and development sector staff, particularly within the scope of development and management of research projects.

Priority IV focuses on improving the performance of tertiary educational institutions, both by creating favorable conditions in terms of the system and organization for effective management of higher education and by evoking stimuli for developing the specializations which are essential for the management of faculties. These are mathematical, natural science, and technical faculties, which currently are not in great demand. The implementation of the objectives of the priority will also be supported by university development programs, which may cover various issues, i.e., the improvement of staff, the organization of internships and apprenticeships for students, establishing new specializations, and e-learning, as well as cooperation with employers and research units and transnational cooperation.

Among numerous objectives under Priority IV, "higher education and research," the most important is "Adapting teaching programs at the higher level to the requirements of the economy and the labor market." In consequence of this, the number of students participating in internships and apprenticeships is expected to increase. In order to achieve this target, research on the functioning of universities, the efficiency and quality of teaching, and their adaptation to the needs of the labor market will be conducted. Moreover, university development programs are planned for implementation, which are supposed to expand this offer to improve the quality of teaching at universities and the cooperation of universities with employers, overseas partners, or the development of e-learning, in addition to raising the qualifications of academic personnel.

Another important priority is "improving the quality of educational proposals from higher educational institutions." In consequence, the number of schools that will implement quality management and control models is supposed to increase. Additionally, the number of faculties which are particularly important, according to the state accreditation committee and the number of development projects implemented by universities are also supposed to increase. The following solutions may help meet this objective: developing efficient models of higher education management, preparing up-to-date curricula (including remote learning), elaborating standards for mutual recognition of accreditation decisions within the European Area of Higher Education, and strengthening the employability of future university graduates.

Another priority is "improving the attractiveness of education in mathematical, natural science, and technical faculties at the higher-education level." Consequently, the percentage of graduates in mathematical, natural science, and technical faculties is expected to increase as is the number of universities offering additional remedial classes for first-year students of the aforementioned faculties and also the number of students in those faculties, which has been ordered by the minister responsible for higher education. Commissioning universities to enroll a determined number of students by the Minister of Higher Education and the implementation of remedial programs for first-year students in mathematical, natural science, and technical faculties is expected to contribute to this as well.

Another objective called for is "improving the qualifications of R&D staff and their cooperation with the economy, as well as marketing and commercializing the results of their scientific research." As a result, the percentage of R&D staff, who have elevated their qualifications for the management of scientific research and commercializing the results of R&D projects may be achieved with the use of various training programs for staff of the R&D sector (courses, postgraduate courses), as well as through projects related to raising the awareness of the said staff and entrepreneurs within the validity of scientific research and development work for the economy.

173

The Implementation of Social Projects by Polish Higher Educational Institutions Illustrated with Examples of Undertakings Realized by Paweł Włodkowic University College in Płock

Strengthening and Developing the Teaching Potential of Universities

The project named the "Academy for Competence Development" is an interesting example of strengthening and developing the teaching potential of a university and enriching its educational proposal. It was elaborated by the Paweł Włodkowic University College in Płock in response to a competition held by the Ministry of Science and Higher Education within the OP HC program sub-measure 4.1.1, "Strengthening and Developing the Teaching Potential of Universities." The project received a recommendation for financing and the school signed the project co-financing agreement. The implementation time of the project falls during the period between 1 April 2010 and 31 December 2015.

This undertaking constitutes a response to the socioeconomic assessment included in the OP HC and in the implementation strategy for Priority IV of OP HC elaborated by the Ministry of Science and Higher Education. The aforementioned assessments indicate that there is a need for the implementation of comprehensive modernization and adaptation actions so that syllabuses prepare university graduates for operating in a dynamically changing employment market. Frequently, the syllabuses on offer fail to fulfill the needs of the employment market in a knowledge-based economy. This results from, inter alia, the existence of an economic barrier caused by high initial costs related to teaching new, attractive professional specializations.

It has been identified that the aforementioned factors also influence the development opportunities of Paweł Włodkowic University College in Płock, which is one of the oldest nonpublic universities in Poland. A quantitative analysis carried out at the university demonstrated alarming downward trends in the number of full-time students compared to extramural students. These analyses gave rise to, inter alia, an idea of elaborating a development project which resulted in a grant in the amount of PLN 11,993,610.60 (100 percent financed), the assumption of which is to enable a more efficient and comprehensive adjustment of the education system to the needs of the employment market and existing economic conditions.

The assumption of this project's enterprise (its primary target) is to strengthen the teaching potential of the University through the implementation of a six-year development program, which will contribute to an improvement in the university's educational offer. It will also constitute a key element in the adjustment of higher education to the needs of the economy and the employment market. It has been assumed that its primary target will be met through the implementation of the following specific targets:

- the adjustment of syllabuses of existing courses to the needs of the employment market and the knowledge-based economy through establishing new specializations;
- the strengthening of practical teaching elements and increasing the involvement of employers in the development of syllabuses through the implementation of cooperation programs between the university and employers;
- strengthening the development of the school through the implementation of a fellowship program for PhD students;
- the adaptation of the quality management model of a university.[7]

New Specializations under Realization

Within the framework of specific target 1, two key specializations have been established in the form of full-time BA courses, which will embrace the total number of 360 students during the implementation period of the project, i.e., a major in Project Management in the Management Department, and a major in Local Government Administration in the Administration Department. While determining the targets of development activities the territorial situation was analyzed particularly, i.e., the fact that such specializations were not offered in the nearest regional environment, which is an important factor contributing to the development of the university.

It has been assumed that these courses will be conducted in three enrollment rounds (60 persons in Project Management and 60 persons in Local Government Administration): Round I, October 2010–September 2013; Round II, October 2011–September 2014; Round III—October 2012–September 2015. It has also been determined that enrollment will be conducted on the basis of a diploma competition and priority will be given to applicants from rural areas and towns as well as disabled persons and members of low-income families.

The feedback provided to date indicates the selection of specializations was proper and considerable interest in such courses has been shown (during the implementation of the project), despite a previous decline of interest in full-time courses. Apart from the selection of attractive specializations, the economic factor has also influenced the prospective participants' interest in the project. Participants of the project have the opportunity of free education due to external financing in the full amount and owing to additional financial resources alloted to the implementation of the cooperation program between the university and employers, the students have the opportunity to take advantage of internships and traineeships that are both professionally and financially attractive.

It has been assumed in the implementation indicators that the project's objectives will be achieved if 75 percent of the students participating in the project obtain BA degrees. At the current stage of the project implementation the assumed indicator is expected to be achieved.

A Cooperation Program between the University and Employers

Regarding the aim of strengthening practical teaching elements, a number of panel meetings with employers have been planned. During these meetings development opportunities in the employment market for specialists in a given field will be discussed. Moreover, it has been planned that the students of newly established specializations (at least 80 percent of them) will participate in a several-week traineeship with enterprises and institutions, and 20 percent of the students will take advantage of three-month internships, during which they will receive salaries to the gross amount of PLN 2,400. It is also important in this form of support to ensure remuneration from employers for traineeship and internship supervisors. The assumptions of such budgeting involve the element of powerful incentives, as well as the willingness to obtain the highest performance during the implementation of internship and traineeship programs, thus allowing their participants to acquire the greatest possible range of substantive knowledge and professional skills; proper motivation (including financial incentives) for further professional development is also provided. While conducting the program of traineeships and internships in their standard forms by the university, organizational and formal aspects are often emphasized, as opposed to their actual effectiveness in terms of professional usefulness.

As far as program implementation is concerned, it is also significant that syllabuses were adjusted to the needs of the employment market. This issue has been addressed in the project through consulting sessions with representatives of employers. Therefore cooperation with the Regional Chamber of Commerce in Płock has been established (it is the main representative of employers within the Płock sub-region), and the programs conducted within the project have been accepted by the chamber.

The expected implementation indicator of the university's program of cooperation with employers is the fact that 60 percent of students will find employment within one year of graduation.

Development of the University's Academic Staff

One of the assumptions of a development program is the development of academic staff in order to improve the quality of teaching as well as establish the conditions for pro–developmental activities of the university. Regarding the aim of achieving the aforementioned assumptions, a competition was held in order to delegate persons dealing with the most prospective areas connected with the current economic processes underway, including regional development and EU structural funds, which are also significant for the university's development. The delegated persons have been included in a four-year fellowship program. The fellowship amount has been determined at a level which allows for their substantive academic development, which would not be feasible to this extent without EU funds. The presumed effect of this form of support is to obtain PhD degrees by the fellowship holders. It is also worth noting that in order to strengthen the substantive aspects of this development action, the university has established a partnership with the Płock Learned Society. This is an association providing methodological and research support, as well as support for doctoral students within their research and development studies and assistance with contacts within the academic environment (aiding in the transfer of knowledge).

The Implementation of an Advanced Quality Management Model

The model of quality management employed for this development project should result in quantitative growth consistent with the quality of teaching. For this purpose, a decision on the implementation of an advanced system for student and university service, aimed at, inter alia, increasing the competence of administrative and office workers, automating activities connected with student service, and streamlining the communication process of students within the university by using modern IT solutions. Nearly PLN 2 million has been alloted to this purpose, including PLN 1 million for the purchase of an implementation service. According to the principles of competitiveness, a contractor has been selected; additionally, a pre-implementation analysis has been conducted at the university. The University XP software has been purchased, which consists of the following modules: Dean's Office XP, Recruitment XP, Recruitment WWW, Scholarships XP, Planning classes XP, Accounting didactics XP, Settlements with students XP, Accounts XP, Questionnaire XP, AWSMail.XP, COK (Electronic Student's Card), COK (ESC Personalization), COK (Student service point), Virtual University, Virtual University—multimedia store, Management Information System, Publications XP, Scientific Achievements XP, Evaluation XP. In order to operate efficiently, the necessary equipment has been purchased as well, i.e., a printer for thicker documents, servers, a system for entering and processing evaluation data, specialist scanners, a system for printing student cards, and the like.

While realizing this module it is worth mentioning that the implementation of a new IT system at the university, which used its own solutions for a number of years, is a very complex process, and it requires a great deal of determination on the part of the university's management as well as the perseverance of its employees, who need to redefine their working methods. It has been assumed that the expected implementation indicator of this action will be a work efficiency increase in the case of 60 percent of the university's staff, and 50 percent of students will be more satisfied with the quality of teaching and student service.

At the present implementation stage of the project named "Academy for Competence Development," it needs to be pointed out that the project has resulted in a quantitative and qualitative impact on the education paths offered by the university within full-time courses. It may also be noticed that the implementation of such projects influences the way in which the university is perceived in its regional environment; i.e., it is perceived as an entity open to new solutions and new challenges of the employment market, which also seeks new forms of development, including the use of external financing. The university, owing to the amount of assets obtained from EU resources, is perceived as a regional leader in northeastern Mazovia.

Increasing the Participation of Higher Education in Continuing Education: Establishing, Opening and Conducting New Postgraduate Courses

Yet another example of development projects implemented by higher educational institutions within the framework of the OP HC involves expanding the educational offer of universities with programs aimed at persons from outside the academic environment (increasing the participation of higher education in continuing education), as well as elaborating, opening, and conducting new postgraduate courses.

A model example of such a solution is the project named "Polish Nationwide Training Program for Sports Personnel," elaborated by Paweł Włodkowic University College in Płock in response to a competition held by the Ministry of Science and Higher Education within the OP HC sub-measure 4.1.1, "Strengthening and Developing the Teaching Potential of Universities. The project received a recommendation for financing, and the school signed a project co-financing agreement. The implementation time of the project falls during the period between 1 March 2009 and 31 October 2014.

The Polish Nationwide Training Program for Sports Personnel: One of the Largest Undertakings Related to the Systematic Education of Sports Personnel in Europe

Within this undertaking it has been planned to train 5,125 persons As much as PLN 24,369,575 has been obtained for this purpose (100 percent of its overall costs). The need for the implementation of this project arose from the analyses of problematic issues, identified through expert opinions elaborated for institutions dealing with sports and sports personnel training. The aforementioned expert opinions indicated, inter alia, the need to prepare personnel for assuming responsible roles in professional sports. They also indicated the lack of a single system for training sports personnel, which produces an extensive variation of their competence levels and reduces educational possibilities at the European level. Additionally, there was a lack of possibilities for raising the qualifications and promotion opportunities of sports personnel, as well as an insufficient performance of instructor/coach specializations.

Moreover, the project implementation on a national scale constitutes an excellent development stimulus for the university's activities, which, owing to the implementation of a nationwide undertaking, has the possibility of promoting its activities as a supra-regional academic center, embracing not only the Płock region, but also capable of conducting teaching and research enterprises within the entire territory of Poland. In order to address the identified problems, the project is aimed at strengthening the university's teaching potential through the modernization of the system for training sports, coaching, and sports managerial personnel in Poland with respect to programs and organization. Its primary target is to strengthen the university's teaching potential through the implementation of the six-year Polish Nationwide Training Program for Sports Personnel, which will contribute to the expansion of the university's educational proposal and will constitute a key element in adjusting higher education to the needs of a knowledge-based economy, taking into consideration the needs of the sports industry. Its specified targets, on the other hand, contribute to the achievement of its primary target, described as the following:

- Implementing and conducting a single program for training sports personnel, which complies with the European standards of five Regional Training Centers in Poland, preventing the variation of qualifications and skills;
- Developing qualifications and raising the competence levels of sports personnel through opening and conducting new postgraduate sports management courses;
- Increasing the participation of higher education in continuing education through the implementation of specialist courses, the core of which will mirror the demand of the employment market for specialists dealing with sports
- The optimization of organizational and financial conditions aimed at developing sports personnel for the needs of the state program ORLIK 2012, as well as training coaching personnel preparing athletes for the Olympic Games and championship competitions (including EURO 2012).[8]

In order to achieve the defined targets, it has been assumed that the project will embrace the entire territory of Poland. Therefore the establishment of five regional training centers in Poland has been planned:

- Płock (main area of activity/recruitment: central Poland), with the seat at Paweł Włodkowic University College in Płock;
  Białystok (main area of activity/recruitment: northeastern Poland);
- Cracow (main area of activity/recruitment: southeastern Poland);
- Wałcz (main area of activity/recruitment: northwestern Poland);
- Wrocław (main area of activity/recruitment: southwestern Poland).

Płock is the seat of Paweł Włodkowic University College. The remaining cities have been selected on the basis of their geographical position; the familiarity with these regions of the project's implementors and their partner institutions constituted another selection criterion.

While elaborating one of the largest European training programs for sports personnel, partnerships established in order to implement the project played a very positive role. One of these such partnerships was a strategic partnership between Paweł Włodkowic University College in Płock and the Ministry of Sports and Tourism. The project constitutes a response to the order of the ministry's representatives concerning the implementation of a comprehensive training program as well as the insufficient financing of sports within this scope. The ministry's representatives are also responsible for the substantive supervision of conducting syllabuses, certifying diplomas, the partial evaluation and monitoring, and assistance with promotion and recruitment. The project also involves the participation of the Eugeniusz Piasecki Academy of Physical Education in the support of a qualified faculty as well as the participation of the Płock Learned Society in scholarly support (including monitoring) of the teaching process.

Postgraduate Course "Sports Manager"

While realizing the component related to elaborating, opening, and conducting new postgraduate courses within the project, it was proposed to establish and conduct a bridge course, "Sports Manager." This course is aimed at obtaining the necessary qualifications for an efficient and creative management of sports organizations and facilities, for managing groups of people, and for organizing sports events. It is also aimed at developing sports personnel for the needs of the state program ORLIK 2012, as well as other sports undertakings.

It is anticipated that the course will be conducted in five parts: Part I in the years 2009–10; Part II in the years 2010–11; Part III in the years 2011–12; Part IV in the years 2012–13; Part V in the years 2013–14. It has been assumed that the postgraduate course curriculum will be conducted under the following plan: in five parts, with 25 persons per group on average, taking part in 16 two-day meetings of 8 classes each, meeting on Saturdays and Sundays, with classes conducted every other week, on average totaling 256 training hours per group. There is the possibility of conducting classes within a different plan if justified. The postgraduate course "Sports Manager" will embrace at least 625 persons in 25 training groups.

While discussing the issues related to conducting the postgraduate course "Sports Manager" within the development project, it is worth pointing out that interest in courses during each enrollment round has exceeded the predicted limit of places for any given part, thus confirming that the initiator of the project defined a need to establish the said postgraduate course correctly.

Courses for Instructors and Second-Class Coaches

The assumption of the development project named "Polish Nationwide Training Program for Sports Personnel" was to conduct instructor courses aimed at educating specialists possessing skills in developing physical education and knowledge about the techniques of sports disciplines, who would be prepared to conduct practical classes in key sports, particularly in football, handball, volleyball, basketball, and the like. In order to meet the demand of sports environments, including those signaled by sports associations, it is also acceptable to conduct courses in sports disciplines that are less popular in Poland.

The classes conducted within the project have been planned according to the following pattern: six parts, four specializations for each regional training center, on average 25 persons per group, each specialization including 16 meetings, with two days of 8 training hours each, meeting on Saturdays and Sundays, once every other week, totaling 256 hours of classes per group. There is the possibility of conducting classes within a different plan if justified. The total number of the participants in the instructor courses will amount to at least 3,000 persons in 120 training groups.

The project also embraces second-class coach courses, which are aimed at educating high-quality specialists possessing comprehensive theoretical knowledge and practical skills based on innovative coaching tools, particularly in sports such as football, volleyball, basketball, and the like. In response to the growing needs of the system of continuing education in sports, it has been assumed that this course will also contribute to educating the future teaching faculty. While trying to meet the expectations of sports environments, including those signaled by sports associations, the possibility of conducting courses in disciplines that are less popular in Poland has also been accepted.

It has been assumed within the project that second-class coach courses will be conducted according to the following plan: six parts, two specializations for each regional training center, on average with 25 persons per group, each specialization including on average 24 meetings, in two days of 8 training classes each, meeting on Saturdays and Sundays, meeting on average every other week, with a total of 406 training hours per group (including 30 hours of training periods). There is the possibility of conducting classes within a different plan if justified. The total number of participants in the coach courses will amount to at least 1,500 persons in 60 training groups.

In the context of conducting second-class coach courses within the development project, it is worth pointing out that long-term development projects are susceptible to unpredictable situations. Such a situation occurred in the case of the Polish Nationwide Training Program for Sports Personnel as well. At the halfway point of the project implementation a considerably serious change in Polish law occurred; it introduced, inter alia, significant organizational and formal amendments within the scope of conducting instructor and second-class coach courses. These amendments resulted, among others, in increasing the required number of classes to be conducted: in the case of instructor courses, up to 250 hours, and in the case of second-class coach courses up to 406 hours. In the case of instructor courses the initiator of the project had planned a greater number of hours from the very beginning, and in the case of second-class coach courses the 256 scheduled hours had also appeared insufficient. This change of law resulted in the necessity of modifying the project's assumptions and consequently finding suitable savings for conducting additional classes. This was possible owing to the economical financial strategy, which allowed the saving of the required amount of PLN 1 million for the implementation of the project in compliance with the new legal circumstances. These are so-called exceptional situations, which are extremely difficult to predict at the planning stage of a project, yet experienced project initiators should always realize undertakings in a way providing a certain margin for error in case of unexpected situations.

The courses are conducted in six parts: I and II part—in the years 2009–10; III part in the years 2010–11; IV part in the years 2011–12; V part in the years 2012–13; VI part in the years 2013–14.

So far, within the framework of the Polish Nationwide Training Program for Sports Personnel courses in the following sports have been conducted: football, handball, volleyball, basketball, classical bowling, sports dancing, sports sailing, field hockey, kyokushin karate, cycling, rowing, and table tennis.

Cooperation between the University and Employers

Regarding the scope of strengthening the practical elements of teaching, activities aimed at including potential employers in the training process of sports personnel have been planned. The project assumptions also include the participation of employers in panel meetings held at each of the regional training centers, as well as in a series of meetings related to the issues of "Sports as a Factor in Local Development," in order to increase the involvement of employers (including those realizing the state program ORLIK 2012) in the implementation of programs training specialists dealing with sports. The participation of employers in standardizing the training syllabus, in response to the problem of the inconsistent education of sports personnel, has also been scheduled. The scope of the teaching syllabuses being realized is determined in consultation with sports environments and sports associations. The issue of the involvement of employers in standardizing the training syllabus has also been raised in this project.

Recruitment

While implementing such a complex developmental undertaking as the Polish Nationwide Training Program for Sports Personnel, special attention needs to be paid to the issues related to the recruitment system which was developed for this project's purposes. In order to enable the participation of the widest possible group of potential support recipients, a specialist online recruitment system has been developed; it is available on the project's website, sport.wlodkowic.pl, owing to which there is the possibility of constant and direct monitoring of the recruitment process, which embraces the entire territory of Poland.

As far as the recruitment process is concerned, it is worth pointing out that the recruitment process has been based on a "first come first served" basis, which results primarily in a limit of available places. However, with regard to the predicted great interest, which was confirmed at the recruitment stage of each of the previous three recruitment rounds, additional enrollment criteria have been introduced in order to support those applicants who are in very difficult situations. It has been assumed, inter alia, that individuals from unfavored areas (residing in small towns or rural areas), as well as persons with low qualifications (applicable to courses). Taking into consideration the project's assumptions, priority has also been given to persons employed within the framework of ORLIK 2012; in the case of postgraduate courses, priority has been given to persons managing sports infrastructure and/or sports institutions or organizations.

Notes

1. http://pl.wikipedia.org/wiki/Polityka regionalna.
2. Final act of the Conference on the Common Market and Euratom, Treaties of Rome, Rome, 25 March 1957.
3. National Development Strategy, accepted by the Council of Ministers on 27 June 2006.
4. National Reform Program, accepted by the Council of Ministers on 28 December 2005.
5. National Strategic Reference Framework 2007–2013, Ministry of Regional Development, Warsaw, May 2007.
6. Operational Program "Human Capital," National Strategic Reference Framework, Warsaw, 7 September 2007.
7. A grant application for the OP HC, Ministry of Science and Higher Education, the project's title: Academy for Competence Development, Co-financing agreement no. POKL.04.01.01-00-448/08-00, Paweł Włodkowic University College in Płock, Płock, 2008, p. 3.
8. A grant application for the OP HC, Ministry of Science and Higher Education, the project's title: The Polish Nationwide Training Program for Sports Personnel, Co-financing agreement no. POKL.04.01.01-00-454/08-00, Paweł Włodkowic University College in Płock, Płock, 2008, p. 3.

A Historical Outline of Education in Płock, 1079–1939

ANDRZEJ GRETKOWSKI AND MARCIN BERLIŃSKI

Looking into the history of Płock and its diocese, one can easily find rich traditions within the schooling, education, and cultural areas. Although Płock got its township rights in 1237, it was much earlier when it became a politically important settlement in the region of Mazowsze.[1]

The fact that in 1075 AD during the rule of Bolesław Śmiały, Płock held a bishopric proves its important position in the eleventh century.[2] Because there is no evidence of a foundational act, it is assumed that the establishment of the bishopric took place after 20 April 1075.[3] It was back then that the time of Płock's greatest splendor began, and it lasted through until the turn of the eleventh and the twelfth centuries. In 1079 Władysław Herman began his rule in Poland.[4] It was during his rule that Płock was proclaimed the capital city of Poland. Apart from that, at the turn of the eleventh century, during the rule of Bolesław Wrymouth, the town also played a role of Poland's cultural center.[5]

At the duke's court, apart from land magnates, many clerics from Poland and abroad also stayed. During that time there were some very important figures staying in the town, such as Bishop Alexander of Malonne, who finalized the building of the Roman cathedral in Płock and funded its door made of bronze. There also was Gallus Anonimus, the first famous Polish chronicle writer.

From Gallus Anonimus's *Kronika* we learn that during the rule of Władysław Herman (whose relics and remains are kept in Płock Cathedral), there was a school in his court. It was for the state's dignitaries, especially those who would prepare Duke Bolesław for his future role as king. Otto of Bamberg (later to become a saint) was the school's principal. That fact is confirmed by Polish historians Włodzimierz Szafrański and Leszek Zygner, who write, "Beside the duke's court there was also a school educating youth and preparing them for holding important official positions in the state. During a short period of time (1080/1081–85) the school was directed by the chaplain, Otto of Bamberg, of the duke's wife, Judyta Maria."[6]

The turn of the eleventh and twelfth century can mark the beginning of Płock's educational development. Over a period of three centuries (from the thirteenth to the fifteenth) there were three schools established in Płock. Each represented a different level of education. Beginning from the lowest level they were St. Michael's Collegiate School (primary level), St. Bartholemy's School (secondary level) and the Cathedral-Castle School (the highest level). Wawrzyniec of Wszerzecze, who completed all three levels of Płock schools, wrote about the structure of Płock structure during those times.[7] He mentioned three schools succesively leading graduates from the lowest, St. Michael's, then to the secondary, St. Bartholemy, and finally to the highest, the Castle School. That school gave to other towns school principals, teachers, and educators. Those schools educated a great many nobles, townsmen, theologians, lawyers, doctors, and priests. Also many senators, members of boards, judges, writers, town councilors, and leaders of the people were educated in those schools. Also some eminent professors of philosophy and liberal sciences were distinguished at the Cracovian Academy.[8]

St. Michael's Collegiate School is said to have been established in 1180. It gave the beginning to the currently existing Secondary School of Stanisław Malachowski in Płock. The historical profile of Malachowski will be given later in this article. St. Bartholemy School was established around the mid-fourteenth century.

The highest level of Płock schools, the Cathedral School, was in existence until the end of the eleventh century. In 1148 it had a scholar-teacher, Zachariasz, who probably was the only teacher there. During the thirteenth and fourteenth centuries there were more teachers, who were the school's graduates, as well as curates. According to priest Tadeusz Zebrowski, in 1483, Bishop Piotr of Chodkowo (together with Duke Janusz II) wrote a request to Pope Sixtus IV asking him to assign two prebends to canons Sandzin and Gumino as doctors or at least bachelors of theology and canon law. The pope gave his permission for that, recommending that they give their lectures in those subjects for clerics, churchgoers, and scholars. However, up until 1495, that plan was not completed.[9]

Scholars, who often held university diplomas, played the main role in the school's activity. They frequently came from Cracow. An interesting fact is that in the notes from 1555 we find information referring to the subjects taught. Those were as follows: theology, philosophy, and law. The list of those subjects may suggest that the Cathedral School had in mind the good education of Płock's future clerics. The Cathedral School lasted until the end of the twelfth century (150 years). Its functions were eventually taken over by the Płock Clerical Seminary.

The Clerical Seminary

The Clerical Seminary, which for many years was the only school of its kind in town, in 1925 led to the beginning of the development of higher educational institutions in Płock. Seminaries were created as a practical response to a Trident Council resolution of 15 July 1563, which obliged bishops to establish clerical seminaries on the territory of their dioceses. The first seminary on the territory of Płock diocese was established in Pultusk. It was established by Bishop Wojciech Baranowski during the sitting of the cathedral chapter on 9 September 1594.

Father Dariusz Majewski recalls the beginnings of the Pultusk seminary: "The location of the Płock Diocese Seminary was selected accordingly to the importance and the size of towns included in Płock diocese. Only two towns could be considered: Płock and Pultusk. Others were too small to be practically taken into consideration. . . . Eventually the selection of Pultusk was decided by the fact that there were already classrooms and apartments for those who would teach at the seminary."[10]

For 139 years the seminary was run by Jesuit priests. On 19 December 1732, Płock Bishop Andrzej Stanisław Kostka Zaluski gave the leadership of the seminary to diocesan priests. The Pultusk seminary existed until 1865.

For a long time during the existence of the Pultusk seminary there was often the idea to create a seminary in Płock. It eventually came into reality on 6 May 1710, when Płock Bishop Ludwik Bartlomiej Zaluski with considerable financial help from Sufragan Bishop Chelmiński Seweryn Szczuki established the Płock seminary. Newly arrived in Płock, missionaries Wincent and Paulo were given supervision over the seminary. At the beginning the seminary it consisted of three buildings: "1. Canon's Stanisław Spinka's curia located at the corner of Canon Market; 2. Lubieński's old house; 3. A new house built by missionasries in 1717. All those buildings were in front of the castle and the moat in the place where currently the tenement house 'Pod Trabami' is located, behind Mostowa Street."[11]

Classes did not begin until seven years that because that was how long it took for the seminary buildings to be prepared. For a long time the school was run by three missionaries and the number of clerics varied between four and twelve. The working day, which lasted at least sixteen hours (from 5 a.m. till 9 p.m.), was filled with prayers, ascetic practices, lectures, studies, meals, and recreation. In the school curriculum there were dogmatic and moral theology, the Holy Bible, canon law, the history of the church, and liturgical ceremony. In 1719 Bishop Zaluski signed a regulation for the Płock seminary, specifying a period of studies of two years.[12]

In 1782 the base of Płock seminary was relocated to the building of the former Benedictine Abbey which functioned there until 1867. The year 1865 marked the date of uniting both Płock and Pultusk seminaries thus creating one diocesan clerical seminary. The decision about moving Pultusk seminary to Płock was dictated by its difficult financial situation.This is confirmed by Father M. Grzybowski, who writes: "The condition of the second seminary in Pultusk, as stated by the contemporary bishop of Płock, Wincenty Chościak Popiel, was miserable: there were few clerics and funds were very limited. Those were the reasons that Bishop Popiel decided to combine those two institutions. He believed that it would be best if the school was located in Płock by his side."[13]

Such a difficult financial situation was to a large degree caused by the politics of Poland's Russian invader after the fall of the January Uprising. In January 1864 the Russian authorities, on the basis of the Czar's order, took over the monastary as well as the seminary's wealth and the school's funds.Three years later, they also took the former headquarters of the Benedictines and ordered the seminary to be moved to the monastery buildings. During the years 1876–83, thanks to the efforts of Płock Suffragan Aleksander Gintowt Dziewaltowski the seminary building was restructured. The post-monastery building was extended and given a chapel, a library, and accommodation rooms and lecture halls for the clerics. In 1895 Bishop Michał Nowodworski made the decision to extend the period of studies in the seminary to six years.

In 1908 Bishop Antoni Nowowiejski took charge of diocese and kept it until 1941.[14] During those years the seminary campus added a residential building for professor priests and a building for the Library and Diocesan Archives. Apart from that, a wing of the main building was extended and seminary students got a new gym. In 1916 the Lower Clerical Seminary building was erected. In order to provide summer holiday rest to professors and alumni, in 1929 Bishop Nowowiejski built a summer cottage in Brwilno on the River Vistula, and it was named after its founder, "Antoniowka."[15]

In 1910 Pope Pius X gave the school the privilege of awarding a Bachelor of Theology degree and in 1925 the ministry board proclaimed Płock Seminary a higher educational institution with full academic rights. After 1924 theological studies were prolonged to six years, consisting of two years of philosophy and four years of theology.

Stanisław Malachowski Secondary School

Marshal Stanisław Malachowski Secondary School is one of the oldest schools in Płock.[16] The contractual date of school's establishment is the year 1180 when a collegiate school was built to fulfill a request of Boleslaw Wrymouth's guardian's wife, Dobiechna.[17] In the second half of the twelfth century there was a trivium-type school opened beside the collegiate school, and it was run by Benedictines and then by regular canons.[18] The first known teacher of the Płock collegiate school was Witalis, mentioned in Duke Ziemowit's document from 1249 as "Vitalis scholasticus Sancti Michaelis." In the contemporary education system, the collegiate school gave the lowest level of education and its students consisted of sons of Płock townsmen, the neighboring nobility, and in a minor number, peasants' sons.

The collegiate-type school lasted in Płock until 1611. During 1611–1773 it began functioning as a Jesuit college. On 24 October 1611 Płock Bishop Marcin Szyszkowski brought from Pultusk to the Płock collegiate school two Jesuits and one rhetoric graduate who started teaching in the collegiate school.[19]

The teaching curriculum included four classes: infima, grammar, syntax, and humanitas, and books were the main didactic aids. In 1612 Bishop Marcin Szyszkowski donated part of his own book collection to the collegiate library.

Father Tadeusz Zebrowski remembers the school's education system, which was in accordance with the Jesuit rules "Ratio Seminarium":

> In the first class, called *infima*, students were taught basic Latin grammar reaching to syntax and the beginning of Greek. Sometimes it was divided into two classes—particularly in larger colleges. Only those who could already read and write could be admitted to the first class. The second class, *gramaticae*, was to broaden the learning of two mentioned languages; Latin syntax was being practiced with the use of Cicero and Caesar's writings. Class three, *suprema classis gramaticae*, was called *syntaxis* in Poland. During that year students discuss the works of Ovid and Virgil and the whole of Greek grammar on the elementary level. Class four, *humanitis*, in Poland called the class of poetry, was direct training for the skill of public speaking.[20]

The school, managed by the Jesuits, lived up to the expectations of the Płock inhabitants, who cared about the development of education in the town:

> From the very start when the Jesuits arrived in Płock, they began teaching, although originally that was not their intent. They were somehow forced into doing it by society, which understood the need of education and was eager to proceed with it. In those days the system of education and upbringing applied by the Jesuits represented a high level. . . . In the mid-eighteenth century also in the Płock school, there were efforts made to reform the program of studies and adjust it to society's new needs. After the dissolution of the religious order most Jesuits who were in schooling still remained there to teach the youth who were keen on extending their knowledge.[21]

The number of students varied between three hundred and four hundred and fifty a year. Most of them came from nobility. In 1623 and 1627 the school welcomed King Zygmunt III, and in 1644 the Płock bishop, Prince Karol Ferdynand, who along with his brother King Władysław for the first time came to Płock to take over the cathedral. In 1656 Swedish king Charles Gustav and his staff stayed in the house of the collegiate school. It was then that the Swedes robbed part of the rich school library.

The year 1773 began the new, twenty-plus-year-long period of the school called the "Postdepartment School of the National Education Committee." On 14 October 1773 the National Education Committee took over the post-Jesuit schools along with their pay, thus creating conditions for state-school development. It is worth mentioning that the National Education Committee, which was created by the Partitional Sejm, was the first ministry of public education in Europe.

The Płock Postdepartment School was organizationally supervised by the Mazovia Department in Warsaw and meritoriously by the Main Crown School—the present-day Jagiellonian University. The school's emblem, the two crossed rectorial scepters of Jagiellonian University was a sign of its relationship with the Cracovian Academy. The Main School's visitors during their inspection evaluated the students' and teachers' level. The best students in academic standing were awarded golden or silver medals of the National Education Committee called "Diligentiae" (For Diligence). On the school's official page we can read: "Polish became the language of lectures. In the school's curriculum there were mathematical-biological sciences, practical classes, and civil and physical education. Lessons were conducted in the former house of St. Michael's Church, especially adapted to be a school.There were three hundred students of various social status studying in six classrooms."[22]

After Poland's second partition in 1793, Płock was ruled by Prussia. During years 1793–1815 the school functioned within the territory of Prussian influence. Later, from 1807 it was within the Duchy of Warsaw (at the beginning, from 1793–1806, as a junior high school under Prussia, and then in 1807–15 as a department school).[23] During the years 1793–1806 most teachers were Polish; however, the number of German language lessons was increased. Until 1804, the school was run by Jakub Ossowski, its principal up to then. But from the following year the German authorities appointed a new principal, the German Fryderyk Roze.

During that time the library added collections of German and ancient literature as well as physics, mathematics, and geography aids. Roze, a distinguished dean, was the initiator of building the astronomical observatory at the top of a gothic tower, as a monument commemorating Nicolaus Copernicus. In gratitude to the school's dean, there was a memorial plaque placed in one of the classrooms, and it said: "To Fryderyk Roze, who was the Płock school's dean in the years 1804–15, friendship, respect, and gratitude. Praise be to those who respect their teachers and youth leaders."[24] Back then there were seventeen subjects taught. Students had to pay a school tuition (24 zlotys per year), which was spent on didactic aids. In 1809, the school was visited by Stanisław Kostka Potocki, the Chairman of the State Board and a director of the Warsaw Principality Education Chamber. He was accompanied by Stanisław Staszic, an enthusiastic protector of the Płock school.

During the years 1815–37 the school functioned as a Voivodship School within the Warsaw Principality (in the Congress Kingdom of Poland).[25] After the Congress of Vienna, Płock came under Russian rule. Direct supervision over schools within the county was given to a curator. There were about fifteen teachers with a dean working there. Between 316 and 480 students attended six groups. The Polish language was used during lectures. In 1821 obligatory school uniforms were introduced.

The school reached a high level of teaching in the 1820s when Kayetan Morykoni was the dean.[26] The best students' names were written into a "Fame Book." Dean Morykoni took good care of the school and the students. He acquired a wide collection of study supplies. The library had 5,000 books and was both a public and provincial institution. In 1820 the school's Mercy Society was created, which collected funds for the poorest students. The November Uprising held back the growth of the school.

After the failure of the November Uprising, a Provincial Secondary School was established and then in 1836–37 it was renamed the Governor's

ANDRZEJ GRETKOWSKI AND MARCIN BERLIŃSKI

Secondary School. At the beginning, the school was supervised by a Scholarly Dictrict in Warsaw, then from 1839 by the Ministry of Education in St. Petersburg. There were five lower and three higher classes with philosophical and technical profiles. Back then in Płock Province it was the only school for males which had the right to issue a matriculation certificate. Until 1872, Polish was an official language of instruction and after that it was officially removed from schools. After the fall of the January Uprising the Russification wave strengthened. The Płock school was not an exception to that rule. Regular searches took place both at school and in dormitories, and students' life was regulated by very detailed rules. Father Henryk Godlewski remembers the situation at school this way: "This secondary school was Russified by the Russian government in 1869. Its history is known to us all because all the older ones of us went through the hardships of that school. This lasted until 1914."[27] Despite numerous Russification activities Polish youth stayed resistant by organizing patriotic societies where Polish books were read. They also protested against removing the Polish language from schools. The greatest protest wave took place in 1905, when school pupils were in attendance. Students were not afraid to introduce their demands and start the protest. As a consequence of those events, 175 students were expelled from school.

After the Russians left the city in 1914, Płock came under German rule. In May 1915, Płock teachers started negotiating with the German authorities to open a high school in the building of the former Governor's Secondary School. As a result, a five-grade high school was opened under the supervision of the Płock School Motherland Society.[28] The situation lasted until the time when the school became state owned in 1921. On 20 September 1921 the school came under the supervision of the state. The ceremony of handing the school over to the state was held five days later. Wacław Jezierski, who visited the school, proclaimed the following act:

> On the basis of an Act from 11 June 1921 the State of Poland regained the rights to own the school for males which had existed in Płock for 700 years and which during the years of the Great War was under the supervision of the Polish School Motherland Society. Therefore I pronounce this school as state run, and I give it the name of Marshal Malachowski State Secondary School. . . . May the honored figure of the "Polish Aristides" surrounded by the halo of the Great Sejm and the May Constitution become a symbol of righteousness, purity of soul and deeds, and civil virtue for Polish youth being raised in these old school walls, and may they always be ready to serve their country.[29]

In the state-run secondary school, there were following subjects taught: environmental science, German language, religious studies, French language, Latin, handiwork, singing and orchestra, Polish language, history, geography, knowledge about Poland, art, caligraphy, hygiene, mathematics, physics, chemistry, and physical education. During the years 1918–34 Mieczysław Olszowski was the school's director. Also during that period the school

190

reached the level of one of the leading scholastic-educational institutions in Płock.[30]

Władysław Jagiełło High School

The founding of the school was directly linked with events which took place in Płock and on a larger scale in the whole Polish Kingdom during the years 1904–5. It was back then that the series of school strikes against the Russified teaching system took place.[31] Under the influence of those events and also the revolution in their own country the Russians were forced to partially loosen their policy toward Poles inhabiting the Polish Kingdom. One of the results was their giving permission to form private schools where Polish language was the language of instruction and to establish Polish cultural organizations. One of these was the Polish Motherland School, whose goal was the organization of schools and libraries as well as giving material help to students. The Polish Motherland School Society was formed in July 1905. One of its first activities was organizing a private presecondary school whose headquarters was located at 28 Królewiecka Street; it was directed by Paweł Topoliński and Alojzy Stodolkiewicz.

In March 1906, a Polish secondary school for males was established under the supervision of Polish Motherland School. It was still located at 28 Królewiecka Street. On the basis of Paweł Topolinski's presecondary school there was an eight-grade Polish Motherland secondary school established. The first director of the new school was Józef Szczepański, a teacher of mathematics and director of trade courses in Warsaw. Classes began on 4 September 1906. Four hundred sixty-five students enrolled in school at that time. In 1909 the principal of the school was Adam Grabowski.[32]

From the start, the school required a high standard of their teachers. It demanded a lot from the teaching staff:

> The teaching staff consisted of twenty people, seven of whom came from the outside of Płock. That was a really outstanding force. Biology was taught by Dezydery Szymkiewicz, one of the most prominent Polish botanists. History was taught by Władysław Horodyski, later a university professor; mathematics by Alojzy Stodolkiewicz, author of many mathematics works; Polish by Czesław Przybyszewski, a distinguished popularizer of Polish books among society; and hygiene by Dr. Aleksander Maciesza, director of the Płock Learned Society during the years 1907–45. The level of teaching was high: teaching and upbringing methods were in accordance with new pedagogical trends.[33]

A high level of education did not go in step, however, with the conditions in which it took place. Those were far from desired. Aleksander Maciesza, teacher of hygiene in the Polish Secondary School for Males described its conditions in following words:

> The Polish school in Płock from the beginning had to be located in the only larger room which was available at Królewiecka Street in buildings which were completely

unfit for school purposes. The rental fees were high. Everyone who had any encounter with the school, mainly teachers and the school doctor, could notice problematic aspects related to its location. Because of the fact that classrooms were small and there were many students, their desks had to be placed very close together and pushed all the way to windows and walls. A greater risk of catching cold, a lack of proper ventilation, incorrect sitting positions both in relation to the desks and to the blackboard— all those aspects started having a negative influence on students' health. Moreover, unfresh air caused by overcrowding of classrooms lowered students' and teachers' ability to focus and work productively. As time passed doctor's checkups could confirm that negative influence on the health of students. There was an increased number of the short-sighted and those with back problems when compared to students attending schools with proper hygiene standards.[34]

In order to improve schooling conditions, the decision was made to build a new school building for the Polish Secondary School for Males. A considerable push to start the building was given by Aleksander Maciesza's wife, Maria Macieszyna, who in September 1910 sent a letter to the Polish Secondary School Supervising Council: "Believing that the development of Polish private schooling is one of the most urgent needs of our society and that everyone should be obliged, within their abilities, to support Polish schools—I declare that I will donate three thousand rubles for purchasing or raising a building for the Polish Secondary School in Płock."[35]

Three years later a Building Committee for the Polish Secondary School was formed. Its leader was Aleksander Maciesza, who made himself familiar with technical solutions present in modern schools. He visited, at his own expense, schools in Germany, Sweden, Norway, Belgium, and Austria.[36]

The building of the new school was begun in September 1912. After one year it was ready to be used. Conditions for studying improved dramatically: "In the new building there were proper hygiene standards maintained, as a result of which staying there will not be harmful for health anymore. Apart from the hygiene aspect, and what's even more important, the new building provides proper pedagogical conditions and much better lecturing conditions."[37]

Along with higher teaching standards went the development of student organizations, among which were as follows:

- Air and Antigas Defense League
  Polish Red Cross
- Queen of the Polish Crown Marian Sodality
  "Jagiełłońka" Sports Society
- Szymon Mohort's Scouts Team
- Various societies: mathematics, physics-biology, photography, Esperantists', radiotechnicians. (The societies' advisers were teachers, and membership was voluntary.[38]

Following the act, from 14 August 1918 the Polish Secondary School became state owned. The Ministry of Religious Beliefs and Public Enlightenment gave the school its name: "King Władysław Jagiełło Royal-Polish Secondary School." A year later the school's building became state owned.[39]

As a result of a resolution passed by the Sejm in 1933–37, called "Jędrzejowiczowska," the secondary school was gradually transformed from having eight grades to four. The first graduates of the four-year secondary school received the so-called small matriculations, which enabled them to pursue further studies in higher educational institutions, which were established from 1937. As a result of school reform, eight-year secondary schools (King Władysław Jagiełło Secondary was one of them) were transformed into secondary schools and higher educational institutions. In 1934, the name of the school became the King Władysław Jagiełło State Secondary and Higher School. During 1906–37 one hundred and forty teachers taught there. There were two and a half thousand students; eight hundred of whom received their matriculation diplomas.[40]

During the interwar period the Secondary School maintained a high level of teaching, producing many outstanding graduates.

Hetmanowa Regina Żółkiewska Girls' Secondary School

The year 1906 is considered the date when the girls' secondary school in Płock was established, and also the Shareholder's School Association was started as well. The association consisted of thirty-nine shareholders along with their leaders, Father Ignacy Lasocki and Stanisław Balinski.[41] A year later the associastion aquired Wanda Thun's seven-grade girls' school at Kolegialna Street. The school got the right to conduct lessons in the Polish language, and the directorship was given to Jadwiga Kotwicka from Warsaw.[42]

In 1908 the director was changed from Jadwiga Kotwicka to Marcelina Rościszewska.[43] For the first five years the school was located in a fairly small building at Kolegialna Street. Because studying conditions were not appropriate and the rent was high, the school's directors decided to purchase a lot consisting of three buildings and a garden at Kolegialna and Misjonarska Streets. Funds for that purpose were borrowed and to pay the debt a loan was taken from the City Credit Association.[44] At the same time the school authorities asked for help in paying off the loan. Money for that purpose would come from both social associations as well as from private individuals. In 1910 the school had 197 female students and their number would consistently increase. During war activities in Płock, apart from the official lessons, there were also secret ones.

During the Bolsheviks' raid on Płock, the school's buildings were used as a help shelter with a hospital, a sewing room, and feeding and wound treating stations for the city's defenders. Prelate Ignacy Lasocki remembered the August events at the school this way: "August 1920— our school simply boils over with feverish work. The Red Cross flag is hanging on the building and it is as if a Samaritan's cape seems to cover the school's buildings. Words by the front door say: 'Polish soldier—this building for you is a hospital, a wound treating stop, a lounge, a commissary, a sewing room, a tea room, a letter-writing office, and a canteen.' The front door is wide open day and night for our fighters."[45]

Less than one month after defending Płock from the Bolsheviks' raid, the girls' secondary school became state run. It was on 14 September 1920 that the school's association handed the school and its all buildings over to the state. Maciej Rataj, the then Minister of Religious Beliefs, confirmed accepting the gift on behalf of the Polish State. Officially the school took the name of Hetmanowa Regina Żółkiewska Secondary School.[46]

From the very beginning the girls' school in Płock led by Marcelina Rościszewska would pride itself with its high level of education as well as the social and patriotic upbringing of its students. A strong emphasis was put on fair treatment and grading of students:

> Equality and friendship and spreading the trend of material or moral cooperation will be the base for social virtues in the future. Here we would like to emphasize the point that even for a moment there should be no permission for any type of partisan treatment or favoring both from those teaching and being taught. Ganator's daughter has exactly the same rights and duties at school as even a princess by origin. There are only female students at this school. The only privileges can be gained by good results and proper behavior at school. Those who are familiar with the child's mental development will understand how unfair an uneven treatment would be. It frustrates and deforms children's characters, both those who are more and those less favored. The period of youth is very sensitive and overcritical![47]

Marcelina Rościszewska ensured the proper social activity of those who were in her charge. For that purpose there were numerous youth organizations for building social character established at school. Some of those were:

- The Zofia Chrzanowska Scout Team, helping, among others, war veterans through collecting donations, preparing Christmas for veterans, or sewing clothes for expatriates' children.
- The "Youth Red Cross Association"—founded as one of the first ones in Poland in the school year 1920–21. It consisted of following sections: income, sanitary, scientific help, correspondence, savings, and social. Among its social activity were deeds such as giving private lessons to poorer friends, feeding poorer students, buying warm clothes and books, sponsoring school trips, sending students with poor health to sanatoriums, and also providing accommodation for the poorest students in the homes of their wealthier friends in the countryside.
- The "State Air Defense League School Association"—three-quarters of all students who donated money for patriotic purposes belonged to it. With those donations there were special training lessons organ-

ized which taught about gas recognition and provided practical exercises with gas masks.

- The Marian Sodality—dedicated to the Annunciation of the Most Holy Virgin Mary, whose aim was the upbringing of students in the spirit of Catholic values.
- Military Preparation—established shortly after the Bolshevik raid on Płock—whose aim was to prepare female students for liaison service in case of war.[48]

Apart from that there were special savings events organized and correspondence with foreign students was maintained (among others from France and the United States), grants were funded and a school chronicle was written.[49]

Superior M. Rościszewska also looked after the high cultural level of her school and the students attending it. There were numerous theater performances and concerts organized at school. There were Moliere's and Friedrich Schiller's plays shown, the number of library books consistently increased, and for many years there were in Płock concerts of well-known music organized (e.g., Mendelssohn's and Schubert's).

The secondary school was well known in Płock and outside of it for its high level of teaching. Professors teaching there were: Maria and Aleksander Maciesza, Stefan and Halina Rutski, Bolesław Jędrzekewski, Maria Gasecka, Henryk Pniewski, Aleksander Rozycki.[50]

The prestige of the school can be confirmed by the fact that its graduates could easily get accepted to universities in Geneva, Lauzanne, and Freiburg. Moreover, it is important to mention the fact that in 1918 on the basis of matriculation exams which were given in front of the Ministry of Religious Beliefs and Public Enlightment commissions the Płock secondary school won second place out of seventy-eight secondary schools, both male and female. That distinction was emphasized by Franciszek Wybult who referred to it in the *Godzina Polski* (Hour of Poland) magazine.[51]

Leokadia Bergerowa School Complex

After regaining independence, the Płock district was one of the largest ones in area in the province. Out of twenty-three districts, Płock was the sixth largest in area. It was mostly occupied by farmlands where small farms up to 5–10 hectares prevailed. Therefore there was a strong demand for creating farming schools for inhabitants of the area.

At the start, there were to be established a few schools of this type. The first school, called the Agriculture School for Males in Niegłosy, was created after a ten-year break in 1919, and in 1921 the Girls' Gardening School of Płock and also the Girls' Agriculture School in Trzepowo were founded.[52]

The County Girls' Agriculture School in Trzepowo was opened in 1923 thanks to the initiative of local social organizations and of the starost. On 9

January during a session of the Płock Parliament the decision was made to open an agricultural school for girls under the supervision of the Ministry of Agriculture.

The school's structure was in compliance with the Sejm resolution of 9 July 1920 about state agriculture schools and with the County Office of the Prefect Departmental Resolution. The resolution stated that over a period of twenty years there would be established a network of schools so that in each of the 250 districts there would be at least one school for males and one for females organized by territorial governments; they would be financed by a loan from the state and located on state property (at least 33 ha for the boys' school and 16.5 ha for the girls' school).[53]

Seventeen hectares were donated to the school from a former farm in Trzepowo as well as old buildings such as a manor house, a barn, and utility buildings. Leokadia and Stanisław Berger—teachers from the Agriculture School in Nieglosy—were in charge of organizing the system of teaching at the school.[54]

Prelate Ignacy Lasocki, who was close friends with Leokadia and Stanisław Berger, recalled the initial conditions where the school was supposed to be located:

> The Bergers were put in charge of organizing new agriculture school, which was much needed here in Trzepowo near Płock, and which was to be located on part of a state farm. My God! How miserable it was! . . . An old, wooden house with holes in it. The few rooms had to serve as a school, a dormitory, the teachers' home, and a kitchen. The buildings were in ruins. Two bony cows and the same number of horses, a few chickens, ducks, a puppy in a dog house, a pig—destined for the table in the future—were supposed to be the exhibit stock of the Ag school.[55]

Thanks to the couple's efforts new buildings were raised: a school building for forty students, livestock buildings (cowshed, stable, pigpen), facility buildings with rooms for laundry, drying, creamery, showers, and four chicken coops with a hatchery. Moreover, school buildings got connected to the sewage system, fields got their drainage, an orchard and a vegetable garden were planted, and in front of the school there was a sports field.

The school was intended for farmers' daughters from the Płock district and the neighboring ones. Candidates were between the ages of sixteen and twenty-six years old. The condition for being admitted was having finished at least four grades of general school or having received proper preparation at home. The first agricultural course at the school took place in the spring of 1923. Studying at the school was free of charge and usually lasted eleven months.[56]

The school curriculum was set in such way to prepare students to handle work on their own farms. There were the following fields included:

- breeding poultry, pigs, cattle, and horses
- agriculture and field farming

- gardening, fruit farming, vegetable farming, and beekeeping
  household section: cooking, baking, cutting fabric for sewing,
  sewing, colored and white embroidery
- general knowledge subjects: Polish, religion, history, geography
  of Poland
- arithmetic, hygiene, economic arithmetic, environmental studies,
  cooperative movement
- legal discussions, gymnastics, singing, music, ethical discussions.[57]

The school earned great respect and its graduates were seen as perfect house-
wives, patriots, and social activists. During the years 1923–29, over 500 students graduated from the school. Among those most meaningful school events
were students' attending the harvest festival at the Polish president Ignacy
Mościcki's home in Spala in 1928, as well as the celebration of the blessing
of Płock airport with the attendance of the head of state.

The school's development was directly related to Leokadia and Stanisław
Berger's involvement: "How much work, sweat, troubles, thoughts, and heart
Mr. and Mrs. Berger put into the Trzepowo School Institute only God Himself
will count and appreciate. . . . And how those 'people,' with the properly selected staff, for decades produced hundreds of peasant girls we could admire
every year at the end of each course during the so-called showing-off," underlined Prelate Lasocki.[58] In the times of the Second Republic of Poland the
school directors were as follows: Leokadia Bergerowa (1923–33), Anna
Władichowna (1933–37) and Henryka Ciborowska-Wysocka (1937–39).

Aniela Bagińska, the present vice director of the Leokadia Bergerowa
School Complex in Płock sums up the school's achievements during the times
of the Second Republic of Poland: "The Girls' Agriculture School during the
twenty-year interwar period was able to skillfully shape the personalities of
its students within a short time of studying. The teachers' efforts, heart, and
involvement put into pedagogy, upbringing, and social work produced impressive results. Girls attending school would take general subjects as well as specific agricultural ones. Theoretical knowledge was supported by practice, and
skills were used on the farm. At school girls would sew, wash, prepare meals,
maintain the garden and livestock, and breed poultry."[59]

The development of education in Płock was suddenly stopped on 1 September 1939 by the aggression of Hitler's Germany on Poland. That date was
particularly symbolic because it is the day when Polish students begin their
school year. Public education returned only after the war in 1945.

In the school year preceding the outbreak of war activities in Płock and
its surroundings there were the following high and professional schools functioning: Władysław Jagiełło First State Secondary and Higher School, Marshal
Stanisław Malachowski Second State Secondary School, State Trade Coeducational Secondary School, Regina Żółkiewska State Girls' Secondary and
Higher School, Stanisław Kostka Private Male Secondary and Higher School,

197

Higher Clerical Seminary, the Organist School, private coeducational gardening courses, Bolesława Jarzabkowna Private Girls' Professional High School, Public Professional Training School, the Regional Płock Society Agriculature School in Nieglosy, and the Girls' Agriculture School in Trzepowo.[60]

Summary

The authors introduced an outline of educational development in Płock during the years 1079–1939. The reason for selecting that period is that 1079 AD coincides with Władysław Herman's coming into power and the establishment of schools for state dignitaries in Płock. The year 1939, on the other hand, marks the beginning of World War II. In the article, the following Płock schools' historical outline was presented: Marshal Stanisław Malachowski High School, Władysław Jagiełło High School, Hetmanowa Regina Żółkiewska Girls' Secondary School, Leokadia Bergerowa School Complex, and the Higher Clerical Seminary in Płock.

Notes

1. The act giving township rights to Płock from Konrad Mazowiecki contained elements of Polish and foreign law; it was preserved in a document by Płock Bishop Piotr I. See B. Czarnecki and A. Krymowa, "Zarys rozwoju przestrzennego miasta do roku 1793," *Dzieje Płocka*, vol. 1, *Historia miasta do 1793* roku, ed. M. Kallas (Płock, 2000), p. 21.

2. Boleslaw II the Generous, also called the Bold (1042–82): Duke of Poland during 1058–76, Polish king during 1076–79, son of Kazimierz Odnowiciel. See K. Jasieński, *Rodowód pierwszych piastów* (Poznań, 2004), pp. 152–57.

3. After the Płock bishopric was established. See G. Labuda, "Kto był założycielem biskupstwa płockiego?," *Notatki Płockie*, no. 1 (1989): pp. 9–11.

4. Wladyslaw I Herman (1043–1102): Polish duke from the Piast dynasty, king of Poland during 1079–1102, younger son of Kazimierz Odnowiciel and his wife Maria Dobroniega. See Jasieński, *Rodowód pierwszych piastów*, pp. 158–70.

5. Bolesław III Krzywousty (1086–1138): Duke of Małopolska, Silesia, and Sandomierz during 1102–7 and Polish duke during 1107–1138. He was the son of Władysław Herman and Judyta Czeska. See Jasieński, *Rodowód pierwszych piastów*, pp. 184–94.

6. W. Szafrański and L. Zygner, "Płock w dobie narodzin państwa piastów," in Kallas, *Dzieje Płocka*, 1:36.

7. Wawrzyniec z Wszerzecza (1538–1614): Canon of Płock and Pultuski, born in Wszerzecz near Łomża. He came from a poor family, probably

of peasant orogin. He received schooling at parish and cathedral schools in Płock. Then he studied in Rome from 1579. In 1582 he got a doctoral degree in canon and secular law at the University in Sapienza. He also held a doctoral degree in medicine. He was a collegiate canon in Pultusk and later of the cathedral in Płock. He left manuscripts, "Information about Mazovia and description of Płock and its paculiarities," and "Lives of Płock bishops." He died in Płock and was buried in Płock cathedral. See A. J. Papierowski and J. Stefański, *Płocczanie znani i nieznani* (Płock, 2002), p. 623.

8. S. M. Szacherska, "Płock za Jagiellonów," in Kallas, *Dzieje Płocka*, 1:154.

9. T. Żebrowski, "Stolica książąt mazowieckich i płockich (1138–1495)," in Kallas, *Dzieje Płocka*, 1:95.

10. Fr. D. Majewski, "Seminarium Duchowne w Płocku w latach 1710–1864," in *Wyższe Seminarium Duchowne w Płocku 1710–2010*, ed. Fr. W. Graczyk (Płock, 2010), p. 13.

11. Ibid, p. 19.

12. Informacje na podstawie oficjalnej strony internetowej Płockiego Seminarium Duchownego:http://www.seminarium.Płock.opoka.org.pl/index .php? page= historia (accessed 9 April 2011).

13. Fr. M. Grzybowski, *Z dziejów Seminarium duchowego diecezji płockiej 1594–1994* (Płock, 1994), p. 17.

14. Antoni Nowowiejski (1858–1941): Archbishop, liturgist, historian, born in a village near Lubien by Opatow, went to secondary school in Radom. In 1873 he moved with his parents to Płock. One year later he started the Płock seminary. In 1873 he was sent for theological studies at the Clerical Academy in St. Petersburg, which he graduated from in 1882 with a master's degree in theology. In 1881 he received clerical blessings. From 1908 he held the position of bishop of Płock for almost thirty three years. In 1930 he got a title of archbishop. In 1940 he was arrested and interned at Słupno by the Germans. Then he was sent to the Soldau Concentration Camp in Działdowo, where as a result of beating, hunger, and exhaustion he died in 1941. See Papierowski and Stefański, *Płocczanie znani i nieznani*, p. 436; A. Suski, W. Góralski, and T. Żebrowski, eds. *Arcybiskup Antoni Julian Nowowiejski (1908–1941): w pięćdziesiątą rocznicę męczeńskiej śmierci* (Płock, 1931); W. T. Mąkowski, *Pięćdziesiąt lat pracy kapłańskiej Jego Ekscelencji księdza arcybiskupa doktora Antoniego Juliana Nowowiejskiego* (Płock, 1931).

15. Information from the official internet page of the Płock Clerical Seminary: http://www.seminarium.Płock.opoka.org.pl/index.php?page=historia (accessed 9 April 2011);. For more about the summer house "Antoniówka," see M. M. Grzybowski and M. Piotrowski, *"Antoniówka": letnisko płockiego seminarium duchownego 1926–1962* (Płock, 2000).

16. Stanisław Małachowski: born 24 August 1736 in Końskie, died 29 December 1809. He was Jacek Malachowski's brother, a member of the Everlasting Board in 1776–80, a great crown referent during 1780–92, and a marshal in the

Four-Year Sejm during 1788–92. He approved of reforms and the passing of the May 3 Constitution in 1791. In the Warsaw Principality from 1807 on, he was a president of the Ruling Commission, the Board of Ministers and the Senate. See *Encyklopedia PWN*, http://encyklopedia.pwn.pl/haslo.php?id=3936918 (accessed 6 April 2011).

17. Collegiate: A church which is not a cathedral that has a chapter of canons, also used to designate a place for priests to pray.

18. Trivium: A section of disciplines which is a part of the seven emancipated sciences (trivium and quadrivium), including grammar studies, rhetoric, and dialect, which were taught in schools of ancient Rome and medieval Europe as basic education. See *Encyklopedia PWN*, http://encyklopedia.pwn.pl/haslo.php?id=4010306 (accessed 6 April 2011). Benedictines/Order of St. Benedict (Ordo Sancti Benedicti): Established circa 529 by St. Benedict from Nurse. The beginnings of the Benedictines in Poland date to the tenth century and last until the end of the eighteenth century. See P. Szczaniecki, *Benedyktyni Polscy—zbiór szkiców i opowiadań* (Tyniec: Opactwo Benedyktynów, 1989); J. H. Newman, *Benedyktyni* (Tyniec: Opactwo Benedyktynów, 1993); *Benedyktyni* website, http://www.benedyktyni.pl/ (accessed 6 April 2011).

19. Jesuits/Society of Jesus: Order established in 1534 by Ignatius Loyola, confirmed in 1540 by Pope Paul III. In Poland they have existed since 1564. Initially the Jesuits' aim was to defend Catholicism and stand against foreign theological indoctrination. Then they continued their preaching, mission and educational activity. See the Jesuits' webpage, http://www.jezuici.pl/wb/ (accessed 6 April 2011); L. Grzebień, *Jezuci* (Cracow, 1999).

20. Fr. T. Żebrowski, "Kolegium Jezuickie w Płocku i Szkoła Przezeń Prowadzona (1612–1626–1773)," in *Małachowianka, Dzieje najstarszej z istniejących polskich szkół, Liceum Ogólnokształcącego im. Marszałka Stanisława Małachowskiego w Płocku*, ed. W. Koński (Płock, 2000), p. 41.

21. Ibid, p. 51.

22. See http://malachowianka.Płock.org.pl/strona,9/ (accessed 6 April 2011).

23. The Duchy of Warsaw: Created in 1807 by Napoleon Bonaparte as a method of establishing a peaceful nation for the Poles with a parliament, government, and army, and also as an ally to the French. In 1809 it was in enlarged to include Austrian territory (around Cracow). It was also part of a personal union with Saxony. The formation of the Constitution of the Warsaw Duchy also occurred in AD 1807. The duchy was liquidated in 1815. See *Encyklopedia PWN*, http://encyklopedia.pwn.pl/haslo.php?id=3928453 (accessed 7 April 2011).

24. Quoted in Fr. H. Godlewski, *Gimnazjum Państwowe im. Marszałka Stanisława Małachowskiego w Płocku, Rys historyczny* (Płock, 1929), p. 13.

25. Congress Kingdom of Poland: A state established in 1815 from part of the Duchy of Warsaw during the Congress of Vienna. It was a monarchy combined with the Russian Empire through a personal union. Its capital was

in Warsaw. The autonomy of the Congress Kingdom, including areas such as government, parliament, army, was supposed to be guaranteed by the Constitution of the Congress Kingdom of Poland. In reality, the autonomy was gradually limited as a result of uprisings against Russian Empire during years 1830–31 (November Uprising) and 1864–64 (January Uprising). See *Encyklopedia PWN*, http://encyklopedia.pwn.pl/haslo.php?id=3927693 (accessed 14 April 2011).

26. Kajetan Morykoni (1774–1830): Dean of the Provincial Płock School during the years 1819–30. He was born in Welcz village near Busko to a noble family. During years 1785–93 he attended the Mankind School in Cracow. Then from 1793 he began studies at the university in Lwów, where for three years he studied law and philosophy. In 1810 he started working in the Department School in Lublin. In 1811 he received a nomination to be professor of Polish literature. In 1816 he became a member of Podlasie Province Commission in Siedlce where he organized the Public Library and Charity Society. On 10 April 1819 he received a nomination for the position of dean in the Płock provincial School. He was one of the initiators and co-founders of the Płock Learned Society which was established in 1820 by the Płock Provincial School. He died in 1830 and was buried at Płock cementary. See Papierowski and Stefański, *Płocczanie znani i nieznani*, p. 412.

27. Godlewski, *Gimnazjum Państwowe im. Marszałka Stanisława Małachowskiego w Płocku*, p. 14.

28. Polish Motherland School: Offically established and opened in 1905 with Warsaw as the Polish Royal Motherland School, closed in 1907, and then reactivated in 1916. It operated until 1939. The school had also a library and a community college as well as literacy classes. See *Encyklopedia PWN*, http://encyklopedia.pwn.pl/haslo.php?id=3959744 (accessed 14 April 2011).

29. Quoted in I. Nyckowska, "Dzieje Szkoły w latach 1863–1939," in Koński, *Małachowianka, Dzieje najstarszej z istniejących polskich szkół*, p. 165.

30. Ibid., p. 66.

31. In Płock the biggest school strikes took place on 5 February 1905 when a delegation of the Male Provincial Secondary School students asked the school director to step out to the school hall in order to read a petition to him: "We, the youth studying in Płock Secondary School for Males after thinking that a) in a Polish town, Russian schools such as this one are an insult to general himan justice and to our national feelings b) the present condition of upbringing does not live up to the slightest expectations of pedagogy, request that our school be transformed accordingly to the following conditions: 1) all subjects should be taught in Polish; 2) teachers should be Polish, not excluding Jewish citizens of the Polish Kingdom; 3) percentage limitations of admitting students to school should be cancelled; 4) our parents should have influence on school matters; 5) female secondary schools should have the same rights as male schools." See M. Szulkin, "Strajk szkolny 1905 r.," *Notatki Płockie*, no. 2 (1956): 9–10.

32. Adam Grabowski (1864–1919): Educator, school inspector, born in Płock, came from a peasant family. In 1889 he graduated from environmental studies at Warsaw University. In Płock he published a sociocultural magazine from 1898, *Echa Płockie i Łomżyńskie*, renamed in 1904 *Echa Płockie i Włocławskie* and founded a provincial Agricultural Society. During years 1910–16 he was the director of the Płock Secondary School for Males (presently Wladyslaw Jagiełło High School). Died in 1919 and was buried at Płock cementary. See Papierowski and Stefański, *Płocczanie znani i nieznani*, p. 196.

33. B. Konarska-Pabiniak, "Szkolnictwo płockie w okresie niewoli narodowej (1793–1918)," in *Dzieje Płocka*, vol. 2, *Dzieje miasta w latach 1793–1945*, ed. M. Krajewski (Płock, 2006), p. 231.

34. A. Maciesza A., *Gmach Tow: "Szkoła Średnia" w Płocku, Sprawozdanie Komitetu Budowy* (Płock: Biblioteka im. Zielińskich, 1917), p. 4.

35. A. Maciesza A., *Gimnazjum im. Władysława Jagiełły w Płocku 1906–1931* (Płock, 1931), p. 51.

36. N.N., *Rola Aleksandra Macieszy w rozwoju medycyny polskiej* (Warsaw, 1979), p. 94.

37. Maciesza, *Gmach Tow*, pp. 14–15.

38. Information contained at the official school's internet page: http://www.Jagiełłonka.Płock.pl/index.php?option=com_content&task=view&id=9&Itemid=11&limit=1&limitstart=2 (accessed 12 April 2011).

39. Ibid.

40. B. Konarska-Pabiniak, "Szkolnictwo polskie w dwudziestoleciu międzywojennym," in Krajewski, *Dzieje Płocka*, 2:701.

41. Ignacy Lasocki (1860–1933): Prelate of Płock Cathedral Capitula, bachelor of Polonia Restituta Badge, one of the most prominent social activists in the most recent history of Płock. He was born in Rycharcice to a landowning family. He graduated from the Clerical Seminary in Płock in 1882. Then he studied in Rome where he received a doctoral degree in law. His clerical blessings he received in 1887. He organized many societies, among which was the Płock Society for Academic Youth. In 1910 he purchased an abandoned Russian army barracks and in 1913 organized an institute for helping children and youth there called "Stanisławówka." In 1907, he incorporated the Shareholder School Society. During World War I he led the Citizen's Committee in Płock. In 1922 he registered a society called "Help and Work" whose aim was to help poor women and teach them professions. See Papierowski and Stefański, *Płocczanie znani i nieznani*, pp. 335–36.

Stefan Baliński (1870–1934): Lawyer, pope's chamberlain. One of the most prominent National Democratic, self-governing, and cooperative activists in Płock. He was born in Szczuczyno in Suwałki region. Graduated from secondary school in Płock and legal studies in Warsaw. He was a member of numerous Polish social organizations and played crucial roles in them. These were, among others, the Charity Society, the Polish Society of Mutual Credit, the Credit Society of Płock, and the Polish Motherland School. He also was active in cultural-educational organizations. It was thanks to him that in 1911 the Society for Looking After Workers was founded. In 1915 he cofounded and was a member of Loan Office Board called "For the time of War" in Płock. In 1917 he became the president of Płock City Council. He died tragically and was buried in the Catholic cementary in Płock. See Papierowski and Stefański, *Płocczanie znani i nieznani*, pp. 37–38.

42. Konarska-Pabiniak, "Szkolnictwo płockie w okresie niewoli narodowej," 2:236.

43. Marcelina Rościszewska (1875–1948): Social activist, director of Hetmanowa Regina Zółkiewska Secondary School in Płock, born in Libava in Latvia, graduated from the Institute for Noble Girls in Białystok where she got her matriculation (high School) diploma. Then she studied in the Lambert Hotel Polish Girls' Institute and then for the next three years at the Sorbonne department of philosophy in Paris where she received a diploma of *mention de géographie*. In 1908 she became the director of the Shareholder School for Females (Hetmanowa Regina Zółkiewska Secondary School in Płock). She was a founder of many social organizations in Płock among which there were the Lwów Defense Committee and the Polish Women's National Service. For participation in the defense of Płock she was awarded the Bravery Cross by state official Józef Piłsudski. She died in Cracow in 1949. See Papierowski and Stefański, *Płocczanie znani i nieznani*, p. 515.

44. Town Credit Societies: Long-term town mortgage loan institutions in the territory of Poland. From 1870 they were established in the Congress Kingdom and later on in the whole of the Second Republic. They were cancelled in 1949–50. See *Encyklopedia PWN*, http://encyklopedia.pwn.pl/haslo.php?id=3988361 (accessed 14 April 2011).

45. I. Lasocki, *Luźna wiązanka wspomnień* (Płock, 1931), p. 95.

46. Konarska Pabiniak, "Szkolnictwo płockie w dwudziestoleciu międzywojennym," 2:704.

47. M. Rościszewska and I. Lasocki, *Rzut ogólny na zadanie szkoły średniej żeńskiej: Siedmioklasowa Szkoła Średnia* (Płock, 1912), p. 4.

48. F. Wybult, *Państwowe Gimnazjum Żeńskie im. R. Żółkiewskiej w Płocku 1920–1932* (Płock, 1932), pp. 13–18.

49. Ibid., p. 17.

50. I. Lasocki, *Luźna wiązanka wspomnień* (Płock, 1931), pp. 77–80.

51. Wybult, *Państwowe Gimnazjum Żeńskie*, p. 8.

52. A. Bagińska, *80 lat Zespołu Szkół im. Leokadii Bergerowej w Płocku* (Płock, 2003), p. 17.

53. Ibid., pp. 16–17.

54. Leokadia Berger: Born on 25 November 1890 in Jackowo, she was the youngest daughter of Waclawa and Leon Grzebski. She graduated from the Higher Gardening School in Warsaw. After that she conducted practical lessons at that school and then studied in Czechoslovakia, where she famil-

iarized herself with the methods of work of a gardening instructor. After returning from abroad she started working as farming and gardening instructor at the Agricultural Sections Union in the district of Płock. From 1917 she cooperated with the Beekeepers Society. During years 1919–23 she worked at the Agriculture School for Males in Niegłosy as gardening teacher. From 1923 she held the position of director in the Agricultural School for Girls in Trzepowo. She died of a stroke on 26 March 1933 at the age of 42. Bagińska, *80 lat Zespołu szkół im. Leokadii Bergerowej w Płocku*, pp. 8–14.

55. I. Lasocki I., *Serdeczne wspomnienie o ś.p. Leokadii z Grzebskich Stanisławowej Bergerowej* (Płock, 1933), p. 8.

56. Konarska-Pabiniak, "Szkolnictwo płockie w dwudziestoleciu międzywojennym," 2:710.

57. Information based on the official website of Leokadia Bergerowa School Complex, http://zsberg.prv.pl/ (accessed 9 April 2011).

58. Lasocki, *Serdeczne wspomnienie o ś.p. Leokadii z Grzebskich Stanisławowej Bergerowej*, p. 10.

59. Bagińska, *80 lat Zespołu szkół im. Leokadii Bergerowej*, p. 47.

60. Konarska-Pabiniak, "Szkolnictwo płockie w dwudziestoleciu międzywojennym," 2:711.

DEVELOPING SCHOOL COUNSELOR COMPETENCIES IN THE PROCESS OF HIGHER EDUCATION

MAREK BOROWSKI

School Counselor Competencies under the Education Law

The image that we create in other people's minds through our reactions—both verbal and nonverbal means of communication—has impact on our relationships with people. Social perception is not free of various mistakes, simplifications, and stereotypes, yet we must not neglect the part that depends on us. One's image is one of those personal resources of an individual that often determines the quality of social relationships. The whole educational system represents a network of relationships occurring at different levels and going in different directions between all members of a school community. The school counselor, being part of this system, through his or her professional and personal competencies co-creates this network of relationships, and has an impact on its range and quality.[1]

The school counselor is a teacher appointed to provide educational care for youngsters at school and outside the school, as well as to coordinate cooperation between the school and the child's family. In Poland this position was introduced to the system in 1975. The special tasks of a school counselor include, among other things, carrying out periodic assessments of the educational situation at school, providing assistance for students by helping them decide about the direction of their further schooling and professional career, coordinating the work of the team for school-readiness assessment, offering educational counseling to parents, helping teachers to solve educational problems, organizing help to tackle school failures and developmental disorders, and providing care for neglected and abandoned children.[2]

In 1975, the Minister of Education and Training officially established the specialty of school counselor, who is a teacher-pedagogue. By the order of the Minister of Education and Training, the work of school counselors can be performed by graduates in pedagogy or psychology, particularly those specializing in school pedagogy or educational psychology.[3] The regulation set high specialist requirements for candidates for this profession. The educational background recommended by the regulation suggested at the same time that among the responsibilities of school counselors there were also independent, complex educational tasks of wide-ranging importance. Performing those tasks called for knowledge of pedagogical science and other auxiliary sciences (psychology, sociology).[4]

The most recent regulation of the Minister of National Education and Sport of 7 January 2003, on the specific qualifications required of teachers, and on the cases in which it is possible for schools to employ teachers without a higher educational degree or teacher training school diploma, states as follows:[5]

§ 1. The following terms appearing hereinafter in this regulation shall be understood as follows:

1. Teacher: The term shall be understood as referring to teachers, educators, and other pedagogical personnel as listed in Art. 1, para. 1, point 1 and 2 of the Teachers' Charter Act of 26 January 1982;
2. Qualification course: The term shall be understood as referring to any qualification course run by a teacher-training facility, teacher-training school, or any other institution, pursuant to the regulations on the types, establishment, transformation, liquidation, and operation of teacher-training institutions;
3. Teacher training: The term shall be understood as referring to acquiring knowledge and competencies in psychology, pedagogy, and methodology as taught in the amount of at least 270 hours and in combination with subject studies (in a specialty) and practical teacher training, as well as undergoing a positively assessed practical training for a period of at least 150 hours. As for vocational and professional subject teachers, the necessary amount of teacher qualification classes shall not be lower than 150 hours. Teacher qualifications shall be confirmed by a diploma or other document issued by an institution of higher education, such as a certificate of completing a teacher qualification course or training at a teacher training school;
4. Subject studies (in a specialty) related to the taught subject or classes: The term shall be understood as referring to subject studies (in a specialty) providing sufficient subject knowledge for the subject or classes taught. The body responsible for deciding whether a given subject of studies is related to the subject or classes taught is the superintendent of the school district's office;
5. Teacher training school: The term shall be understood as referring to a teacher training college, foreign-language teacher training college, vocational school for teachers, technical vocational school for teachers, kindergarten teacher-training school, or primary-education teacher-training school.

§ 2.1. To qualify for the position of a teacher at:

1. teacher training centers,
2. teacher training facilities,
3. psychological and pedagogical counseling centers, including specialist centers,
4. pedagogical libraries,
5. voivodship polytechnic centers,
6. colleges,
7. post-secondary schools,
8. general education high schools,
9. vocational high schools,
10. general education high schools, specialized high schools, technical high schools, post-secondary schools,

a person must have one of the following types of diploma:

1. master's studies in the subject compliant with or related to the subject or classes taught, and teacher training, or

2. master's studies in the specialty compliant with or related to the subject or classes taught, and teacher training, or
3. master's studies in the subject other than the subject or classes taught, and additionally teacher training and postgraduate studies in the subject and classes taught.

A person who has a diploma in higher professional studies in the subject (specialty) compliant with or related to the subject taught or classes and teacher qualifications also qualifies for the position of a teacher of theoretical vocational or professional subjects at the schools mentioned in Art. 1.

§ 3. To qualify for the position of a teacher at junior high schools a person must have:

1. qualifications as specified in Art. 2, para. 1, or
2. a diploma in higher professional studies in the subject (specialty) compliant with or related to the subject or classes taught, and in teacher training, or
3. a master's diploma in a subject other than the subject or classes taught or a diploma in higher professional studies in the subject (specialty) other than the subject or classes taught, and additionally a diploma in teacher training and in postgraduate studies or a qualification course certificate in the subject or classes taught.

§4. To qualify for the position of a teacher at:

1. kindergartens,
2. primary schools,
3. basic vocational schools,
4. basic vocational schools mentioned in Art. 9, para. 1, point 3a of the Act on the Education System of 7 September 1991, in force since 25 October 1991,
5. educational facilities,
6. institutions providing care and education for students studying outside their residential area,

a person must have:

1. qualifications as specified in Art. 2, para. 1, or Art. 3, point 2 or 3, or
2. a diploma from a teacher-training school in the specialty compliant with the subject or classes taught, or
3. a diploma from a teacher-training school in a specialty other than the subject or classes taught, and additionally a qualification course certificate in the subject or classes taught.

The regulation also defines specific qualifications for the position of a teacher-supervisor:

1. at special kindergartens,
2. at special schools,
3. at special education centers,
4. at special education centers for children with moderate and profound mental disabilities,

5. of revalidation and education classes for children and youngsters with severe mental disability,
6. at schools, youth detention centers, and juvenile shelters for the mentally disabled,
7. of vocational and professional subjects at basic vocational schools and secondary schools,
8. of foreign languages and other subjects in a foreign language,
9. who is a speech therapist,
10. who is a teacher-psychologist,
11. who runs group classes through which students can keep their national, ethnic, and language identity.

§ 18. As for the teachers employed before the date of the entry into force of the regulation and those in the course of completing their teacher training, as well as the teachers mentioned in Art. 10, para. 3 of the Teachers' Charter Act of 26 January 1982, it is stated that their work at school or facility, if assessed positively, is accepted as teacher practical training.

§ 19. The amount of hours of teacher training specified in Art. 1, point 3, is not applicable to the persons who acquired their teacher qualifications before the entry into force of the Regulation of the Minister of National Education of 10 October 1991, on specific qualifications required of teachers, and on the schools and cases in which it is possible to employ teachers without a higher educational degree, and who acquired their teacher qualifications in the modes and amounts compliant with the then-applicable law.[6]

In presenting school counselor competencies under the education law I have focused mostly on describing as precisely as possible the requirements that the Minister of Education and Training sets for a candidate for the position of school counselor. The qualifications of school counselors, as defined by law, ensure that educational institutions will employ persons prepared professionally to work in this extremely demanding position that calls for their utmost commitment. Legal, psychological, pedagogical, and methodological knowledge and skills constitute the most basic professional requirements for school counselors in contemporary schools. The complexity of the tasks to be performed by school counselors and their tremendous responsibility for decisions made with regard to students, parents, and teachers prompt schools to incessantly seek high-quality school counselors. This should not result, however, in lowering the qualification requirements for school counselors.

The School Counselor's Personality Traits

The roles that the school counselor plays at school are versatile, ranging from a "guardian," to a "jack-of-all-trades," to a so-called third principal; this is partly a result of the fact that the role of the school counselor is underdefined, and also because it is often not realized why such a person is needed at school. The role of the school counselor is determined by the person's sense of professional responsibility, understood as a kind of awareness contained in the acknowledgment of his or her responsibilities to the surrounding world. There are at least several responsibilities (legal, civil, social, and moral) that are well embedded in the professional role of the school counselor. When developing his or her own image, the school counselor must bear in mind both the scope and the content of his or her own responsibility. Responsibility is an interrelation between a person's actions and the outcome—particularly the consequences—of the actions.[7]

The school counselor should be characterized by traits that would allow him or her to communicate easily with students and earn their trust. By accepting him/herself and other people, the school counselor must put a message of trustworthiness and a friendly attitude across to students. Smiling, speaking in calm voice, maintaining a friendly facial expression, and other nonverbal means of communication have the potential of earning the counselor the students' trust. All people, and particularly children, feel good around those who are composed, determined, and who give others a sense of security. It is important to remember that among persons who would most often contact the school counselor are students who cause behavior problems, who often come from pathological family backgrounds, often with not only inept parents but also with poverty and violence in the family. Such children more than anybody else need contact with people representing positive role models and those who inspire trust. Any contact with students must be based on a unique feel for psychology and pedagogy, resulting from the richness and sensitivity of the school counselor's personality.

Wisdom is an indispensable trait of the ideal school counselor. It lies in the following traits:

- the ability to control one's temper,
- openness to new ideas,
- the ability to investigate problems and cooperate with others in the process of problem solving,
- the ability to listen,
- the ability to approach problems from different perspectives,
- the ability to transfer ideas and experiences from one situation to another.[8]

Tactfulness and earnestness in contacts with not only students but also with parents and teachers ensures that the school counselor's goals can be achieved. Any school counselor should be able to keep discipline when working with students, which consists not only in keeping order in class, but also in maintaining his or her self-discipline at work and in consistency in carrying out a chosen counseling program. The counselor is a person who often happens to coordinate varied actions, who is responsible for organizing meetings, for contacting various people and institutions, and who arranges for different kinds of help for students. Many children who seek help in the office of the counselor are children with problems. The diagnosing and solving of those problems depends on the counselor's knowledge and competencies often acquired during his or her studies and then reinforced by professional experience. The school counselor should have the knowledge and skills necessary to educate parents and other teachers, and to provide therapy and mediation. It is also important for the counselor to diligently document his or her activities, which shall serve as the evidence of his or her professional work and its efficacy.[9]

The School Counselor's Tasks Resulting from the Specificity of the School and Local Environment

The unusual popularity of social rehabilitation, both as a profession and as an academic subject, can be indicative not only of the increase in the awareness of crime threats but also of the newly born need for effective counteractions. Social rehabilitation is seen as a hope for the increase in the sense of security, and it is believed that correction programs for lawbreakers could ensure their improvement.[10]

The first school counselors were employed almost thirty years ago. Initially, they had to cope unaided, working out their own programs and undertaking complex tasks according to the school's needs and based on their own intuition. They searched themselves for their own forms and methods of work. Together with the growing numbers of counselors, standardized guidelines intended to regulate their work, tasks, and responsibilities, and necessary documentation started to appear. As a result of the changes occurring in 1989, current concepts had to be reformulated. Certain tasks were abandoned, some were left unregulated, and yet others were expanded. A departure from the standardization of requirements was being observed, following the dynamics of the surrounding reality. The work and responsibilities of school counselors within the education system are now regulated by the office of the Minister of National Education.[11]

In practice, the following conceptions of performing the school counselor's functions have developed:[12]

1. The conception of work aimed at tackling school failures, stressing the importance of the methodological and remedial approach, corrective/compensating classes and any possible assistance in effectively carrying out the school curriculum. According to this conception, the counselor participates in creating the school's system of learning support and makes efforts at cooperation with psychological and pedagogical counseling centers, with regard to diagnosing school failures. The counselor also helps to organize peer-to-peer help for students in the higher grade and personally gets involved in remedial and corrective/compensating activities by running classes for small groups of students with special learning difficulties. This conception also indicates that the school counselor plays a leading role in raising the quality of pedagogical therapy provided at school, by organizing extra classes and consultations with teachers. The counselor also makes sure that teachers, at least partly, eliminate learning deficiencies, and personally tries to provide learning sup-

port for students in the higher grades. In special cases the school counselor seeks other methods of graduation that are less demanding for students and that are combined with preparing students to work. Such a person should also constantly improve his or her professional competencies and make the effort to promote innovative methods and teaching aids.

2. The conception stressing local, social and intervention activities. The help-oriented school counselor, according to this conception, is most of all supposed to take care of issues resulting from students' living, educational, and social situation, by arranging meetings with parents, both at school and at the students' homes. The school counselor investigates the student's living conditions, checks whether the child's diet is proper and whether the atmosphere at home is favorable for the child's upbringing. The counselor also examines the parents' attitude toward their child, and the child's attitude toward the parents, and tries to provide advice on how to work with a difficult child and how to better and more effectively enhance his or her upbringing and development. Among the school counselor's tasks there also is soliciting financial support, such as sponsoring school meals and inexpensive holiday camps for his or her charges, as well as looking for financial backing for any social benefits available, all of this by collaborating with the institutions and organizations whose mission is to support children and families, and by staying in close contact with the family court and police, and with any possible care and educational facilities, preventive-medical institutions and social rehabilitation centers.

3. The conception according to which the school counselor assumes the role of a coordinator and mediator in learning and educational issues, and an organizer of mass preventive and therapeutic programs. Deciding on this model of work, the school counselor expects to be able to quickly reveal and investigate threats to the child's proper development that have their source in the child him or herself, in the child's family, or in the child's disrupted contacts with peers. Based on those investigations, the counselor makes a diagnosis and arranges for preliminary help. The counselor, according to this conception, coordinates all of the school's social and educational measures, in certain cases getting involved personally, and in other ones coordinating team activities as a whole. Among the school counselor's responsibilities there also is initiating and implementing innovative methods of mass prophylactics, especially drug abuse and AIDS prevention programs, introducing workshop forms of pro-family and sexual education, and taking measures against all forms of social pathology.[13]

These three conceptions can in practice occur in various variants and combinations. The basic groups of tasks would then be repositioned and permeated with one another. The so-called universal variant is most common. It means that the school counselor takes care of everything, but in a limited mode. As a result, the counselor helps some students with learning, intervenes in the local environment, and carries out preventive, psychological, and educational tasks. In this model, the school counselor attends to practically every single difficult school issue.

The final work task assignment for the school counselor is determined by the principal in accordance with the Regulation of the Minister of National Education of 7 January 2003, on the rules of providing and organizing psychological and pedagogical help at public kindergartens, schools, and facilities.[14] In addition, the school counselor's work tasks also depend on the needs of the school, of the students, and of the teachers, as well as on the circumstances of the local environment and the natural abilities of the school counselor.

The regulation of the Minister of National Education and Sport focuses mostly on the directions of the school counselor's work and the scope of his or her cooperation with the institutions, organizations, and persons participating in the process of upbringing, i.e., with parents and teachers.[15] In accordance with this document, any work assignment of the school counselor should include the following tasks:[16]

- Identifying students' individual needs and examining the causes of school failures (this task is particularly important for further work with the child to be carried out at school or outside the school);
- Indicating forms and strategies for providing psychological and pedagogical help for students, including exceptionally gifted students, and responding to identified needs;
- Organizing and carrying out different forms of psychological and pedagogical help for students, parents, and teachers;
- Taking educational and preventive measures targeted at students, and involving parents and teachers, in accordance with the school's educational program and preventive program, mentioned in separate laws;
- Supporting educational and protective actions performed by teachers according to school educational and preventive programs;
- Planning and coordinating the tasks that the school performs for the benefit of students, parents, and teachers, with regard to the students' further education and career choices, in the cases where a professional career adviser is not employed at the school (this task is particularly important for schools in rural areas where students have limited access to information and scarcer opportunities to choose a career that matches their abilities and interests);
- Undertaking actions aimed at organizing care and financial support for students in a difficult living situation (the number of students requiring financial support and care is growing, particularly in rural communities).

These tasks shall be carried out in collaboration with parents, teachers and other personnel of the school, kindergarten, or facility, but also with psychological and pedagogical counseling centers, including specialist centers, and with other schools and entities acting for the benefit of children, teenagers, and families.[17]

Psychological and pedagogical help is a special kind of interrelation between a help-provider and a help-receiver. Within the system of education, psychological and pedagogical help is provided at kindergartens, schools, and psychological and pedagogical centers and facilities, and is targeted at students, their parents, and, to a certain extent, also teachers. Generally speaking, it is intended to facilitate solving problems related to the development, education, and upbringing of children and youngsters.[18]

The process of providing support consists of the following phases:

1. diagnosing the problem,
2. working out the program of help expected to lead to the solution of the problem,
3. carrying out corrective measures.

Psychological and pedagogical help requires taking advantage of interdisciplinary knowledge about humans, including the psychological, pedagogical, but also linguistic, speech-therapeutic, medical, legal, and sociological aspects, which shall serve the comprehensive study of the problem situation and provide adequate help. Professional psychological and pedagogical help is offered by persons who have completed studies in psychology, pedagogy, speech therapy, sociology, and social rehabilitation employed at various ministerial institutions and nonprofit organizations.[19]

Within the system of education, helping measures are taken by the following personnel:[20]

- teachers and supervisors supporting the students in their development and providing help in the case of learning difficulties;
- psychologists and pedagogues employed at kindergartens, schools, and psychological and pedagogical counseling centers and facilities, who support teachers' and parents' educational work and who organize and implement various forms of psychological and pedagogical help for students;
- speech therapists employed at kindergartens, schools, psychological and pedagogical counseling centers, and facilities diagnosing children and youngsters with speech disorders and providing therapy;
- other specialists, such as career advisers, physicians, or social workers employed at counseling centers.

The abovementioned specialists organize and provide various forms of help at kindergartens, schools, and psychological and pedagogical centers. Some of the forms include the following:[21]

1. supporting the educational function of the family,
2. therapy for developmental disorders and dysfunctional behaviors,
3. prevention of children's and teenagers' problems,
4. supporting learning effectiveness,
5. developing social communication skills,
6. providing health education,
7. remedial classes,
8. specialist classes: developmental classes, speech therapy classes, sociotherapeutic

classes, and other therapeutic classes,
9. therapeutic track of learning,
10. remedial track of learning,
11. psychological and educational classes for students and teachers,
12. counseling consultations for parents and teachers,
13. counseling for students.

In addition, the specialists of psychological and pedagogical centers provide specialist help for children, teachers, and parents by diagnosing, counseling, and therapeutic, preventive, and educational activities; they also offer specific counseling forms of help, such as demonstration classes, mediations, support groups, workshops, trainings, supervisions, consultations, counseling, briefings, subject matter help, talks, and seminars.[22]

In addition to this, the mentioned regulation of the Minister of Education commits school counselors to participate in organizing subject classes run by special education teachers for students with disabilities at comprehensive schools, and to provide psychological and pedagogical help in various forms for students following an individualized program or track of instruction.[23] Those two tasks apply to schools in which the abovementioned forms of teaching/learning occur. However, absolutely all school counselors should make sure that the school abides by the provisions included in the Convention on the Rights of the Child. The counselor shall also find it helpful to use the guidelines for the work of a teacher pedagogue / school counselor.[24] The guidelines refer to the specific tasks of the school counselor with regard to general educational tasks, educational prevention, corrective and educational work, individual pedagogical and educational care, and financial support. Counselors' work programs include monitoring how the compulsory schooling obligation is fulfilled by students. School attendance has considerable impact on the acquisition of the knowledge and skills specified by the core curriculum; thus, it can also affect students' promotion prospects.[25]

Social rehabilitation pedagogy, similarly to pedagogy in general, takes on the character of those who practice it. The social rehabilitation reality in a way constitutes a reflection of the theory of pedagogy, as it is shaped by people of certain worldviews, who decide what shall become reality and how. A pedagogical ideology may prove to be even more important for the practicing school counselor than his or her knowledge, including subject knowledge. It is a decisive factor in how the counselor would understand and assess the effectiveness of his or her actions. Who is the contemporary social-rehabilitation pedagogue? What are his or her ideals, beliefs, goals? The pedagogical beliefs of those working in the field of social rehabilitation are related to the manner of and the extent to which those specialists identify with the science of which they are practitioners. Social-rehabilitation pedagogy represents, in the first place, pedagogy, that is the science of educating and teaching, in this case targeted at persons in conflict with society.[26]

Social rehabilitation, as a matter of fact, comes down to pedagogical work, and the persons working in this field are pedagogues in the first place. Those seemingly simple truths bring about important consequences: for example, the fact that in order to provide social rehabilitation in a responsible manner, it is necessary to complete teacher training in the specialty of social rehabilitation. The key term with regard to the assessment of social rehabilitation effectiveness is the concept of "favorable change." The way in which the question about how the favorable change occurs is answered is implied by the specialist's orientation. If the favorable change is being limited to categories related to behavior, e.g., respecting law, and more precisely, behaving in a way that does not lead to lawbreaking, then we use a typically legal criterion of effectiveness, which is the criterion of not relapsing into crime. Social-rehabilitation pedagogy highlights positive changes in the personality as pivotal, considering changes in behavior as the function of personality transformations. Accentuating personality is distinctive of this pedagogical approach, both with regard to taking social-rehabilitation measures and to assessing their effectiveness. The area of favorable changes cannot be limited solely to behavior, as it is possible to fake improvement, for some time refraining from lawbreaking, and then committing a crime at an opportune moment. In addition, social rehabilitation measures aim not only at behavioral changes but also, and even more so, at attitude changes, at correcting the system of values or at changing the person's perception of him or herself.[27]

Training teacher-counselors at institutions of higher education does not come down solely to the process of general education. In the first place it is about preparing them for the difficult job of becoming school counselors. Thus, it is important for the teachers who teach future pedagogues and prepare them to work to reflect on questions concerning educational methods, as it could happen that one day we might realize that we have trained a person of broad knowledge, who is still incapable of performing any tasks that are part of the work of the school counselor. Among the extremely important elements of school counselor training is the system of educating an

Notes

1. Beata Rokicka, *Poradnik pedagoga szkolnego* (Warsaw: Wydawnictwo RABBE, 2009), p. 1.

2. Studio Edukacyjne Eko-Tur (Non-Public Teacher Training Facility), training materials, Warsaw, 2006, p. 2.

3. Ministerstwo Educacji Narodowe (MEN), Regulation of the Minister of Education and Sport of 7 January 2003.

4. Studio Edukacyjne Eko Tur, p. 2.

5. Regulation of MEN, above n. 3.

6. Ibid.

7. Rokicka, *Poradnik pedagoga szkolnego*, p. 2.

8. Ibid.

9. Studio Edukacyjne Eko-Tur, p. 6.

10. Zdzisław Bartkowicz i Andrzej Węgliński, *Skuteczna resocjalizacja* (Lublin: Wydawnictwo UMCS, 2008), p. 7.

11. The regulation presently in force is the Regulation of the Minister of National Education and Sport of 7 January 2003.

12. Studio Edukacyjne Eko-Tur, p. 9.

13. Ibid., p.12.

14. Regulation of MEN, above n. 3.

15. Ibid.

16. Ibid.

17. Studio Edukacyjne Eko-Tur, p. 13.

18. MEN, *Biblioteczka reformy*, "O pomocy psychologiczno-pedagog-icznej" (Warsaw, 2001), p. 2.

19. Ibid., p. 3.

20. Ibid., p. 5.

21. Ibid.

22. Ibid., p. 6.

23. The Regulation of MEN, above n. 3.

24. *Biblioteczka reformy*, p. 12.

25. The Regulation of MEN of 30 April 2007, on the terms and methods of assessment, classifying, and promotion of students and participants, and on conducting tests and examinations in public schools (*Dz. U.* [Polish Journal of Laws], no. 83, Item 562, and no. 130, Item 906; [2008], no 3, Item 9).

26. Bartkowicz and Węgliński, *Skuteczna resocjalizacja*, p. 23.

27. Ibid., p. 25.

THE SYSTEM OF HIRING ACADEMIC FACULTY AT UNIVERSITIES AND ITS POLITICAL IMPLICATIONS

EDYTA BOGDAŃSKA

The purpose of this article is to introduce the Polish situation in the higher education sector and the differentiation between public and private schools. Academics themselves are the driving power for the development of scholarship and higher education. In the Polish higher education sector there are 170,000 workers employed, of whom a hundred thousand are academic teachers working mainly in public colleges and universities (84,000), and only to a limited degree in nonpublic institutions (16,000).[1] The most important is the system of hiring those teachers, which I have described in the following article.

Polish institutions of higher education are divided into two sectors: public and nonpublic.[2] They coexist on the basis of the same resolution from 12 September 1990 and later one from 7 July 2005. The president of the Republic of Poland, Bronislaw Komorowski, has recently signed two resolutions: the Law on Higher Education and About Degrees and Scholarly Titles and about Degrees and Title in the Arts, which will become active on 1 October 2011.

The topic of my assessment will be issues related to hiring of academic teachers:

> on the basis of work contract;
> on the basis of apointment;
> on the basis of a civil-legal contract;
> the dissolution of employment;
> taking up additional employment.

Conditions for hiring academic teachers are to a large extent regulated not by the Labor Law Code but by a resolution called the Higher Education Law. It defines all regulations which should be included in the work contract if it is signed by an academic teacher.[3]

According to the act which came into force on 1 June 2006 and is still in effect, the legislature gave universities freedom to decide about signing contracts with academic teachers. They can be hired on the basis of appointment or work contract (Art. 110). Hiring by appointment can be done provided that two conditions are fulfilled. The first of them is full-time employment, and the second is a declaration of the university as the primary place of work. Those conditions result in a limited number of people hired by appointment, which consequently has made this method very distinctive.[4]

Employment by Appointment

Hiring by appointment can be only in case of signing a full-time contract (Art. 118). The basic condition is signing a written statement that a given school will be the primary place of work—in the implication of the act.[5] The appointment is made by an institution of higher education when the candidate is hired for the first time provided that the candidate took part in a competition. The education statute describes methods of signing contracts and filling particular vacancies.

University workers can be persons who are or who are not academic teachers (Art. 107). Thus we can consider two groups of employees. An academic teacher, as one of them, can have only one primary place of work at a given time (Art. 109).

Research/teaching and research workers are employed at the following positions: ordinary professor, extraordinary professor, associate professor, visiting professor, lecturer, and assistant professor.

Only those who have a professor's degree can be hired for the first of the mentioned positions (Art. 114). When it comes to the position of an extraordinary professor, here only those who have a postdoctoral degree or a professor's degree can be hired. In case of a lecturer's position, the minimum requirement is that the person holds a doctoral degree. As for the position of an assistant professor, the minimum degree required is a master's or a degree equal to that.

The act also defines the minimal required educational degree for being employed in a nonresearch teaching position. It is written in the Article 110, section 2. According to it teaching positions can only be awarded to those who hold a master's degree or a degree equal to that. The same article in section 4 defines requirements for an associate professor. This position can be only given to a person holding the title of a doctor. It is worth mentioning that the resolution from 12 September 1990 cancelled the awarding of the position of associate professor. Only those who received the title before 1990 and did not get promoted to the degree of professor could keep it. The act from 2005 returned this title, and finally a new resolution which will be active from 1 October 2011 will recancel it.

As I mentioned earlier, university workers can be both academic and nonacademic workers (art. 107). The first of the mentioned groups includes the following positions: assistant professor, lecturer, senior lecturer, lector, and instructor. It is estimated that there are 12,825 people filling those positions. Nonacademic employees work as scientific-technical staff, librarians, documentation and scientific information workers, and others. Those account for 74,889 people.[6]

Exceptions

The position of extraordinary professor or visiting professor can be filled by a person not fullfilling requirements described in Art. 114, sec. 2 and 3, provided that he holds a doctoral degree and has considerable creative achievements in scholarly, professional, or artistic work confirmed by the condition described in the statute (Art. 115).

The condition for employing a person mentioned in section 1 for the position of extraordinary professor at a university is having obtained a positive opinion from the Central Commission for Matters of Degrees and Titles.

A working agreement with an academic teacher at a public university can be signed or dissolved by a dean according to the school's statute with the allowance of Art. 121, sec. 4, and in a nonpublic university it can be done by a unit specified in the statute with the allowance of Art. 121, sec. 5.

The procedures before hiring an academic teacher are defined by statute. Appointing somebody for positions of ordinary or extraordinary professor, or somebody to take the function of dean in a public university can be done by the proper minister for education matters on the basis of the school's senate application. That law applies to nonpublic universities unless their statutes say something else (Art. 121).

Employing an academic teacher at a given position requires them to fulfill all the criteria and qualifications in reference to his or her degree or scholarly title as well as academic and teaching achievements.

Conditions for awarding academic degrees and academic titles are described in a resolution dated 14 March 2003. It contains a whole list of requirements related to academic degrees and titles. It also specifies criteria for the same issues in the arts sector. Doctoral and postdostoral degrees can be awarded in the process of a conferment procedure. The conferment procedure for a doctoral degree can be initiated after filling in an application by the person interested. In case of the conferment procedure for a postdoctoral degree it can also be initiated by the employer with the permission of the interested party. Department or academic boards handle the issues mentioned above.

In order to get permission to initiate a conferment procedure for a postdoctoral degree, one has to hold a doctoral degree and have already accumulated considerable academic and artistic achievments as well as have presented one's postdoctoral thesis.

A professorial degree is awarded by the president of the Republic of Poland. Thus, the process of academic promotions leads from obtaining a doctoral degree, through the postdoctoral, and finally to the highest degree.[7]

Dissolution of Work Contract for Faculty Employed by Appointment

A work contract with an academic teacher employed by appointment can be dissolved in the following ways: through mutual-party agreement, through contract termination with prior notice of one side, or through contract termination without prior notice. Contract termination with prior notice for an academic teacher takes place at the end of a school term, provided that there is a three-month-notice period (Art. 123).

According to Article 124, a university dean can terminate a contract in the following circumstances:

1. a temporary inability to work caused by an illness, if the length of the illness exceeds the benefit period, and if there is a statement from a medical doctor about health improvement and the ability to return to work (that period cannot exceed two years);
2. the process of closing the university has been initiated;
3. if the academic teacher received two negative evaluations in a row in a period shorter than one year, which Art. 132, section 1 and 2 mentions;
4. if the academic teacher started working in another place or opened his own private company without the dean's permission, which Art. 129 mentions;
5. if the academic teacher failed to inform the dean about starting another job or opening his own private company, which Art. 129, section 6 mentions.

Terminating a work contract can also happen for other important reasons after getting permission from the collegial unit chosen by the school's statute (Art. 125).

Terminating a Work Contract without Prior Notice

Referring to Art. 126, the dean can terminate a work contract of an appointed teacher without prior notice in the following cases:

1. long-lasting loss of the ability to work in that position, confirmed by a medical doctor's statement in accordance with laws about retirements and disabilities from the Social Insurance Fund, if there is no possibility of hiring that worker in another position which would be appropriate for his health condition and qualifications, or if the teacher refuses to take that position;
2. not providing within the required time a doctor's statement about ability to work in a given position;
3. the employee has committed:

    a. an act defined in Art 115 of the resolution of 4 February 1994 about copyrights and related rights (Dz. U. [2000], no. 80, pos. 904) confirmed by the court's verdict;
    b. legally confirmed (by statement of the discipline commission) theft of an author's rights or misrepresentation about copyrights of a part or whole of someone else's work or artistic creation;
    c. distributing somebody else's work either in original or canabalized version without giving the name or a nickname of the author;
    d. distributing someone else's artistic performance or publicly changing that work, artistic performance, phonograph recording, video recording, or broadcasting without acknowledging the name or nickname of the author;
    e. any other method of violating somebody's copyright or related rights;
    f. forging academic research or research results;
    g. other academic cheating;
    h. a deliberate crime for which he or she has been legally sentenced.

A working contract of an appointed teacher expires in accordance with the law in the following cases:

1. the confirmed fact that the appointment was done on the basis of forged or invalid documents;
2. a legally valid court statement about losing public rights;
3. a legally valid punishment forbidding the person from continuing the work of an academic teacher permanently or for some period of time;
4. a legally valid disciplinary center statement forbidding the person from holding a certain position in the case where the statement refers to duties of an academic teacher;
5. the expiration of a three-month absence-from-work period caused by the employee's arrest;
6. serving time for imprisonment or partial freedom limitations;
7. the expiry of the appointment period;
8. the death of the academic teacher's (Art. 127).

The work contract of an appointed academic teacher employed in the position of ordinary or extraordinary professor expires at the end of the academic year in which the teacher turns seventy, and its expiry is confirmed by the dean. A work contract can be signed with an appointed academic teacher who has turned seventy by the end of an academic year.

The dissolving or expiry of this form of employment with an academic teacher happens according to regulations stated in an act of 26 June 1974, the Work Code (*Dz. U.* [1998], no. 21, pos. 94, with later changes); however, the termination of work with prior notice happens at the end of the school term.

Employment by Civil-Legal Contracts

According to laws relating to higher education it is known that work can be provided in many organizationally legal forms. In the case of academic teachers its base will be a work contract signed in compliance with the Law on Higher Education and the Labor Code resolutions. An academic teacher who works on the basis of this form of employment is obliged to provide evidence of his work directly to his employer (the dean), and he remains under the dean's supervision.

It needs to be remembered that such a work condition differs from other relations which are regulated in the civil code in the particular section of rights and duties. According to civil code regulations work can be provided on the basis of civil-legal contracts, such as freelance contract or specific-task contract. The former, accordingly to civil code regulations, is a precise action contract where the provider is obliged to perform certain legal activity for the receiver. It allows the worker to self-organize his actions, which makes it different from a work contract where the worker is completely subordinate to his employer.

The selection of type of contract is technically up to both sides; however, the freedom is to a large degree regulated by laws in Art. 22 § 1[1] and § 1[2] of the work code. Those regulations state directly that employment in conditions defined in Art. 22 § 1 of the work code is employment on the condition of agreement regardless of the name of the contract. Replacing this form with a civil-legal contract by keeping the conditions of fulfilling duties defined by an obligation contract is an offense against the worker's rights.

Therefore it is not the name of the contract that decides its character, but its content.[8]

Taking Up Additional Employment

1. Art. 129 of the Law on Higher Education says that "having additional employment by an academic teacher at more than one additional employer or having his/her own private company along with an extra job on contract without having obtained the dean's permission earlier is a reason to terminate the work contract with prior notice in a public school which is the primary place of work."
2. Undertaking an extra job on contract by an academic teacher or his deputy in a public university or starting a private company requires getting permission ahead of time from the university's proper authorities. If no earlier permission has been obtained for this activity, the teacher's position is automatically eliminated.
3. Terminating a work contract or the contract's expiry, mentioned in Art. 1 and 2, happens at the end of the month following the month during which the dean learned about the infraction, and in adequate reference to the dean of a military academy, state services, arts, medical academy, or the maritime academy, each minister indicated in Art. 33, section 2, with the exception of Art. 128.
4. Terminating the work contract and the contract's expiry, mentioned in Art. 1 and 2, can be executed or initiated by a dean, and for the dean's position, this is executed by the appropriate higher education minister or the dean of a military academy, state services, arts, medical, or maritime academy, appointed in Art. 33, section 2, on the request of the school's senate with the exception of Art. 128.
5. Art. 1 and 2 treat nonpublic universities the same as public ones unless the statute specifically says something else. It is up to the statute whether there are any limitations and the school does not have to ask anybody's permission for employing any number of positions. This means that working at a nonpublic university as a primary place of employment will allow an academic teacher to also be hired in state universities as additional places of work.
6. An academic teacher notifies the dean about his extra job and the number of working hours or about starting his own company within a seven-day period from when that
7. happens.
   Art. 1 and 2 do not apply to those academic teachers who are employed on contract:

   a. in offices mentioned in Art. 1, section 1 and section 2, points 1, 2, 4, and 4a from the Resolution of 16 September 1982, about state employees (Dz. U. [2001], no. 86, pos. 953, with later changes);
   b. in the academic and professional societies sectors;
   c. in law-enforcement sectors;
   d. in cultural institutions;
   e. under the authorities of the Polish Academy of Sciences and the Polish Academy of Skills.[9]

State universities in comparison with non-state ones show their strong position in the higher education sector when teaching staff is considered. The organizer of a non-state university has to find and select people who could easily be redirected to different activities. If the school is located near other universities, then local staff can be partially employed. In every environment there are people who could be hired for the position of lecturer or assistant professor; however, non-state universities need independent academic workers and PhDs who can be provided in sufficient numbers to form a faculty.[10]

According to Dean Z. Kruszewski, private schooling is "neither a rival, nor a poor relative of state schools."

Multiple Employment

During the time when the resolution of 1990 on institutions of higher education was in effect, academic teachers in non-state universities were mainly people already employed full-time at state universities. The leaders were employees with academic degrees and titles whose work in nonpublic universities was the so-called sine qua non condition of their existence. Many were people with a second full-time job at a private university, and some even had four jobs.

PAN (the Polish Academy of Sciences) institutes also conduct teaching and scholarly research activities. This means that a lecturer at a public university cannot be employed at, let's say, one nonpublic university and one PAN institute, which presently occurs quite frequently. Such freedom can only be given to a lecturer whose primary work place is a private university.[11]

Such dual employment was a response to newly opened private universities and market demand. Moreover, additional work in the nineties caused a considerable increase in academic teachers' salaries, which were rather low in the state universities. Additional employment at a private school provided them with three times the salary that was paid in state institutions, thus being a better motivation for work and a chance to work after retirement, which for many professors was very crucial. Those schools provided a kind of social security related to the future of academic teachers. They allowed for self-conducted research and academic activities, which at state universities was not possible due to the shortage of funds.[12]

The private sector was created as a response to a state education crisis.[13] Presently in Poland nonpublic schools are adjusted to the educational market needs and share the same feature—competitiveness. The profession of academic teacher is not treated as exceptional, and a person can be hired on various conditions.

The project of the new resolution which will come into effect on 1 October 2011 assumes combining two sectors—namely, primary/secondary education and higher education—into one. It is the first attempt of this kind since 1989, and its aim is to integrate those fields.

Presently the government project expects that academic teachers will only have one primary place of employment (Art. 2, section 1, point 33), meaning that multiple employment is limited, but a teacher can get permission from his or her dean for one more job and be employed as staff minimally in the other institution (Art. 112a, act. 2). Moreover, this professional group will be employed by means of an open competition, and their work will be evaluated once every two years, and in the case of professors, once every four years. The rule in the new resolution is that only titled professors will be hired by appointment (Art. 118, section 1). Academic teachers, on the other hand, will be hired by work contracts and this law does not apply to the academic degree of professor. A piece of good news for the academics who don't have the title of professor is that their number of obligatory working hours will depend on their professional activity and not on the number of teaching hours.[14]

According to Prof. Dr. Hab. Maciej Zylicza, changes in the new project will not lead to greater flexibility in academia. In Germany one can be hired for the position of full professor in a university not earlier than six to eight years after the degree was obtained. In the United States such a situation is not possible at all, unless the candidate has received a Nobel Prize. Opportunities that would encourage young people to choose an academic career are few; there should be clear rectuitment criteria and then a detailed evaluation of all academics every two years up until they have attained the degree of professor. Consistent evaluations on the basis of merit should within a few years; this would lead to creating new work positions and raising employees' salaries, which should be proportional to the quality of scholarship and teaching:

I would warn against introducing a required minimum wage for different positions (as proposed by labor unions) because that could lead to freezing the present condition: poorly evaluated academic teachers hired by appointment according to the previous conditions would get guaranteed required minimum salaries and would be able to stay at the university. In the new system, it should not be worthwile for an academic teacher to be employed at other institutions because in the case of low evaluations he would risk losing his primary place of work.[15]

Prof. Dr. Hab. Zbigniew Drozdowicz, historian of philosophy, director of the Faculties of History and Philosophy of Religion, and dean of the Social Sciences Department at Adam Mickiewicz University in Poznań states:

Not in every case does multiple employment have a pathological character. However, it becomes pathological when one professor or PhD works at three or more positions in different universities and doesn't have enough time either for his own academic development or even for proper preparation for the classes he teaches. Only partially the cause for that can be legal regulations which allow for employment in a second position (with obligatory notification of the dean of the first place of work but without having to obtain his permission). In practice the dean's authorities are willing (sometimes for reasons of simple human kindness) to give their permission for more than one employment.

The project assumes that "undertaking or continuing an extra job or starting his own company by an academic teacher who is employed at a public university needs the dean's permission" (Art. 129.1). Deans warn that they will not give their permission for such practices. As a result, many nonpublic universities will experience a shortage of academic staff because presently their staff is mostly employed at state universities as the primary workplace.

Prof. Drozdowicz stated in the Sejm (Parliament) subcomission dealing with these projects of legal reforms that there was a compromise proposed which allowed for extending the *vacatio legis* of that law:

> During this time, let's hope, that nonpublic universities who cannot afford to employ their own teaching staff as the primary work position will simply cease to exist. However, there is another scenario possible, in which the goal of nonpublic universities will be pushing their master's degree teachers to get their doctorates and complete their postdoctoral degrees. On the other hand, there could be a real hunt for professors who cannot or do not want to be employed at public universities anymore. Nowadays those particularly desired by nonpublic universities as workers are retired teachers. However, that relatively simple way of filling the minimal staff requirements may be complicated by a law which will not permit retired teachers to collect both their salary and their pension.

It is right therefore that an academic teacher should be employed at one place only if his wages are stable, and as for nonpublic universities, they should train their own staff. This will not happen instantly because it will require a lot of time and money.

On 18 January 2011 nonpublic schools' representatives organized a press conference during which they expressed their opinions and doubts about the reform of the law regulating the activities of institutions of higher education. At the conference there were such persons as Prof. Daria Nałęcz, dean of Lazarski University; Dr. Krzysztof Pawłowski from the Higher School of Business–National Louis University in Nowy Sącz; and Prof. Wiesław Godzic, assistant dean of the Higher School of Social Psychology.

Deans at nonpublic schools expressed their anxiety as a result of the changes proposed by the Ministry of Science and Higher Education in the project of reforming the resolution called the Law on Higher Education. In their opinion, those changes will lead to discrimination against nonpublic schools instead of producing the necessary element of competetiveness between state and private universities. According to Dean Nałęcz, "The resolution should lead to improvement in the quality of education and these proposals do not indicate such a solution."

Dean Nałęcz also sees many positive changes in the project. She mentioned, among others, the KNOW program, the national qualification frameworks, and departments as the first work position. She emphasized, however, that "whether they will have a positive influence on higher education will depend on the way in which those ideas are applied in practice." Let's keep in mind that the previous method of putting into practice the project requested

225

by the departments is already facing critical opinions from public-university deans.

One of the problems is a lack of guarantee that nonpublic universities will receive weekly grants for students: "The Constitution guarantees free education for everyone on every level," points out Dean Nałęcz, "Additionally the resolution demands that universities provide some educational activities free of charge—for example, exams that students must resit. I am surprised that deans do not plan to cancel these completely, as in many countries often given as examples for us to take after when we think about reforms of our higher education system."

Deans want the State Acreditation Commission (Polish initials PKA) to be a public administration unit. Dean Nałęcz justifies this desire by the need to introduce deadlines for the commission's completing of deliberations to head off the possibility of undermining or calling off its decisions: "We have had negative experiences with the earlier functioning of the PKA," she says. However, let's remember that in most countries similar committees are not power units. The PKA stays away from this type of functioning because that would prevent it from participating in many international unions which gather together acreditation organizations.

There were also some stipulations coming from nonpublic school environments concerning non-constitutional legal solutions referring to academic teachers' employment methods by more than one university: "We should at least get some *vacatio legis* so that we can create our own staff," says Dean Nałęcz. Undoubtedly there will be cases of aggrieved parties bringing suit in front of the Constitutional Tribunal. Resolutions written by MNiSW allow deans of public universities great freedom in giving permission for faculty members' second jobs. Presently 20,000 academic teachers in public universities work two jobs, and those are positions financed by the state budget, and there are 8,000 positions at nonpublic universities, which are financed from students' tuitions.[16]

This can lead to a situation where private universities might be short of staff, which is usually hired first by public universities. A department's response to such a situation might include the possibility of including teachers with master's degrees who have proper experience in the staff minimum to teach in the first-degree studies program.

According to data issued by GUS (the main statistics office) at the end of 2009 there were 100,066 full-time academic teachers employed in Poland. They were ordinary professors, extraordinary professors (among those also extraordinary professors holding academic titles), visiting professors, associate professors (including those who hold postdoctoral degrees), and lecturers (including those who hold postdoctoral academic degrees). That accounts for 82,691 people employed full-time at public schools, and 17,375 in nonpublic schools. Public schools were the primary place of work for 58,088 academic teachers and nonpublic for 588 academic teachers. There are obvious disproportions which will have great meaning in the future functioning of nonpublic universities (GUS, pp. 298–300, table. 40). The supply of academic teachers in the higher education sector is too low in proportion to the number of students.

On 11 November 2009, the number of all university students (including foreigners) was about 2 million (1,268,366 in public schools, and 659,396 in nonpublic schools).[17] Presently in Poland there are 458 universities, 132 nonpublic, and 326 public.[18]

The group of universities is a vast and has an important function in society. Those functions are not only preparing our country's workforce, but also having an important influence on the political context of the flow of information. It is not possible to divide the educational sphere from social processes and occurences. World politics is influenced by teachers even if we do not notice it. Teachers are involved in that area because they continuously remain members of society in which they are active and are brought up. Now we should ask ourselves the following question: "What political content will be passed on by academic teachers who are constantly remaining in a state of anxiety about not only their profession and field of endeavor, but also about the basic aspects of their existence?"

Notes

1. http://www.nauka.gov.pl/szkolnictwo-wyzsze/dane-statystyczne-o-szkolnictwie-wyzszym/.

2. Resolution from 27 July 2005, Prawo o szkolnictwie wyższym [Law on Higher Education], *Dz. U.* (2005), no. 164, pos. 1365.

3. http://e-prawnik.pl/biznes/prawo-pracy/stosunek-pracy/dokumenty/umowa-o-prace-z-nauczycielem.html.

4. http://www.pum.edu.pl/administracja/dzial-kadr/podstawowosc-zatrudnienia-nauczycieli-akademickich.

5. https://legalis.net.pl/index.html.

6. http://www.stat.gov.pl/cps/rde/xbcr/gus/PUBL_e_szkoly_wyzsze_2009.pdf.

7. M. Dąbrowa Szefler, "Zasoby kadrowe i finansowanie szkolnictwa wyższego," in *Szkolnictwo wyższe w Polsce: Raport dla OECD*, ed. M. Dąbrowa-Szefler and Julita Jabłecka (Warsaw: Ministerstwo Nauki i Szkolnictwa Wyższego, 2007), p. 160.

8. http://samorzad.infor.pl/.

9. Resolution of 27 July 2005 Law on Higher Education, *Dz. U.* (2005), no 164, pos. 1365.

10. Z. Kruszewski, "Rola i funkcje uczelni niepaństwowych w przemianach wyższego szkolnictwa w Polsce," in *Przemiany szkolnictwa wyższego*

u progu XXI wieku, ed. Zbigniew P. Kruszewski (Płock: Wydawnictwo Naukowe Novum, 1999), p. 133

11. PAP article from 22 February 2011, http://praca.gazetaprawna.pl/artykuly/ 489332, kleiber_przepisy_dot_wieloetatowosci_w_przyszlosci_musza_ulec_zmi anie.html.

12. E. A. Wesołowska, "Społeczne uwarunkowania wyższych szkół niepaństwowych w Polsce," in Kruszewski, *Przemiany szkolnictwa wyższego u progu XXI wieku*, pp. 151–53.

13. T. Lewowicki, "Nauczyciel wobec współczesnych wyzwań edukacyjnych," in *Modele kształcenia nauczycieli a współczesne potrzeby edukacji i rynku pracy*, ed. Zbigniew Kruszewski, materials from a conference organized by Education, Science and Sport Committee of the Senate of Republic of Poland on 9 December 2003 (Warsaw-Płock: Senat Rzeczpospolitej Polskiej, Szkoła Wyższa im. Pawła Włodkowica w Płocku, 2003), p. 29.

14. Prof. Tadeusz Lut, "Wykładowca tylko na jednym etacie," *Dziennik Gazeta Prawna*, 9 June 2010, http://praca.gazetaprawna.pl/wywiady/447962, wykladowca_tylko_na_jednym_etacie.html.

15. Prof. dr hab. Maciej Żylicz, biochemist and molecular biologist, is president of the Foundation for Polish Science [Fundacja na rzecz Nauki Polskiej]. http://www.forumakademickie.pl/fa/2010/10/jak-to-jest-z-polska-nauka/.

16. http://forumakademickie.pl/fa/2011/02/kronika/.

17. http://www.stat.gov.pl/cps/rde/xbcr/gus/PUBL_e_szkoly_wyzsze_2009.pdf.

18. http://www.nauka.gov.pl/szkolnictwo-wyzsze/dane-statystyczne-o-szkolnictwie-wyzszym/.

Institutions of Higher Education: An Environment Where Science Comes into Being and Knowledge Is Integrated with Wisdom and Learning

ROMUALD DOBRZENIECKI AND
WIESŁAW WOJCIECH SZCZĘSNY

Science formerly was different than contemporary science. Science today is characterized by two substantial features:

1. A close link between research and education. These two components are becoming more and more inseparable due to the system of higher education.
2. Team research. This method of pursuing science becomes a prerequisite necessary for progress and advancement. Science is becoming more and more a collective work. It is not isolated from society. The system of higher education, which is more and more diversified and complex, is becoming a natural environment for science and scientists described in this manner.

Science is such, or at least it seems to be such, if one looks at it from inside. However, one cannot suppose, based on this, that it is *only* such. Science is being constantly reshaped. Research today requires a huge amount of money and interdisciplinary teams. This is a permanent condition. The establishment of facts, research, and scientific thinking are considerably enriched. Science does not only exist, it also constantly generates and steadily reforms the environment of the higher education system.

This article intends to present a modern picture of science seen from inside and outside and the progress of learning about mankind that takes place in new scientific disciplines.

We will then sketch the evolution of ties between subject and method of research as a result of changes in methodology, also known as philosophy of science. For stylistic reasons in this article we will use these terms alternately.

We will conclude our inquiry by presenting *our own* vision of the higher education system as a natural environment for originating science, for scientists performing their research, for getting an education, and for integrating knowledge, research, wisdom, and community life.

Science Seen from the Inside

Clear-cut matters and truisms become at times a good beginning for an article. First of all, the term *science* itself is polysemic; it is chronically ambiguous. Secondly, the term is very unclear in each of these meanings. Therefore, when speaking about science and its nature, methods, qualities, and methodological structure, one may express several kinds of truths. However, the justification of each one of them may seem equally to be the "right one."

There is no discussion, however, about the difference between science as it was formerly practiced (e.g., a hundred years ago) and science today. All we have to do is look through textbooks today to find this difference. The wording and solutions offered today are much more precise than the former ones. New mechanisms of apprehension allow wider and deeper expression of issues of any given field of science. In short, the science of olden times is different than the science today. This is evidence of not only the "quantitative" development of science, but also of qualitative progress. The most convincing arguments for this thesis come from the progress of sciences such as neurobiology, biochemistry, genetics, evolutionary biology, cybernetics, computer science, linguistics, and systems theory. We will put aside all questions of the philosophy of science such as "How did this happen?" "Was the process continuous or 'in leaps'?" "How did new perceptions and new theories appear?" "What was their origin?" "How do they relate to empirics?" "What factors played a significant role in their progress?" We will leave the searching for answers to these questions to the history of science. For the purposes of this article we will use only a few pieces of information relating to history of science and limit them to knowledge of the evolution of mankind.

Each problem that is solved scientifically meets many drawbacks. There are pseudosolutions suggested (e.g., the hypothesis of "the ether" in physics) and serious mistakes are made (e.g., making undisputable assumptions, such as the fifth postulate of Euclid, and even various mythologies).[1] Getting to know the nature of mankind meets more obstacles than just those discovered in natural sciences. Three of them still remain the most difficult to solve.[2]

First of all, man himself has not been satisfied about what science discovered about him. The reasons are similar to the reasons that each one of us prefers "false truths" in his or her portrait to the truth presented in an X-ray picture. *Myths are always more appealing than reasons.*

Secondly, mankind has always attracted the attention of the sciences, various ideologies, and doctrines. In addition to scientists, many ideologists of different orientations and policymakers working for politicians have participated in an attempt to get to know mankind. In this matter scientists have struggled not only with problems but also with lawmakers and the powers-that-be who make decisions about human fates and even their lives (e.g., the cases of Galileo, Giordano Bruno, and the geneticists of the former Soviet Union, as well as the ongoing discussions about the teaching of the theory of evolution in United States). *The problems of science are the only ones that never fought anybody and only gave passive resistance and yet have become more and more complicated and complex.*

Thirdly, science alone has been too "weak" to solve the problem of knowledge of mankind coming from various disciplines dealing with issues of man and his nature. Two disciplines have been dealing for a century with the essence of mankind: physiology (neurophysiology, known today as neurobiology)[3] and psychology as a scientific discipline autonomic and independent of philosophy. What is the nature of this problem?

The science of mankind approaches the issue of unlocking the mechanisms of human energo-mental behavior and deals with its *soma*. Physiology (and, speaking more precisely—neurobiology) has advanced the knowledge of man's nervous system and brain quite far during the last fifty years. This is especially true regarding knowledge of motivational behavior and the description of the dopaminergic mechanism of rewards that creates the basis for neurobiological dependencies. Major dopaminergic paths start at mesencephalon and lead to the forebrain. Most of the dopaminergic neurons in the brain generate the system of motivations. People's motivational behavior is that aimed at reaching their goals and their internal conditions (i.e., hunger, sexual needs), and external agents are drives for this behavior. Physiological deficiencies are the motivation for satisfying their apetite (i.e., searching for food) and for consumptional behavior (like eating). The following terminology convention is accepted: an *incentive* increasing probability of motivational behavior is an *incentive of positive reinforcement*, while an incentive decreasing this probability is an *incentive of negative reinforcement*. We generally accept the postulate that *the quality of a given reinforcing incentive is selective for each kind of activity and depends on the situation*.

Regarding mankind, the selectiveness of reinforcing incentives depends on the cultural understanding of the situation. Since motivation is the dependency of decision making upon emotions (driving agent) and reflection (information agent), the power of motivation depends on energy, and the direction depends on information. There are many kinds of motivation. (I mentioned them in another essay.)[4] Regarding *Homo sapiens* (man), the cultural aspect (an essential context of existence) possesses a reinforcing function.

Behavior that is evoked by given internal and/or external conditions and that is aimed at carrying out particular goals is called "motivational behavior." An incentive that may evoke such motivational beharior is called the triggering incentive.[5] The triggering incentive acts as a positive reinforcement incentive if it increases the probability of reaction. Man by nature attempts to get for himself a positive reinforcement incentive. He will try to avoid a negative reinforcement incentive. We refer here to incentives perceived as aversional.

We have mentioned before that the quality of the reinforcement incentive depends on the context.[6] Various motivational behaviors appear despite a lack of physiological deficiencies. Such is the case of behaviors such as looking for a partner or caring for children. These behaviors are intensified by particular biochemical conditons of the brain such as hormones and easily identified external situations. Incentives that evoke *other* behaviors such as listening to music, exploring unknown environments, pursuing sports, working on research, or participating in rituals are not yet known.[7] It is worth noticing that neurobiologists admit to the fact that they do not know what these incentives are. Scholarship in the arts often drowns its lack of knowledge in empty words or fashionable nonsense, such as "transgression of limits" into "transformative hermeneutics of entangled gravitation" (Sokol and Bricmont 1998).

Science Seen from the Outside

The past work of scientists dealing with man's consciouness and of psychologists can be easily envisioned as a parabola of two teams of laborers digging a tunnel: each team digs at its end hoping to meet and that the tunnel will be ready as a way of commuting from one end to the other. However, nothing like this has happened. To the contrary, the gap created by representatives of both sciences still exists and still is an obstacle to integrating the knowledge of mankind that has developed considerably. Such a development can be called a lacuna in improving the knowledge of man, and especially his brain.

However, what this "gap" (according to some, a void impossible to overcome) is is that the humanists do not know much about the progress made in the natural sciences dealing with mankind, and representatives of physical and natural sciences do not show much interest in the arts or social sciences, especially in psychology that changes into "abnormal psychology" and starts to fight myths that it created. There are much more than the fifty quoted,[8] and it states that psychology is magic and mythology rather than a science in the methodological sense of this word.[9] Here we do agree with R. Zawadzki, when he reminds us that:

> The ideology of reduction in psychology can be considered a peculiar transformation of the cybernetic ideas of the fifties and sixties (Wiener) that were eagerly scooped up for purposes of modifying more-or-less developed versions of the concept of mankind, basing on the simple model of "incentive–reaction." We agree with it when it comes to first attempts of ideas of fifties and sixties (Wiener). If we have no doubts that the psychologist mentioned "knows the works of Norbert Wiener," we have also no doubts that he understood very little of it.[10] Marian Mazur, a Polish cybernetician, rejected psychological terminology as in his opinion it deals with "language history" and cannot bring anything new into understanding steering systems—a theoretical base for integrating knowledge of mankind.[11]

M. Tokarz, the author of *Elements of Pragmatic* Logic, has stated that some people create their own systems of opinions in a way that is highly irrational and impossible to anticipate, even in the simplest situations. We can therefore imagine a person who is *convinced* that p is and at the same time is not a pt. It is similar to some basic laws of logic. I have among my friends a specialist of Polish language who thinks that philosophers are humanists. She thinks that some philosophers are idiots; however, the statement that "some philosophers are idiots" (with an accent on the word "some") is for her too general, impossible to accept.[12] Despite these cases, we must agree that it is not true that humanists are lazy and ignorant and are unable to think reasonably. Just as in any other discipline, the humanities have many reliable researchers and a lot of solid knowledge. And, like anywhere else, there are careerists and people with pseudoknowledge. Those who do not fully understand the specifics of arts and humanities and demand that they disappear or start to resemble hard sciences are the real sinners.[13] Therefore, when we think of integrating the knowledge of mankind in the human sciences we have in mind solid knowledge of reliable researchers. Such things do exist, because "this world is a world of science,"[14] which constitutes the scientific credo of this essay.

From Information via Integration to Wisdom

Since psychology still has problems pinpointing its identity,[15] its subject, its basics[16] and its applications,[17] one can also pose questions regarding the future of psychology as a science: for example, will psychology last to 2026?[18] Psychology has existed as a separate discipline for over a century. Therefore we know its achievements and what we can expect of it.[19] It is therefore understandable to make an effort to find a strong basis for integration of today's detailed knowledge of a mankind existing in various disciplines of science besides psychology. We are of the opinion that system philosophy is such a discipline.

Its key categories are system and information. A system means a set of elements related to one another and working as a whole.

Information in system philosophy is considered to be a nonmaterial factor different from mass and energy. This kind of information is of a structural nature and may be identified with distributing mass and energy within time. Information therefore is neither a substance nor an object. It is a process steering all changes. If these changes have to do with the universe, we deal with cosmic information called an *infon*.[20] It meets two requirements:

1. an infon is a photon of unlimited wavelength (in other words, of frequency of vibrations equal to zero.
2. a photon is an infon moving with the speed of light. In other words,
3. Should there be a difference between the speed of the infon and the speed of light, the quantum of energy changes into the quantum of information (infon).[21]

The last of the postulates can be put as a statement saying that the universe is filled with infons. To put it more descriptively, *information is everywhere.*[22]

Our universe is an entity of constant process, a place continually conveying information. It is an informative world of communication. One can conclude that man and society are informational beings, owing their existance to constant communication and the exchange of information. Information is the essence of existence, an integration of knowledge that is the carrier of universal information. Knowledge, being a carrier of humanistic, social, and cultural information, can be called wisdom.

Therefore, wisdom—the integration of knowledge and impartiality in searching for truth about man and his world—is nonnegotiable and cannot be substituted for by anything whatsoever. In our opinion, an overall market facilitation of research and knowledge would be a submerging of the nonnegotiable characteristics of striving for truth and goodness. In the sharing of information one does not lose it, but—to the contrary—one multiplies human wisdom and goodness.

Speculation thus far leads us to the conclusion that despite various social changes, despite those who negate the progress of science, ever since the beginning of mankind there has been a consistant steady progress of intellectual achievements, of values that are accepted and carried out manifested via new truths, while there is also an increase in the number of their sources. Three major centers of generating knowledge are becoming remarkable: 1) research in schools and institutions of higher education and scholarship, 2) research and innovative planning in economics, and 3) so-called social networks (Facebook, Twitter, and other websites). The last of the three, social networks, is considered to be a crucial source of social self-knowledge and commerce.[23]

Transformations of the Higher Education System, or Where Will Polish Scientists Work?

As we know, effective as of the new academic year (2011–12) there will come into force the new Law on Higher Education of 18 March 2011. This act is the subject of discussion in many social circles as well as on the Internet.[24] We suggest looking at the reforms first from a historical perspective going back to 1951 (we will explain the reason for that particular year in a moment), and then we will start a discussion based on the thesis that higher education reform is based on assumptions known as nondisputable truths while they are only legends and "higher mythology."

The Education Act of 1951 did not distinguish among scientists regarding their employment. One could become assistant, an adjunct, an assistant professor, or a professor in an institution of higher education as well as in an institute or in one of the branches of the Polish Academy of Science (there were not too many of them at that time). This unity was broken as a result of disputes that led to separate acts authorizing three types of "centers": the Polish Academy of Science, higher educational institutions, and research institutes. These disputes stopped very shortly, so what were they about? They were about money, and especially about disbursing of funds between institutions of higher education and institutes. As we know, these funds were mainly for institutes and only a very small part of them was received by institutions of higher education. Of course, the scientists working for institutions of higher education (especially technical universities)[25] were not satisfied and made efforts to change this. They were, however, helpless, as it was said that the industrialization of the country required well-equipped large engine rooms rather than small laboratories for students' experiments in technical universities.

A group of scientists, therefore, presented the surprising argument that departmental institutes were not establishments of science. Science is pursued only at colleges, academies, or universities. It was also pointed out that 300 scientists out of 602 professors and assistant professors working for research institutes in 1967 were also employed in institutions of higher education, and they considered their work for the institutes as an additional one. Therefore these institutes did not have their own employees. Consequently, institutes without scientists could not be considered educational establishments. Therefore, all funds for education should go to institutions of higher education. There is no need to say that all these institutions were state owned. We are saying that institutions without scientists cannot be considered educational ones and that no one can force greater funding by applying tricks of terminology. Increasing funds can only be done by printing more money in order to increase real funds aimed for science and education, no matter how heretical this may sound. After all, money is a carrier of information indicating what is essential for society (and science and education are still of great importance, as proven by information invested).

There is now a question how the situation of scientists in Poland will change after the reform of higher education and particularly of private schools. Two indisputable "truths" still remain, and they are 1) that public schools cannot fail and 2) that public schools are the best ones. Due to ranking, we are able to compare the strong and weak points of schools, says Prof. Witold Jurek, Deputy Minister of Science (12th edition of the League Table of Schools of Higher Education).

This is an essential factor in the quality of higher education, claims Prof. Michał Kleiber, a chair of the league and the president of the Polish Academy of Science. The first two places were taken this year by Warsaw University and the Jagiełłonian University of Cracow. The Warsaw Technical University took third place.[26] Does this mean that these public institutions have the best scholars and that they should receive the most funds? That their graduates are better than the graduates of private schools? Is this what Magda Papuzińska, a journalist of *Polityka*, has in mind when she says, "The Polish higher education system is drifting into an unknown direction," although to Barbara Kudrycka, the Minister of Education, the reform will put an end to the drifting and will lead the Polish schools to the upper echelons of European rankings.[27] We will see about that. So far however, we will be quoting M. Papuzinska.

The number of academic professors is increasing too slowly in relation to the increasing number of students. False: the number of academic professors is not increasing at all. It is true that the reason for it is money. Each new PhD is a threat to the income of the PhDs already employed.

Holding more than one position affects mainly the private schools. False: the reform will end this plague in theory only. Employees have less time for education when becoming teachers (professors are paid more than PhDs for attending seminars and advising new licenciates and master's students). This also relates to giving lectures and conducting experiments.

Academic professors earn little, and therefore they must hold more than one job. As per Ms. Papuzinska, this is hard to decide. This problem certainly cannot be solved based on one legal regulation, although the minimum wages of specialists employed by public schools have increased by 30 percent while a professor will earn at least 4,000 PLN. The Department of Education states that the wages of specialists of public schools showed no increase since 2007.

Studies at public schools are tuition free. Partially true. The reform does not cover this problem as public schools work only partially in accordance with the Constitution of the Republic of Poland. The jurisdiction of the Constitution partially authorizes operations that are not covered by law. The jurisdictional body (consisting of fifteen people: nine professors and one PhD) passed a regulation that paid education is in accordance with the Constitution of the Republic of Poland providing that the number of paying students does not exceed 50 percent.[28]

Due to tuition-free schools young people can study. False. According to the reform, studies at public schools will remain tuition free. The only students that will have to pay tuition are those without aptitude regardless of their financial situation. Ten percent of the best students will not have to pay tuition even if they are rich. *Partially* right (our emphasis).

A positive evaluation given by the Committee of Acreditation means a high-quality education. False. Despite the novelty of naming a Polish Committee of Acreditation and the frequency (every two years), these changes do not affect the functioning of the system. It is only a change made to the structure of the system that results in changes to its functioning. Should these changes be a solution for the problem of optimalization, then even when the naming remains unchanged, there will be an optimalization of the functioning of the system. This case applies to the optimalization of education. But, first of all, one has to know what the optimalization is, then how to optimalize the problem, and finally one has to implement the solution, having proved that it is the best solution.

We will not discuss the problem of schools being short of nmoney and the decrease of population increasing the problem (for us this is neither true nor false). However, due to the fact that the Polish higher education system absorbs annually 9 billion PLN of public funds and approximately 4 billion PLN of private funds, this is a misinterpretation as it is far from optimalization. Secondly, since we do not know the meaning of money (as a unit of information whose carriers are electronic registers), we only know theoreticaly the difference between public funds and private funds and this is a trick played by an old-fashioned term that has disappeared long ago in the global economy and exists only in history.[29] It used to be called "money," while presently it is known as "currency."

The increase in the cost of educating students: Ms. Papuzinska says that this is not true, and that we are putting aside economic arguments based on a legal method of calculating grants. In 2011 this fund will contain—if this is the true amount—230 million PLN (2.4 percent of the total stationary grant). The remaining funds—over 9 billion PLN—will be granted to public schools.

Public schools are preferable to private schools. According to Ms. Papuzinska (and we agree with her), it is only half of the truth. Half of this statement may be true. The professor in a public school says to her co-employee who happens to be a PhD: "What are you worried about? This is only a supplement taken from our pay." This, however, may be true as many specialists working for public schools also work for private schools. It may also be true that public schools are better than private ones in the sense that the diploma of a public university is widely recognized while the diploma of a private school may not be recognized at all. Students are often surprised that it is possible that private schools, other than those of higher education, are better than public schools. We recommend to these students an article written by Marcin Jamkowski and Marcin Rotkiewicz, "A Day of Blossoming Ivy,"[30] where the authors justify the statement "Take a Nobel Prize winner, a president of a corporation, an excellent lawyer, a politician, and it will turn out that every other one of them either studied at or worked for Harvard University."

Conclusion

Finally, "the whole truth" makes it clear that the remedy for all evil in education in Poland is equal access to the state budget for private and public education. The Catholic University of Lublin already uses this solution and is satisfied with it.[31]

Let us also advise that our school already has a team (headed by Tomasz Kruszewski and Romuald Dobrzeniecki) that works on the research project "The Natural History of the Polish Scientist—Continued." This project refers to the analysis of Prof. Marian Mazur, "A Natural History of the Polish Scientist."[32]

Addressing the problem, let us present an incomplete list of questions for which the answers would become a base for optimizing the functioning of the educational system:

1. What is the condition of science seen from the inside? In a systematic approach, science is described as a whole, self-organizing system steered by flows of information.[33] The essential novelty of this definition is using such terms as "steering," "information," and "self-organization." These are terms necessary for a modern definition of science—of which the crucial purpose is achieving new and reliable, "real" information about the subject of research.
2. Who is a real scientist? A theoretist? A researcher and experimentor? A teacher? A master of language and multimedia presentations? An able administrator struggling for funds?

3. Where does the scientist work? How will the scientist—a theorist and discoverer—function? (Arnold Laslo Barbarsi is an example of such "revolutionary." His idea of applying network analysis to foresee human behaviors proved to be too revolutionary for traditional professors and in order to pursue his further career he needed to find a less revolutionary subject.) As a researcher working on solving crucial problems applying to the pharmaceutical industry or the armament industry, or an administrator able to apply for funds for research?

4. How is science to be administered? Science needs administration, but this administration should be aimed at serving scientists rather than managing them. There are persons who, having graduated studies of administration (and who suggest implementing an internal audit for monitoring administration of institutions of higher education and scientists), manage scientists in a manner suggesting that they believe that new ideas occur in "the body part used for sitting" rather than the one for thinking. They are often deans, administrators, or other authorities. Innovative ideas, however, do not originate within specified time limits. They occur when they "want to," especially during late-night discussions.

5. How does one plan in science?

6. For whom does the scientist work? The Polpharma Foundation of Science established an annual contest for financing research projects.[34] Does the scientist working on a receptor for amino acids (e.g., nogo and its role in multiple sclerosis) work for the pharmaceutical concern or does he work for the patient? Does he work for society when trying to find the causes of an illness? Since doctorates are financed by scholarships of the Polpharma Foundation of Science, what happens if there should occur a conflict between the scientific truth and the best interest of the corporation? Will the truth be the preeminent factor or the interest of the corporation? How does this relate to the progress of science and scientific research?

7. What is the scientist responsible for these days (vis-à-vis the market facilitation of scientific achievements)?

Notes

1. J. Kierul, *Od kosmosu Arystotelesa do wszechświata wielkiego wybuchu* (Warsaw, 2007); S. Hawking and L. Mlodinow, *Wielki project* (Inowrocław, 2011); S. O. Lilienfeld et al., *50 wielkich mitów psychologii popularnej, półprawdy, ćwierćprawdy i kompletne bzdury* (Warsaw and Stare Groszki, 2011); A. K. Wróblewski, *Prawda i mity w fizyce* (Warsaw, 1987); H. Szarski, *Cele i kierunki badań naukowych* (Wrocław, 1987).

2. M. Mazur, *Cybernetyka i charakter* (Warsaw, 1976).

3. See A. Longstaff, *Neurobiologia* (Warsaw, 2006), p. xv.

4. See W. W. Szczęsny, *Między dobrem a złem: Wprowadzenie do systemowej antropologii pedagogicznej* (Warsaw, 1995), pp. 46–47. I observe a need for making radical supplements to this essay due to considerable advancement made in neurobiology, which finally gave documented and adequate examples confirming the above mentioned theory of motivation.

5. Longstaff, *Neurobiologia*, p. 440.

6. Ibid.

7. Ibid.

8. Lilienfeld, *50 wielkich mitów psychologii popularnej.*

9. R. Zawadzki, *Magia i mitologia psychologii* (Warsaw: Wyd. Uniwersytetu Warszawskiego, 2008).

10. See N. Wiener, *Cybernetyka i Społeczeństwo* [Cybernetics and Society] (Warsaw: Książka i Wiedza, 1960), originally published in English in 1950.

11. Mazur, *Cybernetyka i charakter*, p. 16.

12. E. Żarnecka Biały, *Mała logika: Podstawy logicznej analizy tekstów, wnioskowania i argumentacji*, 3rd ed. (Cracow, 1999), p. 122

13. See P. Łuków, "Ci okropni humaniści," *Świat Nauki*, February 2007, p. 23.

14. Before the year 1989 the only quotations that were taken into account were those of Soviet scientists. Nowadays, we almost always quote American authors.

15. L. Stevenson, *Dziesięć koncepcji natury ludzkiej* (Wrocław, 2001).

16. J. Trzópek, *Filozofie psychologii naturalistyczne i antynaturalistyczne podstawy psychologii współczesnej* (Cracow, 2006).

17. J. Pieter, *Psychologia filozofowania* (Katowice, 2005); see also J. Brzeziński, "Psychologia stosowana czy stosowanie psychologii związek teorii z praktyką na przykładzie związków psychologii z praktyką edukacyjną," in *Humanizm, Prakseologia, Pedagogika, Materials of conference to commemorate the 100 birthday of Tadeusz Kotarbinski* (Wrocław, 1989), p. 133ff.

18. E. Nęcka, "Czy psychologia przetrwa do 2026 roku," *Charaktery* (2005), no. 11.

19. Mazur, *Cybernetyka i charakter*, p. 43.

20. M. Lubański, "O genezie informacji," *Roczniki Filozoficzne* 50, no. 3 (2002).

21. We are not mentioning mathematics and physics here, but calculations, formulas, and laws of physics are involved. These may be found in T. Stonier, *Information and the Internal Structure of the Universe* (London, 1990), p. 127; see also the quotation in Lubański, "O genezie informacji."

22. Lubański, "O genezie informacji," p. 150

23. W. J. H. Kunicki Goldfinger, "Co to jest informacja i jaką rolę spełnia w kulturze jednostki i społeczeństwie," 1994 (preprint).

24. A Google search for "ustawa o szkolnictwie wyższym" yields 188,000 hits.

25. M. Mazur, *Historia naturalna polskiego naukowca* (Warsaw, 1970), pp. 26–27.

26. Full ranking on www.rp.pl/uczelnie, 2011.

27. M. Papuzińska, "Mitologia wyższa," p. 34.

28. I would like to know how the Members of Jurisdiction understand the opposite?

29. According to Stuart M. Kaufman economists should pay more attention to biology than to physics. There is no doubt that applying knowlede of biology and informatics will start a new era of innovation in economic growth.

30. *Polityka*, 18–24 May 2011.

31. The nineties brought a significal improvement of the situation. The university started receiving funds from State Treasury, there was no more censorship, and the university started to develop it teaching base.

32. See http://pl.wikipedia.org/wiki/Katolicki_Uniwersytet_Lubelski_ Jana_ Paw%C5%82a_II.

33. M. Lubański, "Informacja system," in *Zagadnienia filozoficzne*, ed. M. Heller, M. Lubański, and Sz.W. Ślaga, pp. 46–47.

34. www.polpharma.pl.

Student Self-Governance in Nonpublic Colleges and Universities: Changes and Perspectives, 1990–2011

ALDONA DŁUGOKIĘCKA-KAŁUŻA

There has already been twenty years of student self-governance in Polish non-public institutions of higher education. In 1990 the state monopoly for establishing and opening universities in Poland came to an end. The Act of 12 September 1990 on Higher Education was the beginning of changes giving the opportunity to create institutions of higher education both to natural and legal entities. The first law in Poland that sanctioned the functioning of student government was the Higher Education Act of 1982. Nevertheless, all local governments, including the administrations of nonpublic universities, were given more rights with the act of 1990. It opened a whole new stage of being able to create student self-governance structures and organizations which represent and bring together nonpublic university students in Poland. This process gave rise to very significant changes that, later on, affected the "democratization" of the academic life of students at all nonpublic schools.

The rapid quantitative development of higher educational institutions between 1990 and 2005 translated into a significant increase in the number of college students in Poland. This growth was possible predominantly because of the approval given for opportunities of paid education on a large scale, including those for full-time studies at nonpublic universities. State universities which encounter financial difficulties also try hard to increase their revenues from providing educational services. The economic situation in Poland connected with the ownership transformation of enterprises, foreign capital, and opportunities to run private companies led to a rapid increase in the number of students majoring in the subjects of business and administration. This situation has had a significant impact on the academic training of nonpublic universities, which in the context of the development of student self-governance, means being able to develop self-management and entrepreneurship, broadly defined.

The Functioning and Structure of Student Self-Government in View of the Act of 1990

The first broadly defined tasks and responsibilities, as well as the definition of "student self-government," were introduced by the Act of 1990. According to Art. 156 of the act, student government is made up of the students of a particular university. It takes a form and organizational structure based on the regulations adopted by the school's governing body. Regulations regarding the functioning of student government are effective as of the date on which the senate (the school's legislative body) certifies its conformance with university statutes. As defined in the act, student government is the only representative of all students. It has its own tasks and responsibilities. As pointed out by the act, student government conducts activities within the social and cultural life of students. Contrary to popular belief, student government has a wide range of rights. These rights concern its participation in the distribution of funds, governance, and decisions regarding the curriculum.

According to the law, student self-government has a structure parallel to the structure of the university, which is divided into the following parts:

- school government, which governs all university students,
- departmental government, which consists of all the students of a particular department.

The act also mentions the following student self-government bodies:

- a school/departmental government body, which is hard to define. A reasonable interpretation is that when the act refers to this body, it means the authority having executive power in the relevant student government,
- a school/departmental government legislative body.

The beginnings of the formation of student self-governance were the result of individual initiatives of rather active, entrepreneurial students, who were open to new opportunities. In order to improve the operation of departments at universities and communication with students in each year of study, students elected a year prefect. This function became the first element of the student self-government structure. The election of year prefects elected by general, open or secret, voting at the beginning of each academic year represents the first stage of "democratization" of student self-government. Every student has the right to vote, thus influencing the reality of their academic life. Year prefects acting on behalf of all students before the dean have a significant impact on issues concerning the organization of exam sessions, re-sit sessions, and the work of the dean's office. The possibility of communication between the year prefect and the dean of the school also created the opportunity to exchange opinions and to present the problems of other students. In a great number of newly established, fast-developing universities, the group of year prefects quickly became a strong link between each student and the university authorities. The experience gained in many universities allowed them to expand the structure of student self-government quickly and efficiently. This phenomenon enabled them to organize general elections in order to choose the members of student self-government.

According to student self-government regulations in the first years of their activity after 1990, the most vital organs in the structure of nonpublic college student government are the following:

- an executive board (a legislative body consisting of several members);
- the president of student self-government (the head of the board);
- a vice president of student government (performing the duties of the president during his/her absence);
- an audit committee (for the supervision of the activities of other student government bodies);
- a peer disciplinary board (the authority responsible for giving opinions on disciplinary matters concerning students).

The president of student self-government holds the most representative position, and his/her responsibilities include the following:

1. acting on behalf of students and representing their interests in the Students' Parliament of the Republic of Poland;
2. acting on behalf of students and representing their interests in the Nonpublic College Student Association;
3. representing students before university authorities;
4. summoning and presiding over the meetings of the board;
5. announcing student elections to departmental councils;
6. presenting student projects to university authorities;
7. presenting an annual activity report of the student self-government;
8. processing the applications of departmental councils.

The fully democratic structure of student self-government had an impact on the provision of the act (Art. 156), according to which the student governments decide on the allocation of funds for students' purposes, whereas the university authorities provide the funds for the proper functioning of the student self-government bodies. This provision has become a point of numerous public discussions. The Polish Students' Parliament, representing all students, has repeatedly filed requests for an official opinion concerning the financing of student self-governments at Polish universities. The official reply from the Supreme Council of Higher Education and the Ministry of Science and Higher Education allows student governments to obtain the proper funds from universities, and this has become the basis for many of them to exist at nonpublic universities.

Teresa Bader, deputy director of the Department of Higher Education of the Ministry of Education took a stand regarding this issue during her tenure; on 13 February 2007 she stated, "According to the Ministry of Education, the members of student self-government should be provided with the possibility of using office space, having access to a phone, fax machine, photocopier, and a computer. They should also be equipped with essential office supplies and be able to reimburse students for business trips connected with self-government

243

activity, including meetings and training sessions organized by the Students' Parliament of the Republic of Poland." The ministry also states that in determining the amount of money for student self-governments provided by the university authorities, the following aspects should be taken into account: the roles and responsibilities of student self-government specified in the regulations, including the needs of students depending on their number, location, and the capabilities of a particular institution. The Higher Education Act of 1990, citing the Act on Associations, also granted the right for students to participate in academic organizations, including scientific, artistic, and sports clubs (Art. 158). Furthermore, one of the main assumptions of the act was to give academic organizations associating only students, or students and university teachers, the right to present their ideas to university authorities. Newly established organizations ought to be registered and the open register of academic organizations is supervised by the president of the university.

The Right to Strike

A completely new approach in light of the Higher Education Act of 1990 was Art. 160 on strikes and protests. It states: "A student self-government, student association, or student organization which acts within any given university has the right to protest, yet only if their claims are collective and involve important issues." This provision has served a number of student organizations (including the Students' Parliament of the Republic of Poland) as an "argument" in negotiations concerning the law on student loans and credits in 1998, signed by President Aleksander Kwasniewski. Student protests have never been an actual issue; however, this act gave student organizations and local governments the right of veto.

Students may protest only after being supported by an absolute majority of votes of the university or the departmental authority of the student government, association, or organization. The president or the dean should be notified about a protest twenty-four hours in advance. The act explicitly states that nobody can be forced to participate in a protest, whereas the protest organizer is obliged to ensure that the actions taken do not put anybody's life or health at risk, or lead to property damage and cause a public violation and infringement of the rights of university staff and students not involved in the protest.

The Students' Parliament of the Republic of Poland and the MONSSUN Association–National Student Delegations

The amendment to the Higher Education Act of 27 July 2005 gives the designation of a nationwide delegation of all university students to the Students' Parliament of the Republic of Poland, which generally represents both state and nonpublic university students. According to Art. 203 of the Law on Higher Education of 2005, the Students' Parliament of the Republic of Poland is supposed to:

- REPRESENT students before the authorities of the Polish State
- GIVE OPINIONS on legislation concerning students
- INITIATE projects and activities for the student environment
- CO-DECIDE the position of students and state policy toward youth
- SUPPORT pro-student activities
- SUPPORT international student exchange and actively participate in international student movements

Delegations from the Students' Parliament of the Republic of Poland permanently participate in the actions of public authorities such as the Supreme Council of Higher Education, the State Accreditation Committee, committees of the Sejm and the Senate of the Republic of Poland, and the executive bodies of the Ministry of Science and Higher Education.

One of the most important persons in the Students' Parliament of the Republic of Poland is the the *student ombudsman*, who intervenes in cases of the violation of students' rights and takes a number of preventive actions aimed at raising students' awareness of their rights and obligations.

Student self-governments co-decide how to allocate funds for student financial support and the distribution of grants to youth organizations operating within universities. They have an impact on creating the cultural life of students; they participate in the elections of university authorities. They also influence the activities of the bodies responsible for decisions related to curricula and courses of studies. They deal with the promotion of students and graduates in the labor market and legal counseling.

The supreme authority of the Students' Parliament of the Republic of Poland holds a convention. This regular session is held biannually in November. Every student self-government has the right to send its representatives to the convention. Detailed formal requirements are included in the Electoral Law (Art. 2). The national convention has a very formal character. The allocation of seats is carried out according to the number of students of a given university according to the following rules:

> From 1,000 to 4,000 students—one vote,
> From 4,001 to 10,000 students—two votes,
> From 10,001 to 20,000 students—three votes,
> From 20,001 for each additional 10,000 students—one vote,
> Universities with less than 1,000 students are allowed to make agreements in order to appoint a common delegate.

MONSSUN

Yet another organization which has played a very important role in the development of student self-governance in nonpublic schools is the MONSSUN Association, established in 1994. The establishment of the MONSSUN Association, which initially included five student self-governments of nonpublic schools, allowed them to create a structure representing all nonpublic schools. A very well-organized and fast-developing organization enabled the local governments of nonpublic schools to fully participate in the work of the Students' Parliament of the Republic of Poland.

The position of MONSSUN and the number of nonpublic universities it included positively influenced the participation of representatives of nonpublic schools in the evaluation of proposals for changes to legislation and reforms related to students, courses, and conferences. In the first years of its activity MONSSUN already showed its important and serious role in the context of nationwide student self-governance through its participation in the National Convention of the Delegates of the Students' Parliament of the Republic of Poland. The vast and rapidly growing number of nonpublic universities in the 1990s constituted a powerful representation of student self-governments in the Students' Parliament of the Republic of Poland. It was strongly connected with a growing number of votes and delegates and, consequently, had a greater impact on the results of the elections to the Students' Parliament.

Currently, the association consists of 150 student self-governments of nonpublic universities. Its primary task is to promote nonpublic universities in the national higher education system. In consequence of the cooperation between the MONSSUN Association and the Students' Parliament of the Republic of Poland, it was possible, after a long struggle and several protests, to secure social allowances for students in difficult financial situations. Moreover, MONSSUN is actively involved in nationwide campaigns related to enriching student life. The student self-government jointly with the Independent Students' Association of Nonpublic Schools is not required to pay membership fees. Local self-governments receive legal, economic, cultural, and marketing assistance. Moreover, they may participate in conferences and actively support all nonpublic universities. They also act in close cooperation with the Students' Parliament of the Republic of Poland to create common bills whose mission is to improve the activities of nonpublic schools.

Subsequent Changes in Student Self-Governance:
The Act of 2005 Law on Higher Education

The Amendment to the Higher Education Act of 27 July 2005 brought further changes in the context of student self-governance in nonpublic universities. In accordance with Article 61.1 student self-government participates in the adoption of resolutions by university authorities. Undergraduate and graduate students should constitute at least 20 percent of the senate of each university, within which only one representative of doctoral students is allowed, as the act stipulates. Although 20 percent is not much and the students' votes can rarely affect a particular resolution, the presence of students ensures that no important decisions will be taken without the knowledge of the most numerous members of the university community.

Further provisions of the act give students the possibility to apply for financial aid from the funds allocated for this purpose in the state budget in the form of:

1. maintenance grants;
2. special grants for students who have special needs;
3. scholarships for academic or sports achievements;
4. scholarships from the Minister of Education for achievements in science;
5. scholarships from the Minister of Education for outstanding sports achievements;
6. subsistence allowances;
7. and other grants.

The decision for the allocation of these funds and grants is made by the president in consultation with student self-government.

Further provisions of the act (Art. 179) concern students receiving maintenance grants. According to Art. 179.1, a student in a difficult financial situation is entitled to receive a maintenance grant. The president in consultation with the student government body determines the amount of income per family which entitles students to apply for a maintenance grant, food, or housing allowance. The word "agreement" in legal terminology has a very specific meaning, which includes not only the need to consult about specific solutions, but also requires seeking permission. Therefore, student self-governments have a significant impact on the allocation of scholarships and grants at universities.

According to the Act of 2005 the content of curricula depends on the decision of the Departmental Council; thus, again students participate in the whole process. In order to enact the curricula, the legislative body of a departmental government has to express its opinion on it. Although the opinion of the government is not binding for the departmental council, it should still provide students with greater opportunity to comment on the final content of the curriculum.

A more important privilege of self-government is being able to influence the shape of the Rules and Regulations of the University. In accordance with the provisions of the act, a school legislative body has to agree on the content of the rules and regulations passed by the senate. A student self-government has the right of veto. As a consequence, it might lead to the introduction of completely new rules and regulations. A government veto may be rejected by the senate with two thirds of the votes. One of the privileges of student self-government is the right to approve or disapprove candidates for vice president for students. Sometimes university statutes give student self-governments further rights.

Yet another new approach brought by the act applies to self-government and doctoral students' organizations. Art. 208.1 states that the students of doctoral courses at any given university constitute a doctoral students' self-government. The representatives of these self-governments can establish a domestic representation of doctoral students. They have the right to express opinions and present proposals related to doctoral students. Doctoral students also have the right to join academic organizations, in particular, scientific, artistic, and sports clubs.

Perspectives of Student Self-Government Development: Objectives and Tasks

Currently, according to the list of the Ministry of Education, there are around 300 active nonpublic universities in Poland; 200 student self-governments co-operate with the MOSSUN Association, creating a powerful nationwide student representation. However, due to a demographic low and a significant decrease in the number of students (mostly full-time students) at nonpublic universities, student self-government's role is evolving.

It has become the initiator of activities related to students' professional careers. At many universities self-governments collaborate with the Professional Career Office, local businesses, and entrepreneurship and development clubs. Student self-governments initiate actions promoting personal and professional development from the beginning of university studies.

The functions of student self-government are evolving. Apart from its representative role, the local government becomes the creator and co-participant of social processes. It has an impact on the formation of academic life and decisions concerning students. All this and the demands of the contemporary world become the primary directions of the evolution of student self-governance. The activities of student self-governments affect the quality of the university's promotion and the way it is perceived by the local environment of the city and region.

Student self-governance reform in nonpublic universities in the context of laws since 1990 has allowed for the development of legal representation at the local student self-government level. An ongoing discussion concerning new trends in the area of European higher education is another important change and a step forward.

This is also related to the EU structure, which is open to Polish people and allows them to establish international contacts, exchanges of experience, and membership in European student organizations (e.g., the European Student Convention). The collaboration of student self-governments with other non-governmental organizations is another important element of the development of student self-governance.

The nationwide representation of students in the Students' Parliament of the Republic of Poland, and the MONSSUN Association accepts new challenges, including the following:

- Improving information policy toward student self-governments;
- Training sessions for student self-governments;

- Campaigning for the activation of the student environment;
- Increasing student representation in the Sejm and Senate Commissions;
- Local self-government internship programs for foreign student organizations;
- Transferring and promoting European standards for the quality of education.

Notes on Contributors

Marcin Berliński, MA, is a graduate of Nicolaus Copernicus University in Toruń in the department of international relations, specializing in Great Britain. He is also a PhD student at the Catholic University in Ružomberok, Slovakia, in the Department of Pedagogy, specializing in social work. Berliński conducts classes at the Institute for Postgraduate Education at Paweł Włodkowic University College in Płock, and at the Institute for Postgraduate Education at the Off-Campus Faculty of Social Sciences in Stalowa Wola. He has actively participated in establishing the syllabus for the Social Work course at PWUC in Płock. He has participated in numerous conferences and scholarly symposiums and is the author of over twenty articles, including "Doctor Alexander Maciesza's Achievements (1875–1945) in the Field of Health Education," and "On Alternative Education among Its Representatives—Several Comments."

Edyta Bogdańska holds an MA in administration and is an assistant lecturer in the administration department at Paweł Włodkowic University College in Płock. Currently she is working on issues related to civil service as a particular type of employment in public (governmental) administration. She is the author of several articles. Bogdańska was awarded a scholarship and a certificate by the president of the City of Płock in 2009 for her MA project. Currently, she receives a scholarship within the project "ACADEMY for Competence Development."

Rafał Marcin Borkowski is a graduate of the faculty of law and administration at Cardinal Stefan Wyszyński University in Warsaw as well as the Institute for Postgraduate Education at Paweł Włodkowic University College in Płock in the field of human resources management in an enterprise. He is a participant of numerous training sessions in human resources management as well as a business coach within the ABC of entrepreneurship and business planning. Borkowski is a scholarship holder within the Academy for Competence Development, conducting its activities within the Operational Program Human Capital, co-financed by the European Social Fund. Currently, he is also an assistant lecturer in the Management Department at PWUC in Płock, an advisor on postgraduate courses in human resources management at the Institute for Postgraduate Education at PWUC in Płock, and a teacher of postgraduate studies in Sports Management within the Polish Nationwide Training Program for Sports Personnel in Płock and in Wałcz. He is the author of a number of published articles.

Marek Borowski, PhD, graduated university studies with a major in social policy. He also obtained a PhD in humanities with a major in rehabilitation pedagogy. He works for Paweł Włodkowic University College in its Wyszków branch as dean of the department of pedagogy. He is also a business coach who specializes in the management of organizations. An innovative approach to rehabilitation is clearly visible in Borowski's most important articles: e.g., "The Application of the SWOT Analysis," "A Strategic Approach as an Innovative Element in the Methodology of Resocializing Education," and "The Implementation of an Internal Audit for Monitoring the Influence of Resocialization within the Management system of a Rehabilitation Institution." He has also authored the books *The Reasons for Problems in the Education of Children and Youths and Suicides.*

Aldona Długokięcka-Kałuża graduated in the Department of Political Science and International Relations and the Department of Administration at Paweł Włodkowic University College in Płock. She is a former head of Student Self-Government at PWUC in Płock, a former member of the Students' Parliament of the Republic of Poland, and a former member of MOSSUN. Her professional experience includes communication and public relations, journalism, and administration; she is a graduate of the Polish Community Leaders School. Długokięcka-Kałuża has been living and working in France for the past ten years; at present she holds the position of Director of the Polinka Polish Language School for Children in Toulouse, France; she is the president and founder of the Polish Women in France Association; the owner and president of Aldona Kaluza Consulting, Ltd., and president of the Polish-French Business Center in Toulouse. She is also the author and editor of the *Toulouse Guidebook for Polish Tourists,* a consultant for the guidebook entitled *Essentials for Polish People Visiting France,* and a contributor to *Res Publica* magazine.

Romuald Dobrzeniecki holds a PhD in humanities, specializing in pedagogy, from Nicolaus Copernicus University in Toruń. His scholarly interests are focused on special education issues. He is the author or coauthor of nine books as well as numerous scholarly articles. His studies have been translated into Russian, Lithuanian, and Slovakian. Currently he holds the position of vice president of Paweł Włodkowic University College in Płock

Anna Frąckowiak, PhD, graduated from Nicolaus Copernicus University in the department of pedagogy, where she also obtained a PhD in humanities on the basis of her dissertation, "The Development of Higher Education in the United States Compared to the Bologna Process." Currently, she works in the department of pedagogy at Paweł Włodkowic University College in Płock, where she has acted as dean for scholarly research. She is also interested in continuing education and the education of adults. She is the author of two independent monographs devoted to higher education in Europe and in the United States: *The European Area of Higher Education—Competition for American Universities?* and *Higher Education in the United States—An Educational Mosaic.* She is editor-in-chief of the biannual periodical *Open Edu-*

cation as well as the editorial staff secretary of the *Andragogy Yearbook.* Frąckowiak is also an active participant in national and international scholarly conferences on andragogy, teaching methods, and higher education and continuing education issues. She is a member of the Academic Andragogy Association as well as a charter founder of the Association of Social Gerontologists.

Rev. Prof. Andrzej Gretkowski, PhD, is a theologist, a psycho-oncologist, and an educator. Rev. Gretkowski holds a PhD in humanities, specializing in the field of pedagogy, with a subspecialization in social work. He works as a university teacher and an administrator at Paweł Włodkowic University College in Płock, in the position of dean for development. He also works at the Provincial Polyclinical Hospital in Płock. Rev. Gretkowski devotes the majority of his work and research to the ill and suffering human being, "the autumn of man's life," and to death-related issues, as well as to palliative and hospice care. He is the author of sixteen books, and a coauthor of seven publications, as well as several dozen dissertations, articles, reviews, and comments, including *Family Life Education; The Mystery of Pain, Suffering, and Death;* and *A Tumor Is Not Yet a Sentence: Selected Psycho-oncological Issues.* He has also participated in a great many symposia, seminars, and scientific conferences, held both in Poland and abroad (Spain, Lithuania, Canada, and Slovakia).

Edyta Hadrowicz is a juris doctor, a graduate of the department of law and administration at Warsaw University, and an assistant professor at Paweł Włodkowic University College in Płock in the department of administration and management (first- and second-year degree courses: full-time and extramural courses). Since 2008 she has been conducting classes (including teaching distance education course with the use of a virtual website) and seminars for MA and BA students. Since 2010, she has been proxy for the Teaching Quality Support System at the Department of Administration at PWUC, vice chairman of the Student Disciplinary Board, and member of the Council of the Department of Administration at PWUC in Płock. She specializes, predominantly, in issues of civil substantive law. In her analyses, she also raises issues related to local government, corporate and labor law, nature-preservation law, or the theory of law. She is the author of several scholarly publications in such periodicals as *Local Government* and *European Law in Practice.* She is also the author of a monograph entitled *The Institution of Persons without Corporate Status* devoted to issues of the subjective legal status of so-called persons without corporate status.

Joanna Koprowicz holds a PhD in management. She obtained her degree at the Warsaw School of Economics. Koprowicz's scholarly interests involve human resources management. She is employed as a university lecturer in the School of Management of Paweł Włodkowic University College in Płock. Currently, she holds the position of the dean of this division.

NOTES ON CONTRIBUTORS

Zbigniew Kruszewski, a graduate of the Warsaw University of Technology, is a professor at Paweł Włodkowic University College in Płock in the field of higher education pedagogy. He is the founder and president of PWUC. He participates in scientific research jointly conducted with the State Pedagogical University in Yaroslavl in the Russian Federation. He has published a number of books, e.g., *Higher Education in Płock,* and he has written numerous articles, e.g., "The Functions of Nonpublic Higher Education in Poland," "Nonpublic Higher Educational Institutions in the Polish Transformation," and "Learned Societies for Regional Development." He is president of the oldest learned society in Poland, chairman of the Council of Learned Societies in Poland, a Senator between 1997 and 2005 in the Senate of the Republic of Poland and currently a Member of Parliament in the Sejm.

Michał Luczewski has been specializing in EU structural funds since 2004. He is a coach of the ECF, a certified internal coach for group training sessions; he also holds a teaching certificate as well as an international competence license in EU Funds Management as well as a Proxy for EU Funds issued by TÜV Nord Poland, which constitute a confirmation of personnel competence in EU funds. Luczewski prepares grant applications and coordinates projects, including one of the largest EU programs for educating sports personnel, realized within the project "Polish Nationwide Training Program for Sports Personnel." He also advises and trains potential beneficiaries of the ESF; e.g., since 2006 he has been conducting classes and workshops in postgraduate courses in "Management of EU Structural Funds," focusing on elaborating grant applications within the European Social Fund. Between 2008 and 2011 he was a coach at the Regional Training Center of the ESF in Płock. Luczewski graduated from Warsaw University in the faculty of political science, as well as from Paweł Włodkowic University College in international relations. He completed a number of postgraduate courses, including Management of EU Structural Funds, Regional Development and Spatial Development, Finance and Marketing Management, and European Integration, as well as other courses and training sessions in project management, project accounting, the assessment of projects realized within the OP HC, the principles of equal opportunity for women and men in ESF projects, public procurement law, interpersonal communication, motivational strategies, and the like.

Piotr Nasiadko is a graduate of Warsaw University of Technology. As an American government scholarship holder, he is also a graduate of the University of Connecticut in Hartford. Since 1996, he has been the Director of the Office for International Cooperation of Paweł Włodkowic University College in Płock. He has coordinated international projects, among others, projects realized within the framework of the Leonardo da Vinci and Socrates programs—Erasmus. He has also organized international conferences. He is a trainee of and scholarship holder in international programs in Holland, Germany, Great Britain, Denmark, Belgium, France, and Iceland, among others. Since 2004, he has been elaborating and implementing projects within the European Social Fund. He is an expert with the Operational Program Human Capital at the Ministry of Regional Development and is also an expert at assessing the projects submitted within the Erasmus program as well as within the Scholarship and Training Fund within the Foundation for the Education System. He has been cooperating, for a number of years, with the Institute for Postgraduate Education at PWUC as a co-organizer of the institute, the president's delegate, and currently, as a lecturer. He conducts classes in regional politics and in the management of EU structural funds. He also acts as a key coach of the Regional Center for the European Social Fund in Płock. He was one of the founders of the career services office as well as the Regional Center for European Information in Płock. He supervised the Płock Business School which organized training sessions for the unemployed. For a number of years, he was also a representative of foreign language schools, organizing language courses as well as internships both in Poland and abroad.

Agata Skorek holds a PhD in judiciary sciences, specializng in international public law. She graduated from Nicolaus Copernicus University in Toruń, where she obtained her MA and PhD degrees. She wrote her MA thesis in the department of civil law, whereas her PhD dissertation entitled "The Preeminence of the Human Being in the System of the European Convention on Bioethics" was defended in the Department of Human Rights and European Law. Presently, Skorek is employed as a university lecturer at Paweł Włodkowic University College in Płock, where she also supervises the Ius Publicum Administration Students' Academic Club. Her most important publications are "The Patent Capability of Biotechnological Inventions versus Human Dignity in the Regulations of the European Community," "Genetic Tests in Favor of Third Persons: Comments in the Context of the Fourth Additional Protocol to the European Convention on Bioethics in Genetic Tests," and "Donating Real Estate to a Commune in Light of Judicial Decisions of the Constitutional Tribunal." Skorek also organized the student conference "European Administrative Law in Polish Realities, 2011."

Wiesław Wojciech Szczęsny holds an MA in rehabilitation pedagogy, obtained at Warsaw University, a BA in philosophy from the Warsaw Theological Academy, and a PhD in judiciary science. He is a university teacher at Paweł Włodkowic University College in Płock. He is also the author of many scholarly publications. Szczęsny's most important academic achievements include the preparation of the syllabus for the Theory of Education—funded by an EU grant for the College of Education (Union of Polish Teachers)—and the preparation of a research project concerning the Code of Professional Conduct of Teachers. He is also a coauthor of the research project "The Natural History of a Polish Researcher in Postmodernism—Continued."

Marek Tyrakowski is a doctor of judiciary science and an assistant professor of the Department of Financial Law in the School of Law and Administration of the University of Warmia and Mazury in Olsztyn as well as in the department of administration at Paweł Włodkowic University College in Płock. He was the first to analyze and present the controversial issue of the taxation of the Catholic Church in Poland in a book of the same title.

Kazimierz Waluch is a graduate in French studies at Marie Curie-Skłodowska University in Lublin; he also obtained a PhD in political science in 2002 with a dissertation entitled "The External Cultural Policy of France in Post–Cold War Europe." Waluch was also a scholarship holder of the Ministry of Culture and Communication of the Republic of France, of the Italian government, and of the Tempus program. He was an editor of scholarly publications and publishing series of Information Europe Direct in Płock. Currently, he works as a university lecturer at Paweł Włodkowic University College in Płock. He is a higher education expert in the assessment of projects at the Ministry of Science and Higher Education, and a member of both Team Europe at the European Commission and the Płock Learned Society. He is the author and implementer of numerous externally financed projects. Waluch participated in a great number of Polish and international conferences; he has conducted classes at Polish and foreign universities and institutions of higher education. His scholarly activity includes independent publications such as *Cultural Policy of the European Union; The Culture 2000 Program: A Single Financing and Programming Instrument for Cultural Cooperation: Actions in the Years 2000–2003; The Financing of Culture in EU Programs and Funds; The Activity of the EU Council in the Area of Culture in the Years 1995–2005; Selected European Cultural Networks; and The EU Policy on Culture,* as well as over thirty scholarly articles.

Elżbieta Wituska is a graduate of Paweł Włodkowic University College in Płock in the department of administration. She holds an MA degree in administration, and is also a licensed property manager and a scholarship holder within the Academy for Competence Development, conducting its activities within the Operational Program Human Capital, co-financed by the European Social Fund. Wituska is currently an assistant lecturer in the administration department at PWUC in Płock and the author of an MA thesis entitled "Efficiency as the Criterion of Legal Instruments Applied by a Commune in the Maintenance of Cleanliness and Order Illustrated by the Example of Płock," which was awarded by the president of the City of Płock with a first prize in the third edition of the competition "Diploma for Płock" for the best MA, BS, and BA projects in the academic year 2007–8. Wituska was honored with the second prize in the sixth edition of the competition for the best doctoral dissertations as well as MA and BA projects related to the political system and the activity of local governments, held by the publishing house Wolters Kluwer

Polska. She is also on the editorial team of the monthly *Local Government* and is the author of a number of publications and articles.